NO ALTERNATIVE

The Prayer Book Controversy

The main body and essentials of it...have still continued the same unto this day, and do yet stand firm and unshaken, notwithstanding all the vain attempts and impetuous assaults made against it, by such men as are given to change, and have always discovered a greater regard to their own private fancies and interests, than to that duty they owe to the public.

from the Preface to the Book of Common Prayer 1662

NO ALTERNATIVE

The Prayer Book Controversy

Edited by
DAVID MARTIN
&
PETER MULLEN

BASIL BLACKWELL · OXFORD

First published 1981
Basil Blackwell Publisher Limited
108 Cowley Road, Oxford OX4 1JF, England
Reprinted 1982

British Library Cataloguing in Publication Data

No alternative: the prayer book controversy.
1. Church of England. Book of Common Prayer
– Addresses, essays, lectures
I. Martin, David II. Mullen, Peter
264'.03 BX5145

ISBN 0–631–12974–X
ISBN 0–631–12975–8 pbk

Typesetting by System 4 Associates Limited
Gerrards Cross, Buckinghamshire
Printed in Great Britain by The Blackwell Press
Guildford, London, Oxford, Worcester

Contents

Introduction vii

Notes on the Contributors xii

Acknowledgements xviii

Liturgical Continuity and Change
in the Anglican Churches 1
STEPHEN NEILL

Personal Identity and a Changed Church 12
DAVID MARTIN

Gospel Message or Gospel Manifestation? 23
I. R. THOMPSON

Our Fathers, Often Faithless Too 36
MARGARET DOODY

Cranmer Not Irrelevant 57
RACHEL TRICKETT

Doctrine and Devotion
in the Book of Common Prayer 73
ROGER BECKWITH

Swallowing the ASB 1980 80
GEOFFREY SHEPHERD

Why Language Matters 96
DAVID COCKERELL

Biblical Translation 111
TOM PAULIN

Bogus Contemporary 114
C. H. SISSON

Unwillingly to School – with the ASB 122
CHRIS O'NEILL

Music and Church Worship 125
ANN BOND

A Goodly Heritage 131
G. G. WILLIS

When Prayer goes Pop 135
BERYL BAINBRIDGE

Like Nation, Like Church, Like Book 139
BRUCE REED

Parish, Church and Prayer Book 143
W. H. VANSTONE

The Issue of the American Prayer Book 149
DOROTHY MILLS PARKER

An Australian Prayer Book 162
BARRY SPURR

The Primate and the Prayer Book 175
DOROTHY MILLS PARKER

Prayer and Mammon 179
MARGOT LAWRENCE

Sociology and the Questionable Truth 183
ROGER HOMAN

Letters to the Editor 191
DEREK BREWER

Parliament and the Language of Prayer 203
THE TIMES

Prayer Book Protection Bill: Parliamentary Debate 206
HANSARD

A Warning to the Church 227
C. H. SISSON

Index 231

Introduction

This book arises out of the controversy following the publication of the Alternative Service Book 1980. With deliberate, indeed 'systematic' ambiguity we have chosen the title *No Alternative* because there are so many senses in which the ASB presents no genuine alternative to the Book of Common Prayer.

First, it makes no theological advance. I am not merely referring to the crinoline-and-old-lace arguments embroidered by liturgical synodsmen about meanings and intentions in the Eucharist: a thread of 'sacrifice' here, of 'offering' there and of 'anamnesis' in between. I refer to wider theological issues that have preoccupied the Church over the past two decades.

The 1960s brought a general climate of concern with the 'relevant' and the 'meaningful' which affected a generation of clergy. There were two strands to the resulting theological liberalism: one was doctrinal reconstruction and the other liturgical reform. Both began with the laudable intention of making the Christian faith more accessible to 'secular man' – the great number of ordinary people who rarely attend church services. Yet both frequently fell to the level of iconoclasm, destroying the traditional but offering nothing in its place. Doctrinal reconstruction often gave the appearance of a competition to believe the minimum number of doctrines yet remain vociferously Christian.

Liturgical reform went hand in hand with this development. As fast as the theologians rejected ancient doctrines, saying 'but that I can't believe', the liturgiologists disembowelled the language of the Book of Common Prayer and the Bible in which these doctrines were set. Equally minimalist, they produced in its place the bland literalisms of Series 3 and the ASB. After thousands of hours of quibbling, compromise and revisionary pamphleteering, the Liturgical Commission has at last delivered a dull summa of literalisms, expunging from the language of worship all that poetry and metaphor by which the soul at prayer sensed the inexpressible. In the Book of Common Prayer, by contrast, images of transcendence are built up from the shape of the sentences and the sound of the words.

It has to be admitted that the Book of Common Prayer tended to be woolly when it came to doctrines and definitions. Yet the luminous insistence of the divine presence was almost tangible. The ASB has broken the image. It has done what George Eliot said she could never do, to 'lapse from the picture to the diagram'. A graceless, imageless diagram it is too, a mere caricature of symbolic affirmation. When poetry is removed from liturgy what remains has something of the quality of street directions in a non-existent Kafkaesque city. It is because the ASB eschews creative theological writing that it misses the opportunity to offer a valid theological alternative.

Secondly, the ASB presents no acceptable aesthetic alternative. Indeed, when several professors of language and literature expressed their dissatisfaction with the new forms in the famous issue of *Poetry Nation Review* in 1979, some champions of the ASB went so far as to disclaim any interest in literary beauty. They appeared not only to agree that no beauty would be found in the ASB but to insist that to look for it was a sign of perversion. Supporters of the Book of Common Prayer were derided as 'elitist' by those who praised the 'functionalism' of the new forms and stressed the importance of having 'a language that does its job'. This, oddly enough, at a time when the arts, especially poetry and music, are fast emerging from the artificial restrictions of functionalism and turning to greater freedom of expression.

Thirdly, the ASB gives no worthwhile alternative sound and spirit of worship. The new services are often conducted in an atmosphere of ersatz jubilation epitomized by the difficulties of pronouncing 'The Lord is here'. Wherever the emphasis is laid, the redundant information comes over with jarring theatricality. The ASB seems to encourage ministers to 'put meaning' into the prayers in order to raise them out of the everyday. No such thing was ever necessary when using the Book of Common Prayer where the words themselves are worth their weight in glory. The congregation too is encouraged to display an affected exuberance, particularly at the Peace, creating a raucous chumminess that is no alternative to the peace that passeth understanding that once prepared the heart and mind for the central mystery of the Holy Communion.

The traditionalist has truly been left with no alternative – without even the option of criticism. The process of revision has been so assiduously canvassed that anyone who dissents is liable to accusations of disloyalty, even of uncharitableness. What irony that a lifelong worshipper can be thought lacking in charity if he protests at seeing the language of worship torn from its aesthetic and spiritual roots and supplanted by bureaucratic tedium. Even the ability to choose is rapidly diminishing. Many Anglicans now find themselves in parishes which have taken to the ASB for all services. Even in those where the Book of Common Prayer is available its use is likely to be much abridged and to take place early of a weekday morning. We have come a long way from Choral Communion after the 1662 rite at 9.30 every Sunday and Sung Matins at 11.00. For many of those who are old, disabled or without the benefit of a motor car the Book of Common Prayer has effectively been banned. Traditional Anglicans face a crisis of loyalty to their local churches from which they now feel estranged. Met unsympathetically by the ecclesiastical authorities some have even risked the charge of Erastianism and appealed to Parliament for help. For many in the Church of England, both laity and clergy, the crisis is profound and distressing. The essays gathered in this book demonstrate the range and depth of their reaction.

The first section of the book, commencing with Bishop Stephen Neill and concluding with Professor Geoffrey Shepherd has a focus on the doctrine, spirituality and temper of the Book of Common Prayer. It is particularly concerned with how that spirituality and temper are under threat from the various changes now in train as to how we address ourselves to God and dispose ourselves in His House. Roger Beckwith writes from a traditional Evangelical viewpoint and Ian Thompson from a viewpoint more attuned to 'Prayer Book Catholicism'.

The second section relates the Prayer Book issue to what the Dean of Guildford has called 'the other spiritual disciplines'. Words and Music, the Verb and the Note, are powerful incarnations of spiritual energies. They are not adornments and extras but ways in which we communicate the heights and depths of being. Culture is not some passing pleasure of educated people but the soul in pilgrimage, a divine plummet linking heaven and earth.

The third section, beginning with an article by G. G. Willis, is really about the Church of England and more widely the Anglican Communion, especially in the United States and Australia. The article by Dorothy Mills Parker should be cross-referenced with that of Professor Margaret Doody, which also has a north American provenance. This section is about an inheritance of the English way of life, whether manifest in local parish or evocative national occasion, and it is also about a common bond of all English-speaking peoples. The Book of Common Prayer and even more the Authorized Version of the Bible are links in a chain of being precious to millions who have the privilege of English for their mother tongue.

The final section presents materials which are more specifically part of the fall-out of controversy over the last three years. Margot Lawrence points out how the profits as well as the prophets are mixed up in the deluge of new services and new biblical versions. The main sources of protest have been the universities and press. We have, therefore, included Dr Derek Brewer's analysis of letters to the press, and certain press protests taken from superabundant materials in every serious newspaper. The protest from the universities was essentially made in D. Martin (ed.) 'Crisis for Cranmer and King James', *Poetry Nation Review* 13, and B. Morris (ed.) *Ritual Murder*, both published by Carcanet Press. The final protest was made by vote of both Houses of Parliament in April 1981, so we print extracts from the Parliamentary debate. C. H. Sisson's article in *The Spectator* fittingly concludes the argument.

PETER MULLEN
DAVID MARTIN

The Contributors

Beryl Bainbridge won the Guardian Fiction Award in 1974 for *The Bottle Factory Outing*. Her *Sweet William* (1975) was made into a film in 1980. Recent fiction includes *Injury Time* (Whitbread Award 1977) and *Young Adolf* (1978).

Roger T. Beckwith was born in 1929, graduated in English at St Edmund Hall, Oxford, in 1952, and was ordained in the diocese of Chelmsford in 1954. After two curacies he became worship-tutor at his old theological college (Tyndale Hall, Bristol). He now holds the same post at Wycliffe Hall, Oxford, alongside his research work at Latimer House, Oxford, of which he is warden. His studies are mainly concentrated on doctrine, worship, the Jewish background to the New Testament and present-day ecclesiastical affairs, on all of which he has written extensively. He is a member of the Anglican-Orthodox Commission, and also represented the Church of England for some years in theological consultations with the Old Catholics.

Ann Bond graduated with first-class honours from Cambridge University, where she was Organ Scholar of Girton College and gained the John Stewart of Rannoch Scholarship in Sacred Music. From 1953 to 1963 she was Lecturer in Music and University Organist at the University of Manchester. Now married with two teenage children, she combines a part-time teaching and practical career. She is Organist and Director of Music at Lingfield Collegiate Church, Surrey, and church and organ music critic of the *Musical Times*. She also teaches occasionally at the Royal School of Church Music.

Derek Brewer was born in 1923, and educated at elementary school, the Crypt Grammar School, Gloucester, and at Magdalen College, Oxford. He was an infantry officer during World War II. He held a lectureship at Birmingham University for many years and was a professor in Japan, teaching English literature there for two years before moving to the Faculty of English and Emmanuel College, Cambridge, in 1965. He is now Master of Emmanuel and Reader in Medieval English. He has published a variety of books and articles mostly on medieval English literature and established a publishing firm now incorporated in Boydell and Brewer Ltd. He is also editor of the *Cambridge Review.*

David Cockerell was born in London in 1947. He read philosophy at University College, Cardiff, before researching in philosophy of religion under Professor D. Z. Phillips at University College, Swansea. He took Part 3 of the Theological Tripos at Cambridge, where he also trained for the Anglican ministry at Westcott House. After curacies in Leeds, he is now Vicar of St Faith's Church, Hitchin. He has published articles in *Theology* and *The Modern Churchman.*

Margaret Doody was a lecturer at the University of Victoria, British Columbia (1962–64) where she was subsequently assistant professor (1968–69). She was awarded her DPhil at Oxford in 1968, and then lectured in English at University College, Swansea. She is now Professor of English at Princeton University and is the author of *A Natural Passion* (1974).

Roger Homan is Senior Lecturer in Sociology and Education at Brighton Polytechnic and Director of the Centre for the Study of Religion and Society at the University of Kent. His research has principally been in the sociology of religion and his doctoral study was concerned with old-time Pentecostals. Publications include contributions to *Sociology, Sociological Review, British Journal of Sociology, International Affairs* and the *Sociological Yearbook of Religion in Britain*. He is a lay reader in the diocese of Chichester.

Margot Lawrence has been a freelance writer and editor most of her working life. Her books include *Shadow of Swords*, a biography of Elsie Inglis and *Flyers and Stayers*, the book of the world's greatest rides on horseback, and she contributes to the *Daily Telegraph*, the *Sunday Telegraph*, the *Guardian* and various magazines. She is the widow of Laurence Thompson, the author and historian.

David Alfred Martin is University Professor of Sociology, at the London School of Economics and Political Science. He has been Cadbury Lecturer, Birmingham University (1974), Ferguson Lecturer, Manchester University (1978), Lecturer in Pastoral Theology, Durham University (1979), Firth Lecturer, Nottingham University (1980) and Gore Lecturer, Westminster Abbey (1978), as well as Select Preacher, Cambridge University (1979–80). In 1975 he became President of the International Conference of the Sociology of Religion. His recent books include *A General Theory of Secularisation* (1978), *Contemporary Dilemmas of Religion* (1979), *Crisis for Cranmer and King James* ed. (1979), *The Breaking of the Image* (1980) and *Theology and Sociology* (ed. with W. Pickering and J. Orme-Mills O.P.) (1980).

Dorothy Mills Parker is a freelance journalist, author and lecturer based in Washington, DC, who has written about church-related affairs on the national and international level. She is author of *The Prayer Book Issue* (Society for the Preservation of the Book of Common Prayer, 1978). She is well known in England, where she covered the 1968 Lambeth Conference for the *Washington Post*, and the 1978 Conference and the enthronement of Archbishop Runcie for the *Washington Star*. For several summers she served on the staff of Coventry Cathedral and has written and lectured extensively on their life and work. Since 1970 she has been Academic Secretary to the Dean at Wesley Theological Seminary in Washington. In the secular field she is author of *Lee Chronicle*, a history of the Lees of Virginia (New York University Press, 1957).

Peter Mullen was educated at Liverpool University and St Aidan's College, Birkenhead. He was ordained in 1970 and has worked in parishes in Leeds, Manchester and Oldham. From 1974 until 1977 he was Head of Religious Studies at Whitecroft High School, Bolton. Books include *Beginning Philosophy* and *Thinking about Religion*, besides articles and reviews for *The Times*, *Times Educational Supplement*, *Observer*, *Guardian*, *Theology*, *Modern Churchman*, and *The Music Teacher*. He has broadcast on BBC Radio 4 which also produced his dramatic chorus *St Mark* in 1979. Peter Mullen writes and presents programmes for Yorkshire Television and Tyne Tees Television. He is Vicar of Tockwith and Bilton with Bickerton in the diocese of York.

Stephen Neill was Prize Fellow of Trinity College, Cambridge, before becoming a missionary in South India (1924–44). He was Assistant Bishop to the Archbishop of Canterbury (1945–48) and served on the World Council of Churches (1946–54). Among his academic posts were Professor of Missions and Ecumenical Theology, Hamburg (1962–69) and Professor of Philosophy and Religious Studies, University of Nairobi (1969–73). Since 1978 he has been Assistant Bishop in the diocese of Oxford. He is the author of many books including *Christian Faith and Other Faiths* (1961), *A History of Christian Missions* (1964), *The Interpretation of the New Testament* (1964), *The Church and Christian Union* (1968), *Jesus through Many Eyes* (1976) and *Salvation Tomorrow* (1976). In preparation is a three-volume *History of Christianity in India.*

Chris O'Neill was educated at Worcester College, Oxford, and he trained for the ministry at Ripon College, Cuddesdon. He has been chaplain of Rugby School and is now a chaplain at Charterhouse.

Tom Paulin read English at the University of Hull and went on to take a BLitt at Oxford. He has lectured in English at the University of Nottingham since 1972. His publications include two books of poems, *A State of Justice* (1977) and, most recently, *The Strange Museum.*

Bruce Reed has been Executive Chairman of the Grubb Institute of Behavioural Studies since it was set up in 1969. An ordained Anglican, he is the author of *The Dynamics of Religion* (1978).

Geoffrey Shepherd is Professor of Medieval Language and Literature at the University of Birmingham. He is the editor of the *Ancrene Wisse* (Parts 6 and 7) and of Philip Sidney's *Apology for Poetry*. He has contributed essays to many journals and books including the *Cambridge History of the Bible* and *Chaucer and Chaucerians* (1965).

C. H. Sisson was born in 1914, and is a poet, translator and critical writer. He was formerly an Under-Secretary in the Ministry of Labour/Department of Employment. His books include *In the Trojan Ditch* (collected poems and selected translations), *Anchises* and *Exactions* (poems), *The Divine Comedy of Dante* (translation) and *The Avoidance of Literature* (collected essays). He is an FRSL (1975) and has an honorary DLitt from Bristol (1980).

Barry Spurr was born in Canberra in 1950. He read English at the University of Sydney and took First Class Honours in 1974. He was Organ Scholar at St Paul's College for four years. He went to Oxford on a travelling scholarship and was awarded the BLitt (now MLitt) in 1976. He returned to a lectureship at the University of Sydney and to become Senior Tutor at St Paul's College.

I. R. Thompson (born 1936) is Head of the English Department at Frederick Gough School, Scunthorpe, and a former member of the General Synod of the Church of England. He has written and lectured extensively on the Prayer Book issue and edits *Faith and Worship*, a half-yearly review published by the Prayer Book Society.

Rachel Trickett was born at Lathom, Lancashire, in 1923,

and educated at the High School for Girls, Wigan, and Lady Margaret Hall, Oxford, where she took a First in English in 1945. She has lectured at the University of Hull and at Yale. In 1954 she was appointed Fellow and Tutor at St Hugh's College, Oxford, of which she is now Principal. Publications include six novels, the libretti for two operas composed by John Joubert and *The Honest Muse* (1967), a book on eighteenth-century poetry.

W. H. Vanstone took First Class Honours at Balliol College, Oxford, and St John's College, Cambridge. He was later Vicar of Kirkholt. For many years Canon Vanstone was Examining Chaplain to the Bishop of Manchester and he has been a Canon of Chester since 1978. He is also Theological Chaplain to the Bishop of Chester and author of *Love's Endeavour, Love's Expense* (1977).

G. G. Willis was educated at the University of Manchester (MA 1939) and the University of Nottingham (PhD 1951) where he was awarded his DD in 1969. He trained for the ministry at Lichfield Theological College and served for many years in the diocese of Derby as a parish priest and also as lecturer at Derby Training College. He was a member of the Liturgical Commission from 1955 to 1965 and Lecturer at Cuddesdon College, Oxford from 1962 to 1968. His publications include *Further Essays in Early Roman Liturgy* (1968), *1966 and All That: The Revision of the Eucharist in the Church of England* (1970), and *Series without End or the Supplanting of the BCP* (1974).

Acknowledgements

The Editors wish to thank the following for permission to reproduce certain essays and articles:
The *Times Literary Supplement* for C. H. Sisson's review of the Alternative Service Book 1980, published on 14 November 1980 under the title 'The liturgy's last rites'; Beryl Bainbridge, whose article first appeared in the *Sunday Telegraph* on 16 November 1980; the Society for the Preservation of the Book of Common Prayer for extracts from Dorothy Mills Parker's booklet *The Prayer Book Issue*; *The Living Church*, the weekly national magazine serving the Episcopal Church, published at 407 East Michigan Street, Milwaukee, WI 53202, for Dorothy Mills Parker's interview with the Archbishop of Canterbury, published on 31 May 1981; the *Cambridge Review* for Professor Geoffrey Shepherd's article; *Faith and Worship* for Ann Bond's article; A. D. Peters and Co. Ltd. and the *Daily Telegraph* for 'Prayer and Mammon' by Margot Lawrence; HMSO for the extracts from Hansard; *The Times* for its editorial of 8 April 1981, 'Parliament and the Language of Prayer'; the *Spectator* for C. H. Sisson's article 'A Warning to the Church', originally published on 2 May 1981.

Liturgical Continuity and Change in the Anglican Churches

STEPHEN NEILL

In 1552 the Anglican pattern of liturgical worship was in all essentials settled. This pattern remained in force for almost four centuries. It was the aim of the Anglican reformers that there should be one form of worship for the whole realm, in which all would join. This principle continued to be accepted as Anglicans spread throughout the world. Anglicans, wherever they might be, knew that on any one day they would be doing the same thing, with a few notable exceptions, as all other Anglicans anywhere in the world were doing. It was this acceptance of liturgical uniformity which, more than anything else, kept in being the unity of the Anglican Communion through the period of its growth from an insular body to a worldwide fellowship of churches. For this reason liturgical change is more significant in this fellowship than in almost any other Christian communion.

To say that the pattern was settled is not to say that nothing ever changed. Whatever parliaments and prelates may say, liturgy is in a constant state of change. Local usages grow up and come to be accepted almost without awareness that change has taken place. Rubrics that are found to be inapplicable are quietly disregarded. Forms of service which have held their own for a period are dropped, a notable example being the service for 5 November (Gunpowder Plot), which simply disappeared from the Prayer Book of the Church of England. Some changes, such as the addition of the commemoration of the departed in the Church Militant Prayer in 1662, have clearly been improvements. Some are insignificant. Some have been misfortunes.

One of the early misfortunes was the printing of the ancient book called the Apostolic Constitutions in 1563. Scholarship has now established that this work dates from the second half of the fourth century, its author being possibly also the interpolator of the Ignatian Epistles. Its discovery was a misfortune only because of the strange view that the liturgy in the 8th book really was the liturgy used by the apostles themselves, to which all other liturgies should be brought into conformity. This started the search for a 'primitive liturgy' which has gone on till the present day.

Far more serious was the intervention of Archbishop William Laud in liturgical matters. He laid it down that the holy table must be protected from desecration by altar-rails; these were not the elegant rails to be found in many churches today, but an almost solid barrier, with the openings narrow enough to keep out stray dogs. (I recently saw an example of such rails in a Cotswold church.) He further laid it down that the table must always stand against the east wall, and must not be removed in time of service. This transformed what had been the most corporate form of eucharistic worship in the Christian world into the most individualistic. Cranmer had laid it down that, at the time of Communion, the table should stand in the midst of the church or in the chancel; the communicants came forward to stand around the table. Many of us can remember services in which the priest was separated from the people by the whole expanse of a long Gothic chancel, and the worshippers were scattered through a large church, hardly aware of one another's existence. Only after more than three centuries are we getting back to what our great archbishop planned for us.

The Scottish Prayer Book of 1637 marks the first official departure from the settlement of 1552. The changes are less than might have been expected; almost all are in the direction of the service of 1549, and are well within the

Anglican pattern. More radical changes were made, partly under the influence of the Non-jurors, in the rite of 1764, which became the pattern for the American rite of 1794.

After the turbulence of the Commonwealth period came, almost inevitably, the restoration of Charles II. Once again a laudable effort was made to produce a liturgy which would be acceptable to all faithful people. At the Savoy conference of 1662 neither the embattled puritans under Richard Baxter nor the high-church bishops such as Cosin and Sancroft got all they wanted. The revision was surprisingly conservative. Almost all the changes were for the better, but there was one disastrous misfortune: an Amen was added after the words of institution in the consecration prayer. It is strange that so small a change should have such extensive consequences. The impression was given that the *anaphora* ends with the words of institution, and that the Lord's Prayer is the first act in the post-communion. Cranmer's intention was very different: 'consecration' and communion should be one single act and to this end communion is brought *within* the great thanksgiving; the canon ends, as it always did, with the Lord's Prayer, and this most properly ends with the Amen of priest and people together. So soon was the thought and purpose of the great reformers forgotten.

In liturgical matters the eighteenth century was rather a dull time, the thoughts and adventures of the Non-jurors having fairly wide influence, and the reductionist tendencies of near-unitarians being fought off with some difficulty. It was in the nineteenth century that things really began to fall apart.

The main aim of the authorities was *quieta non movere*. Appeals for shorter services and greater flexibility, and for a lectionary better organized in relation to the Church's year, did meet with some success. But for the most part people did what they thought right, or failed to do what had seemed to be otiose, and what had been done gradually came to be accepted usage. This is well exemplified in the introduction by the evangelicals of early Communion services, for the sake of those who had learned from John Wesley to appreciate more frequent Communion than was offered in the more traditional churches. There is little doubt that this action of the evangelicals was illegal, since the Book of Common Prayer envisaged the celebration of Holy Communion only after Morning Prayer and the Litany had been said. The bishops, however, though they did not on the whole like evangelicals, thought that their desire for fuller recognition of the place of eucharistic worship was on the whole a good thing, and silently agreed to look the other way. In any case there was no intention of any liturgical change.

Trouble began when the Anglo-Catholic wing began to disturb the order of Anglican worship. By omitting the third exhortation and the second half of the words of administration these reformers robbed the service of 1662 of some of its most eucharistic features – and then blamed the service for not being eucharistic. By following the Roman use and inserting the so-called ablutions immediately after the Communion of the people, they totally destroyed the rhythm of the service by introducing a pause where a pause is most undesirable. By treating the Gloria in Excelsis as an optional appendage which may be omitted in Advent and Lent, they produced a liturgy which sounds like Beethoven's ninth symphony played without the Song to Joy. Naturally they turned around anxiously looking for something different and liturgically more adequate. They were so successful that very few Anglican communicants have ever taken part in a celebration of the rite of 1662 bearing any exact relation to what Cranmer intended it to be.

Only in the twentieth century did the church begin to take seriously the reality that in no Anglican church did either clergy or people make any serious attempt to carry out the rubrics exactly. Canon Liddon threatened to leave the Church of England if the Athanasian Creed was recited less than thirteen times in the year. What would he have thought if he could have known that within sixty years of his uttering these dire threats, the Athanasian Creed would almost completely have disappeared from Anglican worship in England, as it had already officially disappeared in Ireland?

The new mood was seen in the abortive revisions of 1927 and 1928. Evangelicals opposed both versions of the book because they seemed to extend some toleration to reservation of the sacred elements after communion; Anglo-Catholics opposed the books because they did not authorize reservation with a view to adoration. The combined opposition led to the twice repeated rejection of the revision. At the time the shock was considerable. But, as days passed and a less emotional assessment of the book became possible, the general opinion was that its rejection was not a great disaster – it was, in fact, not a very good book.

In those days liturgical knowledge was not widely diffused. This century the Church of England has had only two great liturgiologists: F. E. Brightman and F. C. Burkitt. Brightman, scrupulously fair in the presentation of evidence, had never emerged from the rather stiff Tractarian piety in which he had grown up. Burkitt, by contrast, declared that he wished for only one change in the service of 1662, the substitution of 'and' for 'or' between the prayer of oblation and the prayer of thanksgiving; he felt that both should be said. W. H. Frere, later bishop of Truro, was a man of considerable erudition, but he was wedded to a strictly Anglo-Catholic position. E. C. Ratcliff was learned, but, as we now know from Canon Couratin, he was never much in love with the Anglican tradition, and in the last days of his life was preparing to seek admission to the Orthodox Church. Altogether 1927–8 was not a very propitious time for liturgical revision.

For all that, 1928 was a year of considerable liturgical activity. In that year both the Episcopal Church in the United States and the Anglican Province of South Africa received new Prayer Books, the fruit in each case of careful but not radical revision. The notable thing about all these efforts was that they stood firmly within the Anglican tradition. All the principal revisers, whatever their personal reservations, held that the creation of the Book of Common

Prayer was a great achievement, which in its salient features must be preserved as part of the inheritance of the Church of England.

The first example known to me of an attempt to move out of the Anglican tradition was the interesting *Liturgy for India* prepared during World War I by J. C. Winslow, the founder of the Christa Seva Sangh at Poona, and later an ardent adherent of Moral Rearmament, and E. C. Ratcliff, to whom reference has already been made. This was, I believe, used a number of times in India with the sanction of the local bishop; it never caught on, though it provoked considerable interest and raised the question of how far churches in the Third World should be tied to the traditions of Canterbury.

The first official departure was the sanctioning, in the 1930s, of the Ceylon Rite by the General Council of the Church of India, Burma and Ceylon. The diocese of Colombo was in part strongly Anglo-Catholic, and was also under the influence of a number of priests, including Lakdasa de Mel, later Bishop of Calcutta and Metropolitan of India, who felt that an attempt should be made to draw on the ancient pre-Christian culture for liturgical enrichment. As clerical secretary of the General Council, I felt that the matter was being rather lightheartedly dealt with and pointed out the gravity of the issues involved, but, there being no liturgical experts on the Council, the members were rightly of the opinion that it was a beautiful service, and accepted it for use in the diocese of Colombo only.

The Lambeth Conference of 1948 met after a gap of eighteen years since its previous meeting in 1930; only a small number of bishops had been present at that earlier meeting. The agenda was highly charged, with such difficult and controversial matters as the formation of the Church of South India, and there was not much time for consideration of liturgical revision. This was, however, in the minds of many. The disregard of rubrics had been carried to astonishing lengths, and not only by Anglo-Catholics. There were churches in England and in the USA in which the Roman

Mass was said in Latin, with only an occasional glance at any part of the Anglican tradition. But at the same time the work of Gabriel Hebert and Henry de Candole was taking hold; the Parish and People movement was becoming more than a name, and was creating something like a revolution not so much in liturgical structure as in the manner of understanding and celebrating the Eucharist. The day of High Mass at 11.00 with no communicants was almost at an end; the recovery of the Communion of the people as an essential element in every Eucharist was bound to raise a great many questions of liturgical order. For a variety of reasons the attitude of the bishops was cautious. It was recognized that liturgical change was bound to come, and was on the whole to be encouraged, but the resolution (76. i) that Prayer Book revision should take place within the limits laid down by the Book of Common Prayer was passed, if I remember rightly, with little discussion and less dissent.

There can be little doubt that the reason for this caution on the part of the bishops was the immediate and continuing popularity of Gregory Dix's book *The Shape of the Liturgy*, which first appeared in 1945. This is in many ways an attractive book. Dix has read widely; his style is clear, and at times rises to considerable heights of eloquence. But he lacks the temper of the scholar. When he told me that he had read law at Oxford, I instantly understood the problem. Dix is always the advocate, witty and impassioned, highly skilled in making the worse appear the better reason. The learned William Telfer wrote the epitaph of the book, when meeting a colleague in the street in Cambridge, shortly after *The Shape of the Liturgy* appeared, he put the question, 'Would you say that it was a *very* good book?'

Dix is honest with his readers. He tells us that he had not intended to deal at all with the story of Anglican liturgy, for the very good reasons that he regarded it as parenthetical in the history of liturgy, and that to him the Book of Common Prayer, which at his ordination he had promised to use *and no other*, seemed not to be of general interest. It would have been better for his reputation if the 120 pages which in the end he did devote to the subject had never been written.

Dix never had any understanding of the Reformation, and he had an almost pathological hatred for Cranmer, a hatred all the stronger from the fact that honesty compelled him to admit, as many have not admitted, Cranmer's strength and integrity and his brilliance as a maker of liturgies. He starts, however, with the fundamental error of supposing Cranmer to have been a Zwinglian and shows no signs of ever having read Canon Charles Smyth's *Cranmer and the Reformation under Edward VI.* He then goes on to commit himself to the remarkable affirmation that Cranmer was the only man ever to create a liturgy on the basis of the doctrine of justification by faith. This happens not to be true. But if it were, would it be a crime? Dix was an ordained priest of the Church of England; as such he had declared his acceptance of the Thirty-nine Articles of Religion, including article XI Of the Justification of Man. But he shows on page after page that he has no clue as to the meaning of the doctrine, or of its significance in the development of all genuinely Anglican theology. Starting with these disadvantages, it is not surprising that, though he quotes extensively from Cranmer, he gets everything just a little wrong, and produces a caricature and not a portrait.

Unless I have read him carelessly, Dix never discovered the clue to the developments in Cranmer's liturgical work between 1548 and 1552. I think that he is right in holding that there was little development in Cranmer's *theology* during those years, and also in holding that Cranmer never thought that the rite of 1549, beautiful as it is, could be a permanent resting place. What seems to have moved him was not the logic-chopping of Stephen Gardiner, but the criticisms of his friends that not enough attention had been paid to the New Testament evidence as to the nature of Christian worship. Cranmer accepted the principle that the shape of the liturgy must be determined not by the medieval Mass, nor by the Eastern services with which he was acquainted, nor by Hippolytus, with whom presumably he was not, but by the words of Scripture. He was always one to go back to origins. With extraordinary skill he has brought together all that can be gleaned from the New Testament about the way in which the Eucharist is to be understood, at the same time retaining all that seems to him to be truly scriptural from the great liturgical tradition of the west. Hence the passover atmosphere of the 1552 liturgy, and the eschatological elements, which are present, though not over-stressed. Once this is grasped, the shape begins to take shape; the service is not a random collection of fragments, but a great symphonic movement, unbroken from 'Lift up your hearts' to the blessing.

It is sad that so many theological students are recommended to read Dix, and are not recommended to read anything else. It is even sadder that so many of those who teach liturgy seem never to have gone behind Dix to original sources. Hence the assumption in the minds of many, not excluding some of our revisers, that the Anglican tradition is something of no particular value, from which in this day of liberation we should take the opportunity of setting ourselves free. To those of us who hold that that tradition, in its essentials though not in every detail, is a priceless treasure which we hold in trust for the whole Church of Christ, this will appear to be the freedom of antinomianism and not the freedom of grace. This is not the only way of doing the Eucharist, but it is a way which is theologically valid, liturgically satisfying and spiritually edifying. We can part with it only to our great loss.

What then are we to do in the ten years that have been given to us, before the existing revisions become permanent? Above all, it must be made absolutely clear that those who value the Anglican tradition and love the Book of Common Prayer are not blinkered diehards opposed to every kind of change. The trouble was that it came to be accepted, I do not quite know how, that the alternative presented to conservatives was, 'Either you accept the Book of Common Prayer exactly as it stands, or you accept one or other of the new services put forward by the Liturgical Commission and the Synod.' The opportunity for a thoughtful, careful and Anglican revision of the Book of Common Prayer was never given. Clearly there are many things in the Alternative Service Book which can be accepted by all. If the Eucharist is to be celebrated separately from the Divine Office, there is everything to be said for the reintroduction of psalmody, and for a much wider range of lections. And there is great need for revision of the Book of Common Prayer. Many of the rubrics are now obsolete. In places language is archaic; few today would wish to pray for 'the fruition of thy glorious godhead'. A number of words have changed their meanings. What this constitutes is good ground for a revision which shall be Anglican, dignified and theologically and liturgically valid. This will provide plenty of work to be done over the next ten years.

First, we must put Dix on a very high shelf, and forget all about him. Next, much hard study is needed to determine the *theology* we want to express in our liturgy. The idea that liturgy can be changed without a change in theology we now know to be an illusion; change the liturgy and you automatically change the theology. This applies perhaps even more to the rites of initiation than to the Eucharist. Much good theological work has been done since 1945, for instance on the meaning of sacrifice, but this needs to be pulled together and worked out more systematically. In particular, note needs to be taken of recent work on the doctrine of the Holy Spirit in relation to the sacraments.

Once a measure of agreement has been reached on theology, it should be possible to consider the *form* in which that theology is to be expressed. Excessive rigidity is to be avoided, and variety within reasonable limits is to be encouraged. I can see no objection to the introduction of the Peace, if this is understood as a solemn liturgical act and not as the friendly handshake which produces bedlam in the congregation. The fraction is a harmless ceremony, if it is understood as part of the administration and immediately followed by it. But these are details. The question that needs to be deeply studied and weighed is whether the biblical form of the eucharistic service followed by Cranmer is a valid and satisfactory shape of the liturgy. If the answer is affirmative, we have a criterion by which to judge which modifications within that shape are acceptable as recognizably Anglican, and which fall outside the limits of the acceptable.

Last, we have to try and arrive at a consensus as to the style and tone of liturgical language which will convey in 1982 and following years the understanding of the liturgy which we believe to be right and necessary in this age. It is possible today to write English which is dignified and even solemn, and at the same time clear and contemporary. There are a few good modern collects, such as 'Remember, O Lord, what thou hast wrought in us...' (some would object that even here 'wrought' is an archaism, though most people have heard of wrought iron). The assessment of the value of English words is an art in itself. English prose rhythm is a very delicate thing; only those with a sensitive and well-trained ear can handle it successfully. From what they have produced, it does not seem that any member of either the English or the American team had such an ear, witness the massacre endured by the Canticles and the astonishing inconcinnities in the revised Psalter. Surely there are people about who have the necessary gifts and could be brought in to help in matters of style and diction. We may not have a Cranmer today; we should at least have some who can hear his rhythms and understand the brilliance of his workmanship.

So there is plenty to be done in the next ten years. I fear it is unlikely that I shall be there to greet the year 1991. But I hope that that year may bring us a bright and shining new Prayer Book, worthy of our past, relevant to our present and full of promise for our future.

Personal Identity and a Changed Church

DAVID MARTIN

I want here to explore both the relation of liturgy to personal identity and the relation of liturgy to the identity and character of the contemporary Church. My initial focus will be on personal identity but the thrust of my remarks concerns the question of where the Church is going. If it really is the case that the *lex orandi* is the *lex credendi*, then as we alter the form of our prayer, we alter the substance of our faith. As we vary the way we use our bodies, we simultaneously shift the content of our minds. And as we begin to use words like 'aesthetic' and 'culture' as terms of abuse we are ceasing to be a Church and commencing a career as a sect. There may be arguments for some or all of these things, but it is no use pretending that contemporary changes are just cosmetic, or mere pragmatic variations in the means we use which do not infect the ends we desire and achieve. Means and ends are not so easily separated, especially when we are concerned with the speech and comportment of a religious community.

But first let me consider this question of personal identity, how it is nourished and built up. Personal identity is tied in with all these changes at a profound level. Yet many clergy confronted by resistance to their eager manipulations of the

This paper was prepared at the suggestion of the Very Revd Victor de Waal, Dean of Canterbury, and first delivered at a rally in Savannah, Georgia, in March 1981.

service complain that the trouble arises *merely* because of the threat to people's identity. They say that they will only respect such resistance when it can be articulated in theological objections. Of course, they are, in one sense, correct. It *is* a matter of identity, personal and corporate.

People feel threatened and afflicted in the very roots of their being. After all, they are members of the human species, and once they have worn themselves a niche in a naughty world, they do not like being evicted from it. For them there is no such thing as 'mere' identity. When they lose their identity, they have little else to lose, and when that loss is gleefully supervised by once-trusted pastors, their dereliction is complete.

But this natural resistance of those with threatened identities is something much deeper than nostalgia, or conservative attachment to known ways and associations, or ignorance of the theological goodies wrapped up in the new package. It is a sense, sometimes dumb and sometimes acute, of a profound incision and cauterization in religious consciousness. The resisters know that theological positions are being evacuated and others occupied. They recognize that the Church has been hijacked, without much publicity, and sometimes with the acquiescence of people who do not know what trip they are being taken on. Of one thing they are quite sure. They have been told to take it or leave it, and many of them prefer to leave it.

If these linkages between identity and a sense of theological impoverishment are so strong, we have to concern ourselves closely with this precious identity. What is it? What are its sources and its resources? What is the tie between selfhood and liturgy? I used that word 'tie' carefully because the root of the word 'religion' refers to a tie and a bond. So the question is: how are we bonded together?

Our faith and our way of prayer is tied in with all our personal linkages and social bonds. We are incorporated in the Christian body by the giving and receiving of certain signs. These signs comprise gesture, comportment (how we carry ourselves in God's house), the deployment of time, the employment of space and, above all, our speech. Membership is conveyed and established in the giving of passwords. There are some words which will pass and some which will not. If that seems too abstract. I will give two examples of the use of passwords, one from an Evangelical context, one from an Anglo-Catholic context.

Recently I was asked to talk to the ordinands of St John's College, Nottingham. St John's is an evangelical powerhouse of liturgical change in England. At that time it used the Prayer Book once a year, on Ash Wednesday (good for mortification). Over lunch, before my talk, an ordinand got up to give out some notices, largely for the benefit of some prospective ordinands who were up that day for interview. Almost every item in his vocabulary, and his whole manner of speech, operated as a password. He offered his speech to the assembly in a very distinctive way to indicate common membership. Sociologists would say that he was 'passing himself off as' or 'passing for' an evangelical, talking in a way which bespoke his commitment and his identity. (Perhaps I should stress that the sociological use of such phrases as 'passing off as' is not at all perjorative.) Those up for interview were warmly welcomed and told that the community of St John's 'hoped to discern the Lord's will for them'. I did not know whether to be shocked or gratified. I had the same kind of pleasant shock as when I saw pictures of the Bishop of Southwark, a great apostle of relevance, billowing and careening around Wimbledon Centre Court in fourth-century ecclesiastical dress. If I had come hoping to hear the famous 'relevant', 'contemporary' or 'everyday' speech, I would have been vastly disappointed. Naturally, I asked myself whether 'discerning the Lord's will' was all that much more contemporary than 'Dearly beloved brethren, the Scripture moveth us in sundry places...'.

When I came to give my talk I knew that unless I spoke at least some of the passwords, I would never pass muster with them. It is not cynical to say that without some use of words like 'grace' and 'glory' I would not have been admitted to their minds. Such words established my identity as 'friend', an erring brother no doubt, but worth listening to. But, of course, words like 'grace' and 'glory' are precisely part of our so-called archaic vocabulary, and when we use them to speak of faith and hope, we do two things. We establish membership and identify ourselves. We also cut ourselves off from those who use such words for other purposes. The password is an identity card, marking out who belongs and who does not. We cannot throw away those powerful, archaic and necessary words without losing our social being. And indeed, so long as we use them they are not archaic.

My second example is taken from that great Anglo-Catholic church, All Saints, Margaret Street. Here, of course, you need to know the pass-acts as well as the passwords. You must act to pass as well as speak to pass. The world you enter at All Saints is as shatteringly different from Margaret Street as a Japanese temple is from the Shinjuku skyscrapers in Tokyo. It is full of markers which speak of a transition from street to altar. You are put in transit as you enter and you respond with all the gestures of somebody undergoing a profound change. You sign in by marking yourself with a cross. You make a Christian mark, establishing your identity and your right to move freely across the threshold of God's house. The distinctive and glorious speech you adopt in that house is just one of a whole forest of symbols which establish that house for what it is. At the same time, you leave behind the mundane world.

That act of signing yourself in is not only profoundly archaic but profoundly aesthetic. To make the sign of the cross is not only to sign yourself in, but it is to do something startlingly beautiful. The beauty and the meaning are united in the act. The horizontal and vertical lines 'cross' each other in exact mathematical symmetry. As priestly hands trace that vertical and that horizontal, the soul is imprinted with a full, perfect and sufficient satisfaction. The act has physical grace and heavenly benediction in it. The movement of the hands reverts to a still centre, simultaneously physical and spiritual. We are stilled and centred.

Nobody can say that such an act is 'just aesthetic' any more than they can say that graceful words and words of grace are 'just aesthetic'. Exactly the same applies to the lights above the altar. They are the visible reminders of invisible light, which by their clarity, purity and lucidity point to the divine presence. You cannot divide the sense of their beauty from the divinity to which they bear witness. The miracle of light which they represent is a direct analogy of the light invisible. The power and grace of light, like the power and grace of words, carries us across the threshold into the presence of the Most High. Acts, words and lights are sacramental, efficacious signs. They tell us who we are, where we are and in whose presence we stand.

When I arrived to preach at All Saints, Margaret Street, I was met by the wardrobe mistress. She told me she had previously been employed in a hospital and had no idea how complicated Christianity could be till she took up her duties at All Saints. Now, in charge of all this millinery, she loved every minute of it. The service itself had the precision of ballet and the repetitiveness of a musical rondo. The prayer returned again and again, cumulative and powerfully redundant. 'Holy Mary, Mother of God, pray for us sinners now and at the hour of our death.' As repetitive choruses are to evangelicals, so is cumulative incantation to Catholics. Such incantation is not the evacuation of meaning but its reinforcement.

Why then should some churchmen complain of the 'doublets' in Cranmer and his marvellous capacity to add increments of meaning with each apparent repetition? How can they talk, as the Archbishop of York has done, of 'old-fashioned literary grandeur' as though the grace of words were stuck on as a sort of optional extra, a detachable luxury? It is as if they have suddenly become unable to recognize how form and rhythm drive home the stake of meaning and establish identity. You would think they had never listened to the Beatitudes or enquired why 'beautiful' and 'beatific' come from the same word. The verbal roots of 'good', 'beautiful' and 'blessed' are all intertwined together: *Bonus*, good; *bellus*, beautiful; *beatus*, blessed. In the same way, the root of the word 'grace' means that which is pleasing, that which is blessed, and the act of giving thanks. Worship is *ex gratia*: the grace of beauty and the beauty of grace.

What am I saying about liturgy and about identity? First, liturgy anchors us in signs and images which furnish our mental interior. Then by joining together the holiness of beauty and the beauty of holiness, it introduces the imagination to an infinite world. It takes us up to the margin of transcendence. Cut liturgy down to what we already know and our horizon ceases to extend. The everyday as we know it has been reduced to nothing but the everyday. Here lies the point. What is presented as a linguistic tactic is a vast theological shift. When people are profoundly disturbed by the contemporary changes, they are not only threatened in their identity and their associations. They know the presence is no longer 'manifest'. They mourn a lost horizon of transcendence. I would like to stress the absurdity of retaining some markers of transcendence, particularly special dress, while driving the spiritual force out of the words. By flattening the words (or, more usually, deploying sham antique) the revisers lose their soul but do not gain the world.

I will illustrate how a theological issue can lie even in the shift from 'thou' to 'you'. I am not prepared to go to the stake over 'thou', though there are lots of problems in changing to 'you'. One is the way we slide into giving God orders, as in 'You take away the sins of the world', or else into giving Him information about Himself, as in the new Te Deum: 'You are God and we praise you'. But these wretched infelicities apart, we have lost a special approach to God, both intimate and full of awe. 'Thou' invokes the Most High and speaks of the most inward and personal. Some people stress the loss of awe, some the loss of intimacy. All are aware that a distinctive language has been abolished. To invoke 'thou' was different, just as to kneel was different.

The idea behind such changes seems at first glance admirable. They want to do away with the Church as a distinctive enclosure and eliminate the special character of religious diction and action. The threshold is to be removed; the Communion is to be an ordinary meal, with a loaf passed from hand to hand. (That is supposed to make religion natural and normal, though at most lunches I attend the participants definitely do not rip off bits of bread as they pass the loaf around.) They are trying, in effect, to destroy the *sense of a transition*.

Of course, it is right to see religion as concerned with the whole of life, but that wholeness is channelled and made manifest in the holy place. The special place and the distinctive action and diction build up a tension with the merely mundane and create a change in our perception, an alteration in our experience. The core of religion is in the word 'alter', the 'other', and the church represents an *alternative* and an *alteration*. We are altered and changed. This doesn't mean to say that the alteration may not occur outside the holy place. It is to say that the holy place creates a powerful tension between the local and the universal, and gives to the divine a habitation and a name. Thus, when 'you' is used to speak to God, an extra-ordinary intimacy and an extra-ordinary awe are alike destroyed.

This distinctiveness is not just some archaic carry-over, but just one among all kinds of transitions which we daily achieve by special use of speech and space. Your speech and your comportment alter as you cross the threshold of a neighbour's house, as you sing a pop song or auction a whisky bottle. In church the meditative music, the liturgical poetry, the spatial horizons, the orientation of bodies and architecture towards the east, all open up a new potentiality and a fresh way of seeing. To enter into that does indeed partly cut you off from the merely everyday, but *everything* that opens up the soul also takes you away from those who are not opened up.

Modern revisers have only noticed the disadvantages of the enclosure, and ignored its capacity to put the soul in transit. In so doing they really are destroying the power of 'otherness'. They are trying to eliminate and excise the idea of the Holy.

I have gradually shifted away from a concentration on language to the disposition of space and even the way we use our bodies, for example in prayer. I have suggested that the various alterations we have undergone, whether from kneeling to standing, from facing east to facing each other, from heightened language to prosaic language, all carry theological loadings, each one of which implies the destruction of distinctive religious acts and the erasure of a sense of transition in worship. I should also indicate where all this is leading. It is easy to sense the losses, less easy to discern the directions.

Consider standing and facing each other as compared with kneeling and facing east. The standing in a circle is linked, as often as not, with the 'westward position' in which the priest faces the congregation. There is nothing intrinsically wrong with standing in a half circle or with the westward position, and it is well enough known that many such innovations claim ancient precedent. What is unfortunate is the way certain enlargements are being pressed on us as final and definitive. I have actually heard a learned liturgist and personal friend simultaneously claim that the liturgy has varied with time and place and that now liturgical scholarship has finally reached an agreed norm and standard. Yet each position, facing east or west, or sideways, conveys a facet of meaning. Likewise the fashion of standing for all or a very large part of the service, though paralleled in Eastern Orthodoxy, reduces the range and symbolic impact of the bodily postures we use to engage in prayer, quite apart from the fact that there is nothing distinctive about standing.

These shifts are cumulative and reflect pressures within the contemporary Church very far from the context of primitive Christianity in which some of them were practised. The appeal to primitive practices can obscure the pressures of today which make such practices 'take' with a section of the clergy. We have to concentrate not on this highly selective appeal to the third century, but on the social and theological undertow operating *now*.

The direction of the undertow is towards a new version of sectarianism and a Christian variant of the touchy-feely culture. The sectarian element is symbolized in the closed or semi-closed circle, where the faithful set their backs to the world. This is not a transition; it is a closing off and *closing in*. The westward position can be simply the way the circle is closed on the priestly side. The touchy-feely element is symbolized in the easy tactility of the Kiss of Peace, which assumes the right to intrude on another person's defensible space. It is not that the Kiss of Peace (say) is necessarily wrong in itself, especially if placed at the end of a service, though I can do without it at any time. What is wrong is the way enthusiasts promote a whole pseudo-communitarian ideology, and reinforce it with the cult of their own raw spontaneity. That is not worship but self-indulgence. Characteristically such enthusiasts cannot bear old-fashioned personal responsibility. It is no wonder they approve the replacement of 'I believe' by 'We believe'.

The attack on the 'aesthetic' is also sectarian, because it narrows down the range of response evoked by worship, above all feelings of awe, immensity and the numinous created by heightened language and profound music. The jingles of the new liturgy and guitar music may have a place when it comes to creating camaraderie but they allow no approach to the *mysterium tremendum*. All the rich deposits of music and speech which evoke the transcendent, mark out the religious mode of being and mediate the divine presence are being eroded in favour of an impoverished sectarianism and a clerically orchestrated conviviality. Those who have done this think they are reaching out to the world of the everyday and the modern. That is why they have had the impudence to present their sham antique as modern. In fact, they have reached *out* to nothing, least of all the world. They have simply reached *down* to the mundane.

The last element in the shift to sectarianism is less easy to convey, though easy to sense when you actually participate in the new rites. This element concerns the deepest level of personal identity and the subtler levels of change in the Church. It is found less in the new texts themselves than in the social ambience of the way they are used. When you participate, you are aware of a clerically orchestrated communal consciousness, an attempt to suck you in and eliminate your own personal defensible space. The group is intrusive, pushy, hostile to your feeling for the private and intimate.

This kind of communal consciousness was never specifically Christian, in the past, but something which everywhere preceded the emergence of an individual religious sensitivity and personal conscience. The Church, in fact, tried to urge men and women towards a new personal potentiality in the human relationship to God. By the sixteenth and seventeenth centuries, the potentiality was realized and you may find it articulated in the Book of Common Prayer. The 'I believe' is something we take on ourselves personally, even as we also relate to the corporate life of the Church and assume a place in the wider community. It is precisely this personal conscience or sensitivity which is under attack by the partisans of communal consciousness. Somehow the minister (or president) has become an active leader of this communal feeling, not the one who quietly and unobtrusively represents the Christian body. No doubt, we have a clue here as to why many clergy speak of the need to 'get close' to their congregations, to have, as it were, the various instruments in the orchestra under their direct control. When this is successful, we find the Kiss of Peace used as a technique in creating 'communal consciousness', and for driving up the level of group identification. Anyone sensitive to the direct, intimate and personal awareness of God knows that he is being manipulated by a group leader, and intruded upon. You undergo a subtle and impertinent invasion.

That is only one side of it. On the other side you lose a sense of the wider local community and of what Hooker called the whole 'commonwealth'. This may seem unfair since the revisers undoubtedly want to pray for the wider society and to do so more flexibly and carefully than was previously the case. But what they clearly wish to withdraw from is any sense of being embedded in that wider arch of local attachment and loyalty to the 'commonwealth'. Nothing excites their revulsion more than a reference to the maintenance of 'true religion and virtue'. So the Church becomes merely a pressure group, and loses deep alignments with locality and with nation. This is not to recommend alignments which in the past have often been uncritical and unprophetic or to defend a traditional Church-State alliance. It is to say that the revisers are so aware of a menacing secularity in the larger social world that they lose a vital contact with it, either in the neighbourhood or in the national 'commonwealth'.

The Book of Common Prayer is aware of the personal and the corporate, of the Church and the wider commonwealth. That 'commonwealth' by the way is not only our own nation. It is a common wealth treasured and held in trust and affection by all English-speaking peoples. In this matter I refer to the Authorized Version (or King James Bible) as well as to the Book of Common Prayer. What is going on in Australia, New Zealand, the USA and (soon) Canada, is the engineered dispersal of a joint inheritance, by those appointed as its guardians. In order to pursue ecumenical politics, they have both excised the unique character of the Anglican Church and cut a thread uniting all those who have the privilege of speaking English. Both as a group of peoples and as a Church, we have lost character and definition, simultaneously deprived of continuity in culture and profundity in prayer. That is why this essay has concerned itself with the lost markers of identity as well as the muted signals of the holy. From being a Church with roots, possessing identity and conferring identity, the Church of England, *Ecclesia Anglicana*, could end up as a featureless international sect. And then why should we care for her, or love her?

Gospel Message or Gospel Manifestation

I. R. THOMPSON

Behind the current liturgical controversy lies a deep concern about the *language* of worship. Thus Ian Robinson has argued that the new versions tend to reduce what is supernatural to the level of the merely implausible,[1] and Stella Brook has drawn attention to the widespread and deeply held belief that there is irreverence in addressing God as 'You'.[2] According to Neville Ward, much modern liturgical writing is interesting 'and marvellously forgettable'. Although its words provide us with 'pedestrian instant-comprehension ...what is subtle and complex in the life of faith tends to slip through their large mesh.'[3]

I subscribe to these comments for I believe, with Mary Warnock,[4] that they are part of a great argument in favour of the traditional texts. But I also believe that this argument needs to be set in a wider theological context. What may be termed the language failure of the new versions is, I suggest, just one aspect of a profoundly religious and ultimately eschatological failure – a failure which I would attempt to define as a massive over-emphasis on the gospel as statement or message, and a corresponding very serious neglect of the gospel as *manifestation*. A brief analysis of this term in the New Testament may help to explain what I mean.

The English word *manifestation*, as used in the Authorized Version, is a translation of the Greek *phanerosis* (from *phaneros*, visible). The concept may be traced back to the

Old Testament 'theophanies' or manifestations of God, like those in the burning bush or on Sinai, but it is only with the advent of Christianity that the idea seems to acquire verbal precision. In its various forms (*manifestation*, *manifest*, *manifested*) the term is used in the New Testament on no less than thirty occasions. When applied to man and his conduct it is closely associated with the Synoptic teaching of necessary fruits ('every good tree bringeth forth good fruit; but a corrupt tree bringeth forth evil fruit', Matt. 7:17), so that, for example, St Paul can talk of the works of the flesh being manifest (Gal. 5:14). When applied to the Church or the gospel it invariably denotes a visible sign of the power or righteousness of the Kingdom, for example, 'Neither hath this man sinned, nor his parents: but that the works of God should be made manifest in him' (John 9:13). In this sense, all the recorded acts of Jesus may be described as manifestations of his divinity and supernatural power.

Manifestation implies glory – 'this beginning of miracles did Jesus in Cana of Galilee, and manifested forth his glory' John 2:11 – and also, paradoxically, a strong element of secrecy. Manifestations are esoteric symbols, arcane mysteries, either restricted to a privileged circle or displayed more widely in a veiled manner so that their true significance is grasped only by believers (for belief confers insight). The complete manifestation of Christ's own person was granted to just three of the apostles, and the resurrection appearances, except in one instance, were also peculiarly private events. Indeed, the air of mystery which surrounds the resurrection appearances is heightened by the suggestion of initial concealment. Mary in the garden, the disciples on he road to Emmaus, the apostles on the lake, all fail to recognize Jesus when they first see him. And when we turn from private to public contexts the manner of the disclosure changes significantly. Nowhere in public does Jesus manifest himself directly. Always the disclosure is by representative actions or 'mighty works', each of which points beyond itself to some inner mystery or secret of the Kingdom. It is perhaps significant that the so-called nature miracles, which involve more obvious disclosures than the healing miracles, are performed apparently at night and only in the presence of the Twelve. Sometimes the Kingdom is manifested by means which are, on the face of it, quite non-miraculous. Among such episodes we may presumably include the plucking of corn on the Sabbath (by which Jesus manifests his Lordship of the Sabbath), the cleansing of the Temple, the triumphal entry into Jerusalem and the curious episode of the woman taken in adultery, where Jesus stoops to write in the dust. In all these cases we are reminded of the parables: there is the same emphasis on pictorial demonstration, the same intention simultaneously to reveal and to conceal. The consistency of technique is obvious and striking. As the Tractarian writer Isaac Williams observed:

> Our blessed Lord is, as it were, throughout the inspired writings, hiding and concealing Himself, and going about (if I may so speak reverently) seeking to whom He may disclose Himself ... [Likewise] in our Lord's ordinary walk and mode of life among men He very studiously and remarkably concealed His ineffable majesty under the appearance of common humanity, accompanied with great goodness. Though these two points are different, yet they involve one common principle.[5]

In fact, as Williams hints, the paradoxical nature of manifestation stems directly from the paradoxical nature of the incarnation. God, who is pure Spirit, takes flesh and becomes visible; yet being visible He remains still concealed: 'the world knew him not' John 1:10. Paradoxically too, this very concealment holds promise of awesome disclosure: 'we beheld his glory, the glory as of the only-begotten of the Father' John 1:14. According to this view of things the incarnation is the great Manifestation, of which all the gospel manifestations are but particular examples. Recurring elements are: (1) divine grace; (2) outward expression (compare the sacraments); (3) revelation; (4) secrecy. St Paul summarizes all this (1 Tim. 3:16) in the technical expression, 'God was *manifest* in the flesh.'

Yet manifestation is not confined to the gospels. The tongues of fire which accompany the illapse of the Holy Spirit, the speaking 'with other tongues' (Acts 2:24; 10:46; 19:6), the apostolic miracles and visions – these things manifest the Kingdom in precisely the same way as the gospel manifestations and lead us to an understanding of the Church as the continuation or, more exactly, the fulfilment of the gospel ministry of Christ. Through the communication of the Holy Spirit the Church participates in the divine nature; it continues the process of divine revelation and manifests to its members the Christ whom the Father raised from the dead.

In the context of ordinary Church practice it may be helpful to think of manifestation occurring by two opposite processes, expression and impression, which correspond to the two aspects of a sacrament (expression: the outward sign; impression: the inward grace). Manifestation by expression occurs whenever the Church discloses Christ in realistic symbols, that is, symbols which convey what they signify and which render visible the power of the invisible world. Manifestation by impression occurs as the result of grace working in the individual. One remarks, for example, the ability of word and sacraments to implant the divine image in the mind and the heart, and the capacity for grace itself to become visible in its operations. As the Orthodox theologian Vladimir Lossky has written: 'grace cannot remain hidden or unnoticed; acting in man, changing his nature, entering into a more and more intimate union with him, the divine energies become increasingly perceptible, revealing to man the face of the living God...'.[6] These truths are proclaimed especially in the Eucharist, by which the Church manifests Christ under the visible symbols of bread and wine. (As at Emmaus, and perhaps elsewhere among the resurrection appearances, Christ is 'known' – i.e. recognized – in the 'breaking of bread'.) To all this may be added the fact that the Church itself reflects the divine image. In the words of St Paul, it manifests 'a sweet savour (Greek 'odour') of Christ...in every place' (2 Cor. 2:14) and expresses 'the *fullness* of him that filleth all in all' (Eph. 1:23). It does this not just by particular acts but by its very nature. Like the incarnate Word, the Church *is* manifestation. To quote Lossky again: 'all that can be asserted or denied about Christ can equally well be applied to the Church, inasmuch as it is a theandric organism, or, more exactly, a created nature inseparably united to God in the hypostasis of the Son.'[7]

The concept of manifestation is particularly helpful in explaining the mode of operation of the primitive Church in the period following the great persecutions. There is a strong urge to mystery and secrecy (as exemplified by the *disciplina arcani* and the strict privacy of the Eucharist), coupled with a remarkable and growing tendency to give outward expression to the supernatural realities of the faith. The Church pictorializes and sacramentalizes as the gospel manifestations pictorialize and sacramentalize. Partly but not entirely in response to heresy it emphasizes its own Catholicity and 'visibility'. It worships liturgically. It re-enacts, for example, by means of the liturgical calendar. It seeks to embody the vision in music, art and architecture. It evinces a growing interest in such things as monasticism, mysticism, the Real Presence, visible tokens of sanctity. It struggles not just to preach but to manifest the gospel in tangible, complex and symbolic fashion and to invest the tangible with supernatural power. One may surmise that with the passage of time this principle becomes largely subconscious, but the urge to 'baptize' or spiritualize matter, to pictorialize and dramatize, remains very strong (modern European drama begins in the Church). I am not, let me add, seeking to justify every aspect of medieval Christianty, or, indeed, every attempt to manifest. With the waning of the Middle Ages comes the waning of the vision and the Church first begins to walk, and then increasingly fails to walk, a tightrope between visible spirituality and religious carnality. All I would urge is that the instinct to manifest is good and God-given and, when used as it is meant to be used, the means of giving effect to a great gospel principle. Moreover, musically at least, this principle showed itself capable of further healthy development, as the great polyphonic works of Tallis, Byrd, Palestrina and Victoria amply demonstrate.

Indeed, except in terms of some great theological principle like manifestation, how *does* one attempt to account for the extraordinary flowering, over such a long period, of Christian art and music? It is difficult to believe that these things were merely the response of the Church to the problem of mass-illiteracy. Music and architecture, for example, are hardly to be reckoned among the pictorial or storytelling arts. The very scale and energy of this cultural outpouring, and especially of architectural enterprise during the High Middle Ages, cry out for some weighty theological explanation, as does the self-sufficiency of great art, the sense of an artistic masterpiece as valid in itself. A great Christian painting, for exampe, is not merely a didactic device. It possesses, as the iconoclasts knew only too well, a curious power of attraction, a capacity to speak for itself irrespective of any literary or liturgical context. As Lossky remarks: 'An icon or a cross does not exist merely to direct our imagination during our prayers. It is a material centre in which there reposes an energy, a divine force, which unites itself to human art.'[8]

In fact art fulfils all the conditions necessary for manifestation. It possesses to a remarkable degree the capacity to render truth visible or, in the case of music, to embody truth in the physical properties of sound. Through art one is able to demonstrate the relation of the absolute to phenomena, of God to the universe. As in the created world, so in great art, the material is permeated by the spiritual, by those manifestations of the divine energy which, though in a sense hidden, are yet capable of being perceived. For art, like the gospel manifestations, appeals secretly. To appreciate the vision of the artist one must be capable, in spiritual terms, of responding to it. To see a holy icon as just another representation of Christ is, in religious terms, not to see it at all. It is 'perceived' only when it becomes a point of vital contact between Christ and the soul, that is, when it awakens a 'sympathetic' or answering vision in the beholder. At the same time, and because the soul aspires, seeking through grace what is beyond itself, art, like religion, has an educative function: to cleanse and refine the sensibilities, preparing them for higher and higher manifestations of the divine energy. Art appeals to what is latent in man and seeks to draw it out. There can be few Europeans who have not experienced something of the chastening and uplifting power of a great cathedral or who have never been stirred by the glories of sacred music. Evidence of the widespread impact of sacred art is to be found in the extraordinary care which is still lavished (and not just by churchgoers) on our ancient parish churches. Though Wulfstan of Worcester saw church building as a misguided and perverse activity, a labouring 'to heap up stones', ordinary folk tend to think otherwise. Deep within the psyche is an obscure understanding of the worth of such things.

This leads me back to the question of religious language. For if liturgy exists pre-eminently to *manifest* then it requires a language which, like the language of art or poetry, is complex, potent, rich in suggestion and in the ability to enshrine hidden truth. It must be capable, as it were, of manifesting the glory beneath the symbol. As Professor David Martin has written:

> A distinctive language provides one major threshold to a new awareness. We hear, as George Steiner puts it, 'the prayer in the syntax'. It contains images of vision and alteration, a *double entendre*, an intimation of glory. Overhearing that prayerful syntax even the most casual passer-by, obsessed with the utilitarian and the pragmatic, can catch the hint of glory, even if he gives it no philosophic weight. He is momentarily glad that other

> things are here remembered and that all the layers of man's search for meaning are summed up. Perhaps for a brief second the shape of stone, or sense of rhythm, allows him to stand recollected, noticing in himself the emergence of a new being which otherwise is buried in tussle and hassle. In the creation of that moment of recollection language and posture provide the sacramental instruments. A man or woman is overtaken by an interior quiet, made manifold in the rhythm and movement of words. The word is made flesh and the figures of speech allow transfiguration...[9]

It is hardly necessary to remark that the new liturgies have been constructed on linguistic and also theological principles which are diametrically opposed to those we have been considering. The trend is not towards but away from glory, transcendence, transfiguration. Manifestation gives way to 'message' and 'situation worship', the former arguing a one-dimensional view of religious truth, as of something immediately accessible in terms of content and therefore requiring extreme simplicity of expression. From being richly implicit, the language of worship becomes startlingly, often embarrassingly, explicit. However discredited the position of the biblical fundamentalist, here at least the fundamentalist mentality lives on. One notes especially the supercharged statements of the obvious ('This is the word of the Lord'; 'This is the Gospel of Christ') and what can only be described as a regrettable tendency to foster the 'hearty' voice, as in 'The Lord is here', which clearly invites a high fortissimo on the word 'Lord' and 'It is indeed right, it is our duty and our joy...'.

Equally regrettable is the compulsive tendency of the revisers to change relative clauses into main clauses so that instead of saying: 'who art' and 'which is', we now say: '*You* are', '*This* is'. For this represents a break with a linguistic principle which has always, and for very good reason, tended to govern the formulation of Christian prayer. Simplify language in this way and you abolish (and therefore seem to deny) the ontological dimension – the awareness of the eternal, the abiding, of that which is too great and too mysterious to allow, in human terms, of complete predication. The result is to present the religious experience as something almost childish and infra-rational. The very syntax of Series 3 kills manifestation stone dead.

A similar tendency to treat religious truth as mere 'message' is observable in the new translations of the Bible. The gospels in the New English Bible (NEB), for example, attempt to mediate religious epic in a style that is anything but epic. The consistent hint of underlying glory, which is so notable a feature of the gospels in the Authorized Version (and also, I would add, in the original Greek[10]), is sacrificed time and again to a misplaced desire for 'accessibility'. It is a desire which is nearly always self-frustrating. Instead of revealing what is latent in the gospels, the new versions set out mindlessly to destroy it. They violate the very conditions under which, in such contexts, revelation is alone possible. For manifestation does not hide in order to obscure; it hides in order to reveal. The 'hidden' element in the gospel manifestations is not a negation; it is a dimension. Always the glory is there – for those who have eyes to see and ears to hear. Particularly it shines forth in the majestic quality of our Lord's utterance: 'Never man spake like this man'. What modern translation can do to that utterance is well demonstrated in the following passage from Ian Robinson's book *The Survival of English*:

> In the NEB Satan tries to establish a feudal system with Jesus as a vassal, but Jesus says, after the manner of the Victorian damsel, rebuking the importunate villain, 'Begone Satan! Scripture says...' (Matthew 4:10). A similar girlish gush ends the first chapter of the Sermon on the Mount: 'You must therefore be all goodness, just as your heavenly Father is all good' (Matthew 5:48). There is also something very Victorian-governessy here:

'Then I will tell them to their face, "I never knew you: out of my sight, you and your wicked ways!"' (Matthew 7:23).[11]

One is obliged to ask: can these be the accents (or even the remotest echo of the accents) of the incarnate Word? The question surely answers itself. Whatever else may be postulated about Jesus, one thing is tolerably certain: he never spoke like this. The failure of style here is also a failure of the religious imagination, a failure to *visualize* Jesus. Something has gone wrong not just at the theological level but also, one feels, at the devotional level as well.

Such failures are serious, not least because they may be seen as symptoms of a widespread failure to manifest which seems increasingly to afflict Western Christianity. For manifestation is the guarantee of the Church's authenticity, the means by which religious truth is objectively demonstrated. Through manifestation the Church declares itself to be what it is: the living vehicle of divine revelation. Conversely, failure to manifest not only drives the religious experience inwards so that it becomes highly subjective, it also allows a serious element of philosophic disharmony to intrude itself into the Christian position. Forgetting or unlearning that most basic of truths, that the natural world is also, in some mysterious way, the repository or manifestation of the supernatural, the worshipping community comes gradually to envisage the cosmos as other than it is (commonly as a kind of clockwork mechanism) and employs new aids to worship with little attempt to evaluate the intrinsic worth of such aids. Spiritual discernment gives way to pragmatism and utilitarianism (if people 'respond' to it, if it helps to put the message across, then it must be 'good'). False 'icons' are thus substituted for true ones and secularism increasingly invades and destroys the domain of the sacred.

I began by referring to the two aspects of manifestation – the divine and the human – and some attempt must now be made to bring these two aspects together. Manifestation, in the sense in which the term is used in the New Testament is, I suggest, a vital aspect of the moral universe, for it witnesses to the inevitable process by which all things declare themselves to be what they are. Just as God manifests His goodness in Christ and in creation, so, for better or worse, man too manifests his own moral nature. As the Jesuit poet Gerard Manley Hopkins argued:

> Each mortal thing does one thing and the same:
> Deals out that being indoors each one dwells;
> Selves – goes itself; *myself* it speaks and spells,
> *Crying what I do is me: for this I came.*

Thus too:

> ...the just man justices;
> Keeps grace: that keeps all his goings graces;
> Acts in God's eye what in God's eye he is –
> Christ – for Christ plays in ten thousand places,
> Lovely in limbs and lovely in eyes not his
> To the Father through the features of men's faces.[12]

Through grace, redeemed humanity struggles to manifest the good, the light, the necessary fruits of the new life. Always the urge is to express, to release into the visible world that which is within. Indeed the Christian is commanded to manifest his works: to let his light shine before men, though, as with the divine manifestations, such light will shine secretly in an unbelieving world and the works themselves will have about them an element of deliberate secrecy. It needs to be argued that the rediscovery, at all levels, of the secret element in religion is the way back to manifestation, to a proper concept of the sacred, and to the fullness and mystery of the Christian life.

NOTES

1 Ian Robinson, *The Survival of English* (Cambridge, 1973), pp. 35–9.

2 Stella Brook, *The Language of the Book of Common Prayer* (London, 1965), pp. 53–4.

3 J. Neville Ward, *The Following Plough* (London, 1978), p. 113.

4 Mary Warnock, 'Ancient and Modern', *PN Review*, no. 13.

5 Isaac Williams, *Tracts for the Times No 87: On Reserve in Communicating Religious Knowledge*, pp. 6–7. He adds:

> It is evident that in some sense even now the manifestation of Himself must be according to some law of exceeding reserve and secrecy, for our Lord has said that if any man will keep His commandments He will love him, and will manifest Himself unto him; that He would "manifest Himself to His disciples and not unto the world." Now as it is too obvious that many do not keep His commandments, therefore to many He is not manifested. So that to us all, even now, our Lord observes this rule of concealing Himself even in His manifestations: and therefore all His manifestations in His Church are ways of reserve. (p. 114)

6 Vladimir Lossky, *In the Image and Likeness of God* Oxford 1974), p. 59.

7 Vladimir Lossky, *The Mystical Theology of the Eastern Church* (Cambridge, 1957), p. 187.

8 ibid. p. 189.

9 David Martin, editorial, *PN Review*, no. 13, p. 3.

10 On this point we may note the judgement of John Donne, Dean of St Paul's 1621–31, and on any reckoning a major poet and theologian. Commenting on the tendency of some pagans to undervalue the Scriptures because they knew them only in inferior translations, he remarks:

> ...howsoever the Christians at first were fain to sink a little under that imputation, that their Scriptures have no Majesty, no eloquence, because these embellishments could not appeare in Translations, nor they then read Originalls, yet now, that a perfect knowledge of those languages hath brought us to see the beauty and the glory of those Books, we are able to reply to them, that there are not in all the

world so eloquent Books as the Scriptures; and that nothing is more demonstrable, then that if we would take all those Figures, and Tropes, which are collected out of secular Poets, and Orators, we may give higher, and livelier examples, of every one of those Figures, out of the Scriptures, then out of all the Greek and Latine Poets, and Orators; and they mistake it much, that thinke, that the Holy Ghost hath rather chosen a low, and barbarous, and homely style, then an eloquent, and powerfull manner of expressing himselfe.

11 Ian Robinson, *Survival of English*, p. 35.

12 Gerard Manley Hopkins, 'As kingfishers catch fire, dragonflies draw flame'.

Our Fathers, Often Faithless Too

MARGARET DOODY

Faith of our fathers, living still
In spite of dungeon, fire and sword...

So we sing in hope, at this point of crisis in the Anglican and Episcopal Churches, hoping that the faith will still survive this most startling onslaught, the attack from within. What we are seeing in this crisis is a recurrence in a most extreme form of a temptation to which we have nearly succumbed before. I think that today we might usefully focus on another period in the history of our Church, a phase of trouble which seems to me to offer a parallel to our own. Not all of our fathers were always faithful.

There are several reasons for looking at our history at this point. For one thing, as an academic I of course believe that something can be learned from history. And our oppressors – those who are bearing down on us with such force with their new prayer book – not only think they have history on their side, but are also convinced that we – their victims – know nothing of history and are incapable of analysing it, incapable of seeing their own activities in the light of history, of causes and connections. It is time to remind them that we do know something about it, and can subject their doings to an historical analysis that goes beyond the moment. They are naturally much happier with a skewed historical view which

A slightly shorter version of this paper was given as an address at a rally in Savannah, Georgia, in March 1981.

gives the utmost value to the 'modern', the 'contemporary' and 'relevant'; they like to treat the present as an island of time sundered from the past and are always inviting us too to take that dangerous and phantasmal ground. Such a view offers countless opportunities to repeat old errors; history is then really a trap, an invisible labyrinth in which the fancied 'progress' is along old dead-end passages, 'in wand'ring mazes lost'.

> After such knowledge, what forgiveness? Think now
> History has many cunning passages, contrived corridors
> And issues; deceives with whispering ambitions,
> Guides us by vanities.[1]

It is also good to get clear in our minds the fact that what is 'with it' for one or two generations can seem palpable folly a hundred years later so that we are not rendered helpless by appeals to progress and to fashion. There have been various phases in the life of the whole Catholic Church when doctrine was rescued only under protest from those who thought they had social and intellectual fashion on their side. I intend to consider here only one of those phases, a recent one in the long view, because it is part of the history of our own Anglican-Episcopal Church, and because what happened then is very close to what is happening now. Our sister Churches, Roman Catholic and Protestant, of course have similar temptations and problems, but it is our particular duty to contemplate the temptations and flaws in the Anglican and Episcopal Churches, to see the sins typical of our own tradition.

The historical parallel may soberly hearten us. The faith was in a parlous state before in our Church in England and America, but it survived. Fashionableness tried to subvert doctrine, but did not ultimately succeed. Yet the price was heavy, and the matter was not over, as the recurrence of problems in our day now makes clear. It may do some good to point out to those in power in our Church at present that their beliefs and practices bear a striking resemblance to beliefs and practices that they themselves would officially condemn. In our present affliction we can see a recurrence of a particularly Anglican and Episcopal pattern of concealed sin and high-class folly.

The period of crisis in the past to which I allude is the period stretching from the late seventeenth through the eighteenth century. Church history of that period shows us a time of unacknowledged perversion of doctrine in the name of good social and moral intentions. There is not sufficient time to go into all the origins and processes of this cracking-up. My summary will inevitably be a crude sketch. Briefly, the history can be described as follows.

During the English Civil War of the 1640s and its aftermath, Anglican theology underwent a crisis of confidence. Partly because of what was seen as perversions of the doctrines of grace and faith in various Protestant sects in mid-century, grace became an embarrassing concept. Increasing emphasis was placed on duty, good will and good works. I refer you to Dr C. F. Allison's excellent book, *The Rise of Moralism* (1966) for a full analysis of the problems of the later seventeenth-century Anglican theology. We may see in what happened yet another exhibition of the constant temptation of English-speaking peoples to swerve towards the Pelagian heresy, the belief that a Good Man pulls himself up to being Even Better Man by his own bootstraps. As Dr Allison points out, 'sin' became identified with particular transgressions only, with the *phenomena* of sin, and the individual was exhorted to behave well *before* approaching God. Goodness then tends to become 'virtue'; human-centred virtue can be seen in individual actions which are measurable, capable of being reckoned up. With another slight turn of the wheel, Christianity could be seen only as the book of rules for right conduct. Jesus Christ as Person became only a model of behaviour. Christ in His divinity, His Godhead, was seen primarily, even only, as a lawgiver. The doctrine of Atonement goes by the board. John Locke thought that

Christ came to give human beings 'a clear knowledge of their duty'; Christ gave us 'a morality'.[2] Locke was only one of the many writers (including divines and philosophers) who repeated this idea. Now that we have a morality we can get on with it, and be good. As Allison points out, the definition of Christianity as a morality is dangerous and untrue.

> Morality is deprived of its roots, and is disastrously separated from orthodox Christian dogma. This was the origin and curse of the moralism which now is ascendant in the West. It exhorts a power of freedom that fallen man does not possess; it is a religion of control...and not of redemption, and it ends in despair rather than in hope.[3]

The possibility of lurking despair was not, of course, seen by the exponents of what seemed the bright new refreshing doctrine of world-pleasing and world-suiting works. The bishops appointed by King Charles II (who had an eye for picking the right men for the job) were, naturally enough and in all good conscience, interested in making the Established Church a good organ of social order. So too were their successors, picked by the pragmatic and Protestant King William III (1688–1702). It should be noted that a number of churchmen who made headway in their careers under Charles II attained their highest preferment under William. Most of these had taken the oaths of allegiance to the intervening monarch, Charles's Roman Catholic brother James II (1685–88). When James was overthrown and William came to power in the Glorious Revolution of 1688–89, a small number of clergy felt that they could not take the new oaths as they had made solemn oaths of allegiance to the previous king (who was still alive) and they would thus be breaking their word. These conscientious Anglican clerics are known as the Non-jurors (i.e. non-swearers). They were deprived of their benefices. The most famous of them is Bishop Thomas Ken,[4] hymn writer and author of *The Practice of Divine Love.*

His upright and consistent conduct through four reigns is an encouraging example during some rather sorry times and Vicar-of-Bray manoeuvrings. The Non-jurors, who took things like oaths seriously, were not Latitudinarians.

After the excesses of the Commonwealth period, 'grace', 'enthusiasm' and 'mystery' were associated with sects politically dangerous to the state. Not only that – the Church's leaders saw a good new world potentially arising from the proper practices of a Christianity which placed no impediments in the way of what men of the new era wanted. The divines who flourished at the end of the seventeenth century were neither hypocrites nor Machiavellian manipulators. Many, like John Tillotson (1630–94) who became Archbishop of Canterbury (1691–4), were great preachers, and their sermons continued to be given from many English pulpits through the next century. They and their successors did their best to give the English Church a new tone, a forward-looking manner, getting rid of encumbrances and falling in with the 'truths' which the world around them, their society, was pointing out. We should be tender to and forgiving of our present ecclesiastics – though we should have to look hard to find any Tillotsons preaching among them – remembering their predecessors, who were entirely sincere in opening the door to the Deists, and then in following those same Deists whom they had partly brought into being. Never underestimate the appeal of contemporary fashion. The with-it has a perfectly genuine appeal to men who truly mean well.

These divines and those who thought like them I shall call Latitudinarians, using the traditional term – men of latitude, who regarded beliefs and forms of worship as things indifferent. What these Latitudinarians saw in Christianity was what many men around them wanted to see. The era was a time of unprecedented economic expansion, from the end of the seventeenth century right through to the 1770s. It was the era which saw the emergence of the British Empire. The dominant public social and philosophical emphasis was on the practical and the socially useful. Christianity had to be rescued, had to be made to fit in with a world that was rational, forward-looking and practical. The theology was a theology of works.

One trouble with a theology which bases everything squarely on 'good works' alone is that the definition of 'good works' is likely to be supplied by the dominant and articulate classes of contemporary society, and by local and temporary trends. The divines saw a splendid opportunity to insist on rules of right behaviour, and right behaviour became socially useful behaviour. Christ became less important, even something of a stumbling-block (to the Greeks foolishness), for his conduct is hard to square with the genially useful. Christ then became increasingly remote. We see instead in the works of Tillotson and others the benevolent God who has made sure that following his rules is easy, conformable to our natures, socially desirable *and* socially and psychologically comfortable. As Tillotson says, in a sermon typically entitled 'The Precepts of Christianity not Grievous',

> There is nothing in all these Laws but what is most reasonable and fit to be done by us, nothing but if we were to consult our own interest and happiness...we would choose for ourselves; nothing but what is easy to be understood, and as easy to be practis'd by an honest and a willing mind.
>
> Now the practice of all these is suitable to our nature, and agreeable to the frame of our understandings; proper to our condition and circumstances in this world, and preparatory to our happiness in the next.... Our very natural reason...is an enemy to all these sins, and a law against all these vices.
>
> And as the practice of all piety and virtue is agreeable to our reason, so it is likewise for the interest of mankind; both of private persons and of publick Societies.... Some virtues plainly tend to the preservation of our

> health, others to the improvement and security of our estates, all to the peace and quiet of our minds, and, which is somewhat more strange, to the advancement of our esteem and reputation; for though the world be generally bad...yet I know not how it comes to pass, men are commonly so just to virtue and goodness, as to praise it in others even when they do not practise it themselves.[5]

This sounds very nice, but it has one slight defect, namely that most of it is not true. God's law is not always easy to be practised. The pleasing notion that the good man gets along very well socially is often contradicted by experience. But unpleasant experience was rationalized away by countless divines (and Deist philosophers) who repeated the rational and pleasing idea. If the good man gets along cheerfully and well, then Christ is an embarrassment, an irritating anomaly. How did our Founder, far from advancing his peace, reputation and esteem, lack sufficient contrivance to keep out of gaol? And why did he lack the elementary social sense that keeps a man from getting messily executed?

An unconscious sub-text of all such preachments is the Practice of the Distance of God. Basil Willey has captured the tendency in a nice phrase when he writes of the eighteenth century's assurance 'of immunity from disturbing contacts with the transcendental'.[6] Martyrs are unnecessary in polite society, and sacraments barbarous. If we go along in our own good grooves, there is no way for Christ to come to us, and no need that he should do so. In fact, the preachments urge him to keep away as far as possible, entering into the picture only as a kind of brand name of respectability stamped on our morality. What the divines were preaching was a good comfortable doctrine. It was especially good for the rich and successful. Over and over again they, and the Deist philosophers, address themselves to *gentlemen*, in the serene belief that God himself must approve of gentlemen, even that God must be one. Richard Steele in *The Christian Hero* (1701) spends considerable effort in defending Christ and St Paul as gentlemen, admitting as a kind of obstacle to belief the fact that 'the Heathen struts, and the Christian sneaks, in our Imagination.'[7] His enterprise supplies an egregious example of the with-it which soon becomes anachronistic, even comic; Steele now seems much more antiquated than St Paul.

But the dominant social ideal of the eighteenth century was the gentleman, the landed gentleman imitating God in caring for his estate and being glorified. The gentleman is educated, urbane, benevolent and powerful. He represented a new phase of the aristocratic ideal. The world offered a new model of the good, and of the good man, which official Anglicanism, in order to be 'with it' felt almost irresistibly compelled to accept. The 'gentleman' seemed so indisputably right. How could Christianity, without making itself look peculiar, bring itself to question him? The Good Man as Gentleman is so strikingly God-like, dispensing justice, dispensing favours, making the earth yield her fruits by smiling upon them. He is God-like, not Christ-like; no need for any agonies in his garden. The whole idea of goodness in this period becomes associated with what is god-like, powerful and serene. The good works are so clear, and heavenly approval so certain. As Pope (with a touch of blasphemy) describes the good man in general:

> Earth smiles around, with boundless bounty blest,
> And Heav'n beholds its image in his breast.[8]

Anglicanism, tumbling over itself to fit in with the new age and its dominant fashions, insensibly became a religion made to fit the upper and upper-middle classes. It is of course notorious that our Church in this period became an avenue of employment for younger sons of gentlemen, that livings were pocketed in lieu of estates and that most of the real work of the real Church was done by underpaid curates. God, the gentlemen's god, taking his cue from the contemporary world, did not see much wrong with this. God became the gentleman's polite deity, approving benevolence, hospitality and land improvement. (God was oddly slow to say anything against slavery or against the land enclosures which deprived the poor of their means of living and sent them thronging into the new slums of London.) God would not be so ungentlemanly as to impose duties which did not pay off, or deprivations or afflictions without immediate use. There is no salvation outside the social sphere, and no good without visible usefulness. New philosophers (Deist and agnostic) clarified this cheerful system of morality:

> Celibacy, fasting, penance, mortification, self-denial, humility, silence, solitude, and the whole train of monkish virtues; for what reason are they everywhere rejected by men of sense, but because they serve no manner of purpose; neither advance a man's fortune in the world, nor render him a more valuable member of society; neither qualify him for the entertainment of company, nor increase his powers of self-enjoyment? We observe, on the contrary, that they cross all these desirable ends...We justly, therefore, transfer them to the opposite column, and place them in the catalogue of vices....[9]

So says the philosopher David Hume in his *Enquiry concerning the Principles of Morals* (1751). Virtue has by now been equated with what men of sense (or gentlemen of sense) really do. The old 'monkish virtues' do not fit in to the picture. Presumably Christ's life according to such a scheme is vicious, or at least quite wrong-headed. We knew in the eighteenth century what virtue is. 'Personal Merit consists altogether in the possession of mental qualities, *useful* or *agreeable* to the *person himself* or to *others*.'[10] Broad-thinking Anglican divines of the eighteenth century could not go quite all the way with David Hume, as they had to make a bit of room for revelation, or an apology for

Christianity, but they went as far as they could. Hume, after all, was only following Tillotson and similar divines. They too believed in the useful, the agreeable and the social. Christianity is only right action, that is, actions and attitudes which contemporary fashion believed in.

Official Anglicanism at this point was, as now, nervously in love with the world. It believed, just as now, that the world, the outside world of progress and rationality, really had all the answers, and that episcopal Christianity had to conform to that world, or it would perish. The approved social forms and formulae and norms of the time were somewhat different, of course, from those in vogue now, in the 1970s and 1980s. I am not accusing those presently in charge of the church's organization of talking about gentlemen, or favouring livings for indigent younger sons. But although the symptoms may be different, the temper is strongly similar. The message is this: *Be ye conformed to the world or the game is up*. At its best, such a Christianity becomes unwittingly a mere elegant decoration of the social and economic system. At its worst, it is a slave to every contemporary fashion, centreless, veering at the mercy of any wind that blows strongly enough to catch it. The world, far from being our adversary along with the flesh and the devil, is now our guide, philosopher and friend. The world is implicitly submitted to as the *real* source and end and test of truth, to which Christ too must submit. Whatever in Christianity does not fit in must be overlooked. Christianity is tested by social usefulness and agreeableness.

An inevitable concomitant of this frame of mind, then and now, is an increasing secularization of practice and ritual. The sacraments become, like Christ, a practical embarrassment. Their 'usefulness', or even reality, is dubious. In eighteenth-century churches, churchgoers were confronted with the tables of the Law at the east end of the building, overpowering the Communion table. The crucifix was absent. Crucifix and Communion were felt to be disturbing, puzzling, even of uncertain significance. The Law makes sense. The

Eucharist, commonly called the Lord's Supper, was celebrated less and less frequently, and in the works of many Anglican commentators became merely a commemoration. This sacrament had suffered a grievous blow in being used for political purposes. Taking Communion in an Anglican Church twice a year was, after the Restoration of 1660, a test for eligibility for political office. It is doubtless deeply true that the sacrament of the Eucharist undergoing this distortion was surrounded by an aura of unease. The unease arising from deep abuse combined with the new practicality and sociable emphasis to displace or remove the sacramental. Churchgoing was treated pragmatically, in terms of the pleasure it affords and its social use. It was thought to keep the lower orders up to the mark, create a good 'cheerful' social atmosphere and unite the community in reminding all of their duties. In Joseph Addison's words:

> It is certain the Country-People would soon degenerate into a kind of Savages and Barbarians, were there not such frequent Returns of a stated Time, in which the whole Village meet together with their best Faces, and in their cleanliest Habits, to converse with one another upon indifferent Subjects, hear their Duties explained to them, and join together in Adoration of the Supreme Being.[11]

No mention, you see, of any contact with Christ. The idea of the sacramental provides a disturbing element which must be tamed. Bishop Hoadly in *A Plain Account of the Nature and End of the Sacrament* (1735) explained away the sacrament of Holy Communion (which had become 'the' sacrament) in a rigorously memorialist account, thus paraphrased and endorsed by Henry Fielding the novelist:

> What could tend more to the noble purpose of religion than frequent cheerful meetings among the members of a society, in which they should, in the presence of one

another, and in the service of the Supreme Being, make promises of being good, friendly and benevolent to each other?[12]

In this overwhelming bright rush of trouble-free piety, this irresistible modern and right-minded wave of eighteenth-century 'cheerfulness', the orthodox Anglicans might almost be counted a secret Church within the Church. Samuel Johnson, Christian, Anglican, sacramentalist, recognizably belongs to the Church of Donne and T. S. Eliot. And he counted himself as converted by the *Serious Call* (1728) of William Law, a Cambridge MA who would not take the oaths of allegiance to King George I and thus remained outside the Church organization. Much has depended in the past on the work of the laity in keeping the faith alive while our faithless fathers in power rushed into agreeable heresies.

Yet those who then kept the Church alive had what is now being taken away from us – the Book of Common Prayer. The Latitudinarian divines, partly for political reasons, never quite dared to tamper with the Book of Common Prayer itself, though they might write commentaries galore to de-mystify and de-mythologize it. There was indeed some thought of revising the Prayer Book quite drastically around the time of the American War of Independence. Benjamin Franklin and Sir Francis Dashwood collaborated in writing a revised, abridged and unsuperstitious Book of Common Prayer. In the Preface to his *Abridgement*, Franklin urges the appeal of new shortness and cheerfulness: 'the younger sort...would probably more frequently, as well as cheerfully, attend divine service if they were not detained so long at any one time.'[13] Franklin's and Dashwood's revision cut out almost everything that might be offensive to a Deist, including most of the Psalms, which Franklin detested (he had a Deist's aversion to the concept of a chosen people). Most of the Confession went out. Absolution was entirely omitted. The Apostles' Creed was reduced to four lines. The *Abridgement* (a project partly in earnest and probably partly in jest) was published in 1773. It did not catch on. The Episcopal Church was at that time spared the infliction of a Prayer Book devised jointly by America's leading Deist philosopher and England's founder member of the Hell-Fire Club. (The Hell-Fire Club which met at Dashwood's Medmenham Abbey devoted itself to 'philosophical' discussions, strange rituals in monastic costume and bizarre sexual orgies; how much of the accounts of their carryings-on is true is difficult to estimate.) But some of the ideas in Franklin and Dashwood's proposed revision would have had great appeal recently at Minneapolis, and a defender of the new American Prayer Book cites Franklin, without analysis but with approval, in a paragraph designed to prove that revision is a good thing.[14]

Providentially, those who went about instituting a Prayer Book for the now separate Protestant Episcopal Church in America understood the Prayer Book tradition and the Catholic Faith. And during the whole period I have been dealing with, the Church went on, in England and America. The Church was itself, despite attacks and weakening interpretations, in the life of its services, in the life of the Book of Common Prayer. In every parish church the words were said, the liturgy enacted; the sacraments were celebrated in prayers and ritual which went above and beyond contemporary cheerful notions. But the successors of the sociable and cheerful divines, at this moment having power in their hands without restraint, now see, and very logically too, that the way to make their doctrines stick for good is to take the Book of Common Prayer away from us, leaving a 'revision' which is in fact a rewriting of the whole doctrine according to their beliefs.

We see on both sides of the Atlantic these revisers coming down upon us in their zeal. These new Latitudinarians are different from the old ones, naturally. They are aware of the revived Catholic (and Orthodox) tradition in the Anglican and Episcopal churches since the early nineteenth century. So they come sprinkling their discourse with sprigs of St Basil, assuring us that this time they have it right. But their nature is the same. They too believe that Christianity must conform to the world or go under. They too are in favour of what is socially useful (in contemporary eyes) and submit Christianity to the revelation of the world, as the final test, and make the world the source of truth.

Of course, there are obvious differences, and these revised churchmen would be most annoyed if they knew they were being compared to the clergy of the Restoration and the eighteenth century, whom they would claim, most probably, to contemn and condemn. But they are truly *remarkably* like them. Undoubtedly, they are unlike their predecessors in not being fond of the word 'duty'; we are not going to be subjected to sermons on sobriety and benevolence, and certainly not on chastity. But they, too, are graceless moralists who appeal always and finally to the well-being of the community and to contemporary notions of good behaviour and virtue. They come to us talking of tolerance and peace, and are against pollution of the environment. I too am against pollution, and I am certainly not suggesting that tolerance is not a good thing. It is a virtue, just like sobriety and benevolence, which the eighteenth century saw as good things. But these are necessary by-products of Christianity, not the reasons for it. Once implicitly adduced as the *reasons* for Christianity, the basis of it, they become shallow simulacra of themselves, pieces of prudential conduct, or easy attitudes which have nothing to do with Christ. The new moralists approve loving your neighbour, and think (like their predecessors) that this is an easy matter – which it is not. 'Inasmuch as ye have done it unto the least of these....' How am I going to see the face of Christ in all? In the sick man who repels my natural reason aesthetically, in the human individual industrialist who makes products I disapprove of, in the drug-flown mugger who tries to kill me? How am I to reach out to that transcendent charity if Christ has dissolved in the glowing mists of my conscious virtue, my serene right-mindedness? If Christ is merely the rubber stamp endorsing my own opinions? Christianity is reduced to a moralism, mere morality, the rather thin list of any virtues that happen to catch our fancy at any time. Sobriety is good, (but we all know what its negative side is) not that that is our temptation at the moment. Benevolence can turn into harsh paternalism in the flick of an eye. Fashionable virtues do not save. They cannot even be counted on, finally, to make the better society.

My point is that these new zealots for 'revision' of the Prayer Book are laying upon us a dubious and shaky doctrine which shares the old worst traits of Anglicanism gone bad. These new men, like the Latitudinarians before them, lay claim to reason and progress, and also insist that obedience to Christ is an easy matter; cheerful too. In fact, it is not so much a matter of 'obedience', an old-fashioned idea, but we find Christ is going along with us, and we are going along with him, and everything is marvellous, and Heaven beholds its image in our breasts. Would you seek for evidence that such are their beliefs? Look at the new Prayer Book.

These churchmen too are rational anti-sacramentalists, without altogether knowing what they do. (The Restoration and eighteenth-century divines supposed that they had at last got hold of the 'right' and 'reasonable' meaning of 'the' sacrament, had tidied things up.) Would you seek for evidence? Look at the new Prayer Book. The sacraments are absent. God does not, Christ does not do anything so unruly, so ungenteel, as to touch our human lives. Christ himself is not 'incarnate by the Holy Ghost of the Virgin Mary'; his human existence was merely brought about, vaguely, 'by the power of the Holy Spirit', a different proposition. The new Latitudinarian Prayer Book offers us the Practice of the Distance of God. Ritual and God's power are far asunder. Confirmation is no longer a sacrament, conferred through the laying-on of hands; it is a mere renewal of baptismal vows, depending on the candidate's statement. Marriage is no longer a sacrament, but a (rational) covenant. The priesthood as sacramental office has been taken away. Consecration no longer has anything to do with the laying-on of hands, but is enfeebled to a mere petition. The priest is no longer commanded to drive away heresy – logically enough, as any priest who goes along with all this is already *in* heresy. The priest (or 'president') is not given the power to bind and loose. Confession may be heard by a layman, and there is no Absolution. Everywhere we see the signs, again, of our assured 'immunity from disturbing contacts with the transcendental'.

Those who offer us this sweetly reasonable doctrine (they do not see, as Allison does, the despair that is its underside) would not have us dwell on anything unhappy. They give us the lightest and easiest expression of penitence, evidently believing along with Shaftesbury and other eighteenth-century Deists that man is innately good and naturally moral. This in a century which has seen some of the most grievous results of human sin and some of the most terrible human suffering known in history! We are allowed to grumble mildly at the sins of others, those others who are strangely outside this new dispensation of enlightened and cheerful virtue. We are allowed to tell God what to do. But we do *not* say 'There is not health in *us*' nor do we call ourselves 'miserable offenders'. They would not have us have the bad taste to groan over our own state of sin. That is for old-fashioned people of a gloomy cast of mind. They *will* keep us cheerful. Holy Communion is not now to be suppressed by being celebrated infrequently (as in days of yore); it is to be celebrated constantly and lightly – lightly, wantonly and ill-advisedly. It is Eucharist made Easy, all done in the jolliest manner. The designers of the new Prayer Book ensure that things are kept on an even, happy-making tone, without any chance of real drama, of inner struggle or seriousness. They ensure this by the flat, banal and disjointed language, the distortions of the rite, even by the perpetual busy-ness of the doings and the congregation's hopping about from page to page, from section to section. It does not take a literary critic to realize that the printed format is a defiantly discontinuous text, insisting on disintegrated and non-dramatic reading, and claiming that continuity, drama and devotion are invalid. Nothing of importance is to happen in this service. The business of the Peace (that handshake all round) makes sure that thoughts and devotions get interrupted, and we cannot try to concentrate on Christ. We are once again being invited into church for 'frequent cheerful meetings among the members of a society, in which they should, in the presence of one another, and in the service of the Supreme Being, make promises of being good, friendly and benevolent to each other'. Not, you observe, in the presence of God, but primarily in the presence of each other, and secondarily in the service of that vague Supreme Being. Christ does, of course, often get a mention in the new book, but the theology is basically good-works and Supreme-Being theology. Christ did something rather embarrassing and painful, but we, chock-full of cheerfulness and living in polite society, can be assured of not doing the same. If that is all there is to the sacrament of Holy Communion, the Anglican and Episcopal Churches can erase themselves within two generations. There are better places for cheerful meetings, and, if that is all it boils down to, better ways of spending one's time. There is nothing in these services for those in affliction, nothing here for sin and sorrow.

The Latitudinarian version of the English church, the construct and concept of our faithless forefathers, was (as we can see with hindsight), a church for the rich, the healthy and the comfortable. So too is this one. Our new reformers would be the first to cast scorn on the blatant importance of the idea of 'the gentleman' in treatises of the older period. But what do they offer but a counterpart? The new services are really services for the enlightened professional person, somewhat educated and abreast of the times. This ideal member of the congregation is also in good health, with good prospects and without any serious spiritual ache. These are not services for St Augustine or St Theresa or John Donne or George Herbert or Samuel Johnson or Simone Weil.

'We're pretty good as we are, aren't we?' is the notion behind the Communion service. O God, we are B plus or A minus if not straight As. For all the pious contemporary chat about the oppressed – and our oppressors assume at the moment a mighty superior tone on this matter – no use has been made of the experience of those in our midst who have lived in suffering and sorrow. The whole history of the black Christians in America, a history of affliction, and of the transcendent touched in affliction, has been ignored. They were never consulted in the making of the new American Prayer Book. Sometimes spirituals are included in services, but it is evident that their meaning has not been heard.

> Were you there when they crucified my Lord?
> Oh! Sometimes it causes me to tremble, tremble, tremble,

as the spiritual goes. No. Those who take part in this new service were *not* there when they crucified our Lord, and nothing causes us to tremble.

> And in my prosperity I said, I shall never be moved
> (Psalm 30:6).

Our pastors and masters remain unmoved when they hear the cry from Church members who protest that we live in affliction with this new book which gives us another doctrine. This new Prayer Book is a last-gasp version of enlightened moralism, so enfeebled that no one will pretend to instruct us in our 'duties' (that word is so unfashionable now) but will hope to distract us into being well-meaning and useful members of society, without any private 'enthusiasm'. They have taken away the sacraments. They have taken away the language of the sacraments and the language of worship – and with these they have taken the spirit. They have taken away the vital organs and call us in to sit with the corpse.

We are in affliction. We are mourning a loss. We are mourning a loss of belief, of meaning, in the Anglican and Episcopal

Churches. We are not lamenting as antiquarians the loss of a few pretty words. We are mourning Christ, who has been entombed in a dead and deathly antique Latitudinarianism. That the tomb is painted on the outside with a bright confident smile, that we are constantly assured again that all is 'easy' and 'cheerful', good for and in the world, and all without any necessity of old 'monkish virtues' either – none of this can console us.

> Save me, O God; for the waters are come in unto my soul.
> I sink in deep mire, where there is no standing: I am come into deep waters, where floods overflow me.
> I am weary of my crying: my throat is dried: mine eyes fail while I wait for my God. (Psalm 69:1–3)

This Lenten time is a good time to acknowledge our affliction, to feel and know its full weight, and to turn to God for help. Our Lord burst through the tomb. We know he cannot be held in these little temporal chains that seek to bind and tame him.

> In the juvescence of the year
> Came Christ the tiger....[15]

But we must do our part by fighting against this new Prayer Book, fighting in all fairness and openness and (so far as lieth in us) with courtesy, but fighting all the same. We are not fighting, as our oppressors insist, for archaic words, but for living truth. We know that this new-model Prayer Book itself represents a perverse and archaic version of Christianity, a recrudescence of eighteenth-century aberrations and heresies. It foists upon us the recurrent old sins of Anglicanism dressed up as the newest and best in doctrine and practice. We must encounter it with all our true prayer, and with all our hearts, and with all our intelligence. There is no other way. Their book is not the faith. The organization which foists it upon us is not ultimately the Church, though it represents something which keeps trying soothingly (while using all the mechanisms of power) to make itself into the Church.

> Thy word above all earthly powers,
> No thanks to them, endureth.

The Anglican and Episcopal Churches survived before, despite the copious writings of bishops and the activities of powerful political machines. And if it be the will of God, they will survive again.

NOTES

1 T. S. Eliot, 'Gerontion'.

2 See John Locke, *The Reasonableness of Christianity* (1695), especially paras. 166–74.

3 C. F. Allison, *The Rise of Moralism* (London, 1966), p. 207.

4 I had not noticed until the day of the symposium at Savannah that that Saturday, 21 March, was the day on which we remember Bishop Ken. It seemed heartening to recall that there had been Anglican bishops who not temporized with their consciences and broken an oath, despite risk to their jobs and pressure from the organization.

5 John Tillotson (Archbishop of Canterbury), *Works*, ed. Thomas Birch, 3 vols (London, 1752), Sermon vi, 'The Precepts of Christianity not Grievous', vol. I, p. 57.

6 Basil Willey, *The Eighteenth-Century Background* (1st edn. 1940; Harmondsworth, 1962), p. 123.

7 Richard Steele, *The Christian Hero* (1st edn. 1701; London 1710), p. 15.

8 Alexander Pope, *An Essay on Man* (1733–34); the Twickenham edition of the *Poems of Alexander Pope*, 6 vols (London New Haven, 1964), III i, ed. Maynard Mack, epistle IV, lines 371–2, p. 164.

9 David Hume, *An Enquiry concerning the Principles of Morals* (1751); see Hume, *Enquiries*, ed. L. A. Selby-Bigge, 3rd edition (Oxford, 1975), section IX, part I, para. 219, p. 270.

10 Hume, *Enquiry*, para. 217, p. 268; see Willey, *Background*, p. 123, for comment.

11 Joseph Addison, *The Spectator*, 4 vols (London, 1967), vol. I, *Spectator* No. 112, Monday, 9 July 1711, p. 340.

12 Henry Fielding, *The History of the Adventures of Joseph Andrews*, ed. Martin C. Battestin (Boston, 1961), I, xvii, p. 68.

13 Benjamin Franklin, Preface to Book of Common Prayer in *The Writings of Benjamin Franklin*, ed. A. H. Smyth, 10 vols. (New York, 1899), vol. VI, pp. 166–7. For further comment, description and discussion see Alfred Owen Aldridge, *Benjamin Franklin and Nature's God*, Durham, NC, 1967), especially chapter 13.

14 Marion J. Hatchett, *Commentary on the American Prayer Book* (New York, 1980), p. 9.

15 T. S. Eliot, 'Gerontion'.

Cranmer Not Irrelevant

RACHEL TRICKETT

This essay is not intended to be contentious or polemical. It is not a counterblast to the Alternative Service Book, nor a protest against changes in the liturgy, nor a re-statement of the arguments for the literary superiority of the Book of Common Prayer and the Authorized Version of the Bible. Its intention is to describe, and by describing perhaps help towards explaining, why the Book of Common Prayer has not seemed to one particular Christian an irrelevant or partisan document, and why, over almost thirty years as a practising Anglican, someone who was brought up a Nonconformist, familiar with an extempore liturgy, and committed to the principle of participation between the congregation and the minister, should have come to love and rely on Cranmer's liturgy as a source of spiritual and devotional support.

I was raised a Congregationalist. My father, an Independent Methodist minister, because his chapel was not within walking distance, preferred that his children should be brought up in the Congregationalist or Independent discipline rather than as Wesleyan or Primitive Methodists, because the Congregationalists, like his own sect, affirmed the necessity of individual chapel self-government. In spite of this distinction, the co-operation between all these sects in the area of Lancashire where I was bred and lived until 1970 was close, and each of them advanced against the Anglican Church and its liturgy the argument that a fixed order of service and a traditional series of responses suffered from the defect of 'vain repetition'. In the 1930s when I was a child less was heard of the evils of 'priestcraft' – the authority of the priesthood and the priest's exercise of this authority, which was symbolized in his position when celebrating, his back to the congregation and isolated from them as he ascended the sanctuary steps to consecrate the elements. But though the passionate rejection of 'priestcraft' which my grandfather and great-grandfather had vehemently maintained against Catholic and Anglican alike had been gradually dropped, at least publicly, in the more tolerant and Laodicean atmosphere of the 1930s, protests against an unspontaneous and rigid form of service, traditional, repetitive, superimposed by a printed rite, still remained current.

It seems to me strange today to find that in most Anglican churches the priest celebrates as did the dissenting minister in mine and my father's chapels, facing the congregation; that as the minister came down from the dominating pulpit to join the deacons and the flock on the same level for the sharing of the Lord's Supper, so the priest (now referred to in Rite A as 'the President', his function seeming no longer sacerdotal, nor even that of one who administers the sacrament, but rather as the chairman of the meeting) comes down to an altar frequently set up in the nave.

In the past, the answer to our nonconformist jeers of 'vain repetition' from Anglican and Roman Catholic apologists was a vigorous counter-accusation that the informal, unmysterious 'love-feasts' or 'Lord's Suppers' of our chapels were no more nor less than memorial services. The old title 'love-feast' as I find it in my grandfather's and great-grandfather's Independent Methodist circuit calendars, and the more common later title of 'the Lord's Supper' (as opposed to the Last Supper) themselves scarcely suggest the formal solemnity of an obituary or memorial service. And in their intimate domestic atmosphere these services sorted better with the simplicity of action and word than our new Anglican rites with their occasional anachronistic pomp of vestments and aromatic oblations of incense. No one, listening attentively to the minister pronouncing over the small cubes of National Loaf (our daily bread during the war), and the small glasses of Ribena, (the common drink of a largely teetotal congregation) the Pauline injunction, 'for as often as ye do eat this bread and drink this wine, ye do show the Lord's death, till he come', could seriously have mistaken the occasion as some purely formal or commemorative gesture.

Similarly when I became an Anglican, I began to realize how the formal responses, the traditional statement of the human condition in relation to our Creator and Redeemer, were infinitely more than 'vain repetition'. Vain only if not attended to, or if not understood; and not understood only if never explained or expounded. So we got each others' liturgies and the devotion generated by them badly wrong: it is very likely that we still do, for we are creatures of prejudice however much we pride ourselves on our tolerance and ecumenicism, and to clergy and laity alike prejudice is a shorter cut to apparent unanimity than expounding or explaining.

The supporters of the Book of Common Prayer are often accused of failing to recognize the peculiar warmth and feeling of community, the positive spiritual qualities that the new rites, especially Rite A, can produce in many congregations, just as the use of a vernacular Mass for Roman Catholics has evoked a sense of co-operation and release that Protestants discovered almost four centuries ago at the Reformation. The supporters of the ASB equally cast doubt on the effectiveness of the Book of Common Prayer in strengthening the faith and devotion of contemporary believers. They admit that churchgoers who are familiar with the 1662 liturgy may be affected by a nostalgic emotion which warms the imagination to a superficial degree, but feel that this itself may be a positive hindrance to more objective, adventurous thinking, or to seeing the faith in the light of present needs.

Professor Hanson of Manchester University in an article

for *The Times* published in December 1980, expressly condemned the nostalgic associations of the traditional customs of the season, carol services, cribs and Christmas trees, and used the surprising instance of the prevalence of traditional forms in the Orthodox Churches of Eastern Europe. At this time, he contended, thousands of Russian and Eastern Christians would be consoling themselves by vain repetition of the ancient rites and liturgies associated with the festival. If I interpreted his article right, this seemed to him a sad instance of the bondage of the Church in a persecuting society, an occasion for sympathetic regret which should encourage the faithful in a non-persecuting and indifferent society to relinquish such supports and grow into the more adult habit of affirming the faith through new and experimental forms, severing the links with the past, stripping our services of all nostalgic, familiar and muffling associations for the sake of discovering anew the basic elements of truth in the Christian revelation.

Upholders of the traditional forms too often, in contrast to Professor Hanson, seem to reject the idea that 'the Lord hath yet more light and truth to break forth from his word' – a particular tenet of the scriptural Protestants in whose discipline my own faith was nourished. At the risk of sounding a trimmer, it seems to me that both extremes are wrong. There has been, and is, much sympathy for Professor Hanson's view among the clergy. Professional men, professionally trained in new ways, become impatient of the conservative and apparently obscurantist attitudes of their parishioners. The better educated among the flock seem patronizing and behind the times; the elderly and less well educated seem ignorant and obstinate. Hope lies with the young and middle-aged, the former unacquainted with traditional forms, the latter bored by them, and both willing to give a trial to something new. The novelty that the Church can now offer, the latest model in technology, is hoped to make the most cost-effective and immediate contribution to need, and to serve until the next series or model is devised for an endlessly changing society. Among parishioners there is a sullen resentment of change, or an indifferent belief that what the Vicar says must be right, a refusal to exercise the difficult art of judgement, and sometimes a genuine feeling that they have not enough expert knowledge to do more than acquiesce in counsel from the professionals.

So both sides continue to misunderstand each other. The traditionalists often are reluctant to admit that the Christian revelation can truly manifest itself through what seems to them the maimed, impoverished language of the new rites, whereas there is undoubtedly evidence that it *can*, even if not in its fullness. The opponents of tradition are stirred to abuse, one correspondent in *The Times* referring to the Book of Common Prayer as 'a gilded corpse', and are often willing only to concede, as an act of contemptuous charity for the elderly, an 8.15 Communion in the middle of the week according to the rite of 1662. These also are refusing to admit that the Christian revelation can truly manifest itself through the grace and stately cadences of Cranmer's prose, whereas there is evidence today (not only from past centuries) that it *can*, though again, not in its fullness.

But this is not merely an argument about language and changing attitudes in society. The truth is that much of the anxiety felt in clerical circles about the continued use of the Book of Common Prayer is theological. Again and again Cranmer's emphasis on the doctrine of the atonement in the Communion service, on the burden of original sin, on the need for penitence and redemption is condemned as excessive; it is impossible in these more psychologically enlightened times for it to be repeated in a public service with sincerity, and dangerous in its neglect of the more important elements of community with God and with each other. The elements that are found to be lacking are the assurance of some sort of perfection (though with little reference to grace), the insistence upon our common uplifted humanity and our obligation to 'go forth into the world' to do God's work. But equally, the new rites conspicuously omit concepts of human imperfection, divine judgement, individual responsibility of the soul towards God and the second coming and all its apocalyptic connotations.

Ritual gestures reflect this dichotomy. The custom of facing the east for the Creed is rejected (as of the priest facing the east and representing his people in the enactment of the sacrifice), without acknowledgement of its old significance (in honour of the belief that the Lord's second coming would be, like the rising of the sun, from the east). Genuflection is out, because the act of humility in worship may emphasize a sense of human unworthiness rather than a belief in human regeneration. We may receive Communion standing because in the primitive church, it is averred, this was sometimes the habit to symbolize the renewed nature of the communicant after Confession and Absolution (though not before the symbolic reception of the one perfect, sufficient sacrifice given for the redemption of our sins). This justification for the practice teeters uncomfortably, to my mind, on the verge of Manicheeism, Gnosticism and the notion of the *Perfecti* for whom all things were possible, and no holds barred. Cranmer's liturgy certainly lacks any notion of perfectibility except through grace and Christ's sacrifice or of community except of the Church as 'the body of all faithful people', or of the missionary zeal of going forth into the world to do God's work. It speaks rather of leading a new life after redemption, in general rather than specific terms, leaving to each individual the decision as to what that may imply.

The peculiar mingling of theological purism and pedantry and a modernist desire for community produces in our new series an odd mingling of the Catholic and the Protestant, which, it may be maintained, is the essence of Anglicanism. But much of what the new rites aim at is the familial intimacy of the old dissenting communities with their emphasis on the chosen, the children of God, forced to meet together in their own homes or chapels, unacknowledged, unrecognized, unaccepted at large. It is hard for an established

Church, the spoiled child of the nation, to assume this role. Like a spoiled child the Anglican Church today cries petulantly for more and more of its own way, asking to lay hold on the privilege of a persecuted or dissenting minority while in fact it accepts the alternative privileges of a legal and national authority. There are many sincere Anglicans, clergy and laity, who would prefer to be disestablished, to become a sect, to associate themselves with the church universal, as if their connection with the English constitution were a hindrance to this freedom. It was easier, undoubtedly, for Cranmer, and even for the bishops who devised the Prayer Book of 1662, to assume that establishment did not mean association with a predominantly non-Christian state which would embarrass their spiritual pretensions. Circumstances have changed so radically in the last 150 years at the least that this position must be seriously and carefully reconsidered. I believe that one way of thinking seriously about this is to examine the value that the Book of Common Prayer has had over the centuries to a broad section of the community, ranging from devout believers to agnostics. Apologizing for this lengthy preamble, I hope, too, that my own experience of the devotional power I have experienced from this rite may, in a small and purely personal fashion, suggest why its retention as more than an archaic relic might widen the range of Christian influence in a non-Christian society, and strengthen the sense of continuity, identity and individuality which is necessary not only in a country and its people but, in the last resort of greater importance, in the search for truth which is the common responsibility and the highest concern of every one of us.

The old Sunday diet on which I was nourished – 10 a.m. Sunday School, 10.30 morning service, 2.30 Sunday School and 6 p.m. evening service – furnished the day so thoroughly that it left every later, easier, subsequent seventh day (or first if you prefer it) empty and uneasy. I did not find the fullness fruitful; often rather boring, irritating and frustrating. But it acquainted me with the Scriptures, with the exposition of Scripture (often in interminable sermons, some brilliant, some good, some downright bad), with the primitive poetry of hymns and the weekly chanting of the Psalms, not from Coverdale's Psalter, but from the Authorized Version. When I became attracted to the Anglican liturgy I began to attend Matins, a service now seldom communally celebrated, as I was unable to communicate, and because in those days the central morning service on Sunday was Matins and not a family Eucharist. Matins is a curious mixture of monastic offices, and used to be envied the Anglicah Church by liturgically minded Roman Catholics, but often, it must be admitted, was endured by the regular congregation as the inevitable burden of appropriate church attendance. It seemed to me always less devotionally effective than Evensong, but the evening is a more romantic time (like early morning, when the chaste unsung Eucharist attracted and still attracts larks as opposed to owls or nightingales, if you can so divide human personalities). But two aspects of the interminable psalmody of Matins struck me before I became an Anglican. First, the Te Deum, greatest of all Christian hymns, portentous transitions of which reflected in the various musical settings, affirmed the necessity for adoration ('We praise thee O God, we acknowledge thee to be the Lord') and the universality of the claim 'All the earth doth worship thee, the Father everlasting', and then progresses through its series of acclamations to conclude in a humble prayer for support, 'In thee O Lord have I trusted; Let me never be confounded'. I do not suppose when I first began to sing the Te Deum regularly that I was absolutely clear about the exact meaning of that last phrase, but I was aware of an enormous significance here, of the possibility of confutation, of being confuted, routed, confused, refuted, disproved. 'In thee O Lord have I trusted': I was thrown back on the earlier words, the idea of a trust, faith, confidence in some promise or security or defence against the humiliation, the doubt and dread of being scoffed at, silenced, proved wrong. A hope, at least.

In Lent this beautiful hymn was relinquished for the Benedicite, that quaint catalogue of praise which reminded me of seventeenth-century rhetorical poetry with its lists of delights, pleasant but not especially effective. Then the Benedictus which recalled to me the idea of trust 'and to remember his holy Covenant'. What Covenant? Those who had not been instructed in the Old Testament must have made little of this unless their Sunday School had acquainted them with it. But again the words insisted on the oath or promise 'which he sware to our fore-father Abraham': any Jew would know, I soon realized, the meaning of the promise or covenant. To my Jewish friends the idea of the promise, the covenant, the bond was real enough, even to non-believing Hebrews. Sometimes in place of the Benedictus we sang the Jubilate Deo and the words of the second verse remained in my mind like an echo: 'Be ye sure that the Lord is God; it is he that hath made us and not we ourselves; we are his people and the sheep of his pasture.'

Of course from Scripture lessons we knew about the chosen people; comparative religion classes had taught us all about this sort of thing among ancient tribes. But I was never taught at school the importance of that verse; apart from its place in Matins it never came home to me until I had to study *Paradise Lost* at college and consider Satan's claim to be self-generated, his inability to accept the fact that he was a creature. But any ordinary churchgoer who sang, yawning over it, the Jubilate Deo at Matins, had at least ringing in his memory those words 'it is he that hath made us and not we ourselves', a basic tenet of the Christian faith.

The notion of oneself as a created being, not a self-generated or evolving being, is more difficult for anyone in the post-Darwinian period to entertain than it was previously. Each of us has two conflicting instincts: one which sees our-self as self-sufficient, self-justifying and self-condemning; the other which feels a helpless inability to achieve the 'obscure sense of possible sublimity', the imperfect perception of perfection which inspires every effort in art, achievement, or virtue. 'Be ye therefore perfect', we are admonished, but one part of us answers with St Paul, 'The things that I would do I do not; the things I would not do, I do.' These conflicting instincts exist in all of us. We know that we are going to die; we do not really believe it. We want to be happy and to give happiness; we know that, even if we think we have a right to felicity, we shall more often be frustrated, and in trying to make others happy more often than not will fail, and we know that others will fail to make us happy, too. We want some sort of rough answer to this dilemma of desire and denial. Perhaps, by a slow evolution of sensibility, a progress towards greater understanding, we may gradually improve. The theory of evolution in the nineteenth century gave hope here, a hope harshly dashed by the facts of twentieth-century history. To accept the optimistic theory of gradual perfectibility demands either an acceptance of the survival of the fittest, which involves a ruthless elimination of the unfit, a preference of the ends over the means, an acquiescence in brute force while at the same time hoping for an eventual elimination of this process through acquired wisdom as well as power, a manipulation of our own instincts. Or, on the other hand, we may assume an apparently pessimistic acceptance of the *status quo*, a refusal to admit the possibility of change or improvement, amelioration or progress. Many modern Christians shrink from this apparent acceptance of stasis and would rather risk the doctrine of inevitable change and development.

They do this, because, by not doing so, they put the dilemma back upon the concept of an omnipotent Creator and are confronted again by the age-old problems of sin, predestination, free will, the problems of evil and of pain. Cranmer's liturgy, with no doubt unenviable confidence, confronts these; our new rites prevaricate and avoid the issue. It is no part of my intention to enter into theological discussion on these matters. I am not a professional theologian, and my answers, such as they are, to these problems are not the result of logical analysis but of the relation of my faith to my personal experience. The insistence on original sin and the necessity for redemption in Cranmer's eucharistic liturgy seems to me nearer to my experience of life in the twentieth century than the outline of doctrine in the new rites. It is a fact that the remarkable success of Calvinism in the fifteenth and sixteenth centuries was not that it seemed extreme and restrictive as it does to us, but, like Marxism in Europe in the nineteenth century and in the Third World in the twentieth century, it had the appearance to scrupulous and conscientious souls, troubled by the necessity of frequent confession in the old religion, of a liberation, a new freedom, a release. It had all the power of freeing, not of binding. The assurance of salvation through grace, the burden rolling off Christian's back at the foot of the cross, the sense that the debt had been paid, once for all, the release from the threat of countless purgatorial penances, the rejection of uncomputed payments for Masses for the departed soul, the freedom from the imposition of good works to recompense what must seem incapable of compensation, failure, guilt, a sense of irretrievable imperfection: all this Calvinism cancelled at one bold stroke. C. S. Lewis, in his perceptive introduction to the *Oxford History of the Literature of the Sixteenth Century*, writes of this together with the period's fascination with the idea of magic, separated now from its orthodox connection with miracle and Christian ritual; he makes us see the age of the Reformation and the Renaissance with new insight. It is easy today, looking back, to recognize the bonds which that apparent liberation forged; less easy to look at our own ideas of a new freedom with the foresight which can predict the limitations they may impose. So too Cranmer's insistence on sin and redemption which may seem inevitably morbid to us, may be understood as releasing to him and to those who supported him.

But the Book of Common Prayer of 1662 was devised after a century had passed in which the ill effects of this new movement had most obviously and tyrannically manifested themselves as far as the established Church was involved. The state had suffered under the sects, the Major Generals, the bickering Presbyterians, even Cromwell's magnanimous tolerance – his reception and toleration of the Jews, his support for every liberation of Protestant and free thought in Europe, his impassioned plea to the sectarians, 'I beseech you in the bowels of Christ, think that you may be mistaken', are cancelled out again by his conviction of the need to subjugate Catholic Ireland, to send out his Ironsides ruthlessly against all opposition, religious or constitutional. 'God's Englishman' was disinterred and hanged in public as a regicide. For modern Christians it is valuable to look back at history, and not to regard it as irrelevant to the faith. For we believe that God revealed himself in time, and we are presented with the time-ridden problem of proclaiming an absolute and eternal revelation in a time-ridden world, the history of which shows us all too clearly that every effort, however, sincere and well-conceived, ended in failure.

The Book of Common Prayer, as devised and proclaimed in 1662, retained (to the distress of many at the time and many later) Cranmer's insistence on human depravity and the need for redemption, but suceeded in retaining what, of his devising, seemed capable of retention throughout varying circumstances and diverse social and spiritual situations. It survived as the main liturgy of the Church of England until this last decade, through innumerable changes in society, religious emphasis and intellectual speculation. No essential reason has been advanced why it should not still survive. For this is not a matter of language, which can be adapted, or of theological emphasis to which (as in the case of the 1928 version) the rite can be adjusted. It is a matter of the basic affirmation of the Christian doctrine as accepted by the majority of believers in this country.

A learned and literary Christian, in favour of change but distressed by the linguistic failure of the new rites, said agitatedly in discussion, 'What I can't forgive Cranmer is his meddling with the canon of the Mass.' This is characteristic of the narrow and pedantic attitude of those Anglicans who are against sincere change, but for superficial shifts to suit superficial social alterations. Cranmer's rite did meddle with the canon of the Roman Mass, but with extraordinary inspiration. To one who came from a dissenting sect, the pattern of the 1662 Communion service is one which reflects a deep truth of human experience.

It opens with the Lord's Prayer, followed by the great Collect declaring the omniscience of God the Creator and beseeching him to cleanse and purify those who desire to communicate. There is no Mass of the Catechecumens here; it is supposed that all those present desire to communicate and can be prepared by God to do so. This is followed by the Commandments; the old law, not rejected but, as the service demonstrates, superseded by the mercy and grace of God who recognizes our inability to fulfil that law. This is followed by the prayer for the state and its governors, then the reading of Scripture, the Epistle and the Gospel and the Creed. In this each individual, though one of a whole congregation, expresses in the word *credo*, I believe (now superseded by the adoption in Rite A of one primitive ritual which, suiting our modern desire for uniformity, can be substituted, *credimus*, *we* believe – but how do I know that you do, or you, I?). After the Creed come the notices, banns of marriage, excommunications, and, most important, the sermon, the exposition of the Scriptures. This is followed by the offertory with a selection of texts. Next follows the intercessions for 'the whole state of Christ's Church militant here upon Earth' – prayers for our human condition in general; these are too often now interpreted as an occasion for intercessions for precise occasions, inappropriate often to a public ritual, and reminiscent to a born Nonconformist of the interminable extempore and often personal and prejudiced prayers of the occasional preacher. The following exhortations have been neglected for a good many decades, and as these are polemical, controversial in many respects, but most especially forbidding, they are totally ignored in the new rites. What can be said for them is that they militate against a too easy acceptance of the most sacred rite of the Church which, today, we tend to believe should be not only frequent but common. Without suggesting that the exhortations should be revived, it seems to me that there is room in our practice to remember the attitude of such devout Anglican Christians as Dr Johnson who refused to communicate more than once a month on the grounds that the preparation for this solemn sacrament could not be made by busy people without time for meditation; he did not consider it a festival that was open, like the market place, to anyone at any time.

At this point the central section of the office begins. The priest invites the congregation, if they desire to communicate, to make humble confession. It is this confession which has most baffled the modern liturgists. Are we worthy of God's wrath and indignation? Are we conscious of manifold sins and wickedness? Do we earnestly repent? Is the burden of our sins intolerable? The Confession in Rite B is perfunctory. Rite A attempts a little more solicitude. But what is the argument against 1662? The use of the word 'intolerable' may be explained. It is not slang; it means unbearable; we cannot carry that load. 'O Lamb of God that bearest away the sins of the world' – *Qui tollis peccata mundi*. This is the central tenet of the Christian faith; without it the whole structure of the doctrine disintegrates. Catholic and Protestant throughout centuries, while battling about exactly how Christ bears our sins in the sacrament, have never disagreed over the belief that our imperfections cannot be rectified except through the redemption on Calvary. Why then is this confession considered excessive or morbid? It simply expresses, not sentimentally or emotionally, but exactly, what Christians are supposed to believe. And many Christians feel a deep spiritual deprivation in not being able to confess this in their liturgy. 'Miserable offenders' as a phrase has apparently also offended because not everyone can say it sincerely. Nor could the Pharisee when he prayed with the publican. But it was not thought necessary to praise his more familiar version as against 'Lord have mercy on me, a sinner'. If we must change, why not change to the words of Scripture rather than substitute our own perfunctory admission that we have not done good? The point of the confession is that we cannot do so without God's help. And in the age of the concentration camps, of the H-bomb, Vietnam, Ulster, universal terrorism, universal disorder, why should we resent a confession of our own part in all these as miserable offenders against that truth of perfection which is what our faith asserts?

'And bring you to everlasting life', the priest says in the Absolution. We think little of everlasting life now, being so fixed on temporal existence. So, after the comfortable words, the declaration that it is very meet, right and our proper duty that we should at all times and in all places give thanks unto God, we proceed to the prayer of humble access, and on to the prayer of consecration. Cranmer certainly omitted here any reference to the resurrection and ascension of Christ and to his second coming. It seemed to him that the Lord's Supper should stand alone in the centre of the ritual and that the words of the institution should be acknowledged by the people by a simple Amen. I am among those who are glad that the statement of the resurrection and the ascension and the second coming should be added here. But then I do not want them on pedantic or archaic grounds, but on the grounds that they are lacking in this rite as not in the Nonconformist Congregational service I was brought up on. It echoes still in my mind, 'For as often as ye do eat this bread and drink this wine ye do show the Lord's death *till he come*'. The repetition of the Lord's Prayer afterwards in the 1662 rite has the simplicity which makes this service more familial than the new version before Communion: 'As our Lord Jesus Christ has taught us, we are bold to say.' It does not seem boldness, but humility to repeat the prayer after receiving. And at the reception, I miss in the new rites another statement which, for me, is a reason for my acceptance of the faith: 'Preserve thy body and soul unto everlasting life.' This is what I want. Who does not? The new rites, in courtesy to those who reject transubstantiation, include beforehand the words 'Feed on him in thy heart, by faith, with thanksgiving', but this does not substitute for me those more essential, less theological words which promise me, as our Lord promised, that my body and soul shall survive. There is nothing in common practice today outside Cranmer and 1662 which, as I receive the sacrament, reassures me of this.

Then comes Cranmer's great innovation – the offering of ourselves 'our souls and bodies to be unto thee a reasonable, holy and lively sacrifice', the prayer that we may be accepted, 'not weighing our merits [what a relief!] but pardoning our offences'. The whole tone lightens and leads into the Gloria, the great cry of acclamation after the redemption has been enacted through the sacrament. To have the Gloria here is to affirm that sense of joy and liberation which the Reformation brought to so many. It was as bold an innovation of Cranmer's as of our new liturgists to make such a change. He pushed the Lord's Supper back into the centre of the enactment, prefaced it with our acknowledgment of our unworthiness, brought the Lord's Prayer first and afterwards, orchestrated the whole ceremony to underline our creatureliness, our unworthiness, to remind us of the promises, to insist on our imperfection, to affirm our redemption, our own resurrection and preservation, body and soul unto everlasting life, to burst then into the paean of praise for this glorious release and to end with the Peace. Certainly Cranmer tampered with the Catholic Mass as our reformers have tampered with him. To many Christians, Cranmer's innovations still represent a pattern of human experience which matches our own. The reason why so many still want to retain a central position for the Book of Common Prayer is neither purely aesthetic nor nostalgic, but, as it was originally devised, and as our modern liturgists claim for their revision, because of its relevance to life, and its truth to human experience.

Doctrine and Devotion in the Book of Common Prayer

ROGER BECKWITH

The much derided tribute which, earlier this century, was commonly paid to the Book of Common Prayer as 'our incomparable liturgy', had an august pedigree behind it. When the poet George Herbert in his last illness requested a visitor to pray with him, and received the inquiry 'What prayers?', he replied, 'O Sir, the prayers of my mother the Church of England: no other prayers are equal to them.' The great Dr Johnson, in June 1784, went so far as to say, 'I know of no good prayers but those in the Book of Common Prayer.' John Wesley stated, 'I know of no liturgy in the world, ancient or modern, which breathes more of solid, scriptural, rational piety than the Common Prayer of the Church of England.' Charles Simeon claimed that 'no other human work is so free from faults as it is.' It would be easy to multiply such statements, made in the past by distinguished representatives of all schools of thought in the Church.

One cannot reasonably doubt that men as learned as those named had some acquaintance with the other liturgies with which they compared the Book of Common Prayer, so much to its advantage. Liturgy is not a new study in the Church of England. What is even more certain, however, is that they had a deep and long-standing acquaintance with the Book of Common Prayer itself, and that experience had ever more firmly convinced them of its great and enduring worth. Such testimonies are, in fact, disinterested evidence that its compilers had been successful in achieving their known aims.

It is not by any means always that a book tells its readers as plainly and frankly as the Book of Common Prayer does what its aims are, and puts them in a position to judge for themselves how successful or unsuccessful it has been in achieving them. The English Prayer Book, however, since its first compilation in 1549, has carried two little explanatory essays, both probably written by Archbishop Cranmer, which expound its purpose very fully. The first is Cranmer's old preface, now entitled 'Concerning the Service of the Church', and the second is the statement 'Of Ceremonies, why some be abolished, and some retained'. What is now called 'the Preface' was added by the 1662 revisers, and explains, equally clearly, their moderate policy of Prayer Book revision, and the different fields in which they had found it necessary, after the lapse of some generations, to make limited change.

The principles laid down by Cranmer, and often underlined by the 1662 revisers, in these essays, can be summarized under the following eleven heads.

1 *The Centrality of the Bible*. The Prayer Book was designed to reinstate the public reading of the Bible and the public recitation of the Psalter, in a regular, orderly and comprehensive manner ('Concerning the Service of the Church'). A knowledge of the Bible could in this way be restored to the Church through its public services. Moreover, biblical principles of worship, such as those laid down by St Paul in 1 Cor. 14, must govern the way that services are drawn up and conducted ('Of Ceremonies'). The services should contain nothing contrary to the Bible, and the most accurate translations should be used for the passages read from it ('Preface'). In practice, the Prayer Book services not only conform to the teaching of the Bible (avoiding the errors of the Middle Ages) but often embody its very language, positively teaching what the Bible teaches.

2 *The Glory of God.* By worshipping in this manner, showing respect to biblical revelation, the Prayer Book hopes to 'please God' and promote 'the glory of God' ('Of Ceremonies'). Hence, the services themselves regularly ascribe glory to God, and the Absolution at Morning and Evening Prayer prays 'that those things may please him, which we do at this present'.

3 *Spirituality.* If pleasing God involves some change in inherited custom, one must not be afraid to make the change, since Christ's religion is not a ceremonial law, but one which serves God 'in the freedom of the Spirit' ('Of Ceremonies'). 'Reverence and devotion' are a prime consideration, and words and phrases in services will from time to time need to be modernized in order to promote these ideals ('Preface'). The repeated stress that the services themselves lay on sincerity and on penitence is a mark of the same concern.

4 *Edification.* The essay 'Of Ceremonies' quotes St Paul (1 Cor. 14) as making 'edification' – the building up of Christians through their understanding – the aim of all that takes place in the congregation. For this reason, it says, ceremonies must not be either meaningless or (in the light of biblical teaching) positively misleading. It is on the same grounds that the Book of Common Prayer abolishes the use of Latin and substitutes the vernacular ('Concerning the Service of the Church'). The presence of explanatory exhortations in the services, and especially the revival of sermons in them, after the medieval neglect of preaching, are in the same interest.

5 *Simplicity.* As an aid to edification, the Book of Common Prayer greatly simplifies the existing worship of the church. The burdensome multitude of ceremonies is reduced to modest proportions ('Of Ceremonies'). The complicated and perplexing directions governing the services are made few and plain ('Concerning the Service of the Church') – so few,

in fact, that the 1662 revisers find it necessary to add to them quite considerably, but only where they consider the officiant to lack sufficient guidance ('Preface'). As a result, the use of the services is, on the whole, a very straightforward task for anyone willing to follow the guidance given.

6 *Congregational Participation*. The preface 'Concerning the Service of the Church' directs the parson to say the daily services, whenever possible, in church and not in private, and to have the bell rung, in order to gather a congregation. This regulation is motivated by a concern, which appears throughout the Book of Common Prayer, that worship should be more congregational. The aims of edification and simplicity, just mentioned, greatly assist congregational participation, but the rubrics give further assistance by providing the congregation with much more to say or sing, by bidding the minister make his words audible and his actions visible, and by requiring the laity to receive Communion more often than in the past and to be given the sacrament in both kinds, not in bread alone. Even the title, *The Book of Common Prayer*, probably means common to clergy and laity alike, and not confined to the clergy, though it may also mean common to the whole nation, and not confined to the area of a particular local 'use'.

7 *Unity and Concord*. Before the Reformation, there were a variety of local adaptations of the Roman liturgy, called 'uses', obtaining in different parts of England and Wales. The Sarum use was the most widespread, but the Prayer Book aimed to go beyond any merely local use and establish a single national use ('Concerning the Service of the Church'). The goal here was, of course, a religious and not just a political unity, and the same goal of Christian 'unity and concord' or 'peace and unity' is set forth as a reason for not abolishing traditional ceremonies unnecessarily ('Of Ceremonies') and for being cautious about making changes at the 1662 revision ('Preface'). The services also express this ideal, for instance

where God is addressed as 'the author of peace and lover of concord' (Morning Prayer) or where the invitation to draw near with faith is addressed to those who are in 'love and charity' with their neighbours (Holy Communion).

8 *Order.* The essay 'Of Ceremonies' quotes 1 Cor. 14 in yet another connection – to show the need for order in worship. Along with edification, this is certainly one of the main lessons Paul has for the headstrong congregation at Corinth. Cranmer applies his lesson to justify the requirement that authorized forms of worship should be respected, and not arbitrarily altered by individuals, and also to justify the maintenance of a certain number of ceremonies, though fewer than before. In the same vein, the preface 'Concerning the Service of the Church' directs that doubts about the interpretation of the rubrics be referred to the bishop, and if necessary to the archbishop. The use of liturgical worship (i.e. set forms of worship) in the Book of Common Prayer services is itself an expression of this principle of order, and the careful way the services are planned makes them a particularly favourable example of the principle.

9 *Frequency.* The encouragement given to the daily use of Morning and Evening Prayer ('Concerning the Service of the Church') is a specimen of the principle that worship should be regular and frequent. The rubrics give further directions about the services to be used on Sundays and holy days, and also require the laity to receive Communion at least three times a year. Though today this seems seldom, it was a threefold increase of the medieval norm.

10 *The Independence of National Churches.* The essay 'Of Ceremonies' ends by pointing out that the Book of Common Prayer is only claiming to order the worship of its own nation. It is not passing judgement on the way worship is ordered in other nations, where the circumstances and needs may call for reform to be conducted differently, but it is,

on the other hand, claiming the right to order worship for its own realm, without being obliged to obey directives from Rome or to follow examples set in Zürich or Geneva. The point is echoed in the Thirty-Nine Articles (Article 34).

11 *Respect for Antiquity.* Though far from being the leading principle on which Cranmer sought to do his liturgical work, as it is often alleged to have been, respect for antiquity was undoubtedly a potent influence on his thinking. In the interests of unity and concord, he was ready to maintain any existing custom which was edifying, and to resist unnecessary innovations, but especially was this so in the case of *ancient* customs, entitled to 'reverence...for their antiquity' ('Of Ceremonies'). The Preface to the Ordination services shows the same attitude. Then again, where edification demanded change, Cranmer was always happy if there was an edifying ancient custom which he could revive, like the ancient pattern for reading the Bible and reciting the Psalter ('Concerning the Service of the Church'). The opening of the Commination service is a parallel case.

Of course, the Book of Common Prayer is showing some marks of its age, three centuries after the 1662 revision. If those who prepared the new services had adequately appreciated all these eleven principles underlying the book, and had in addition followed the moderate method of revision outlined in the 1662 'Preface', words and phrases could, where appropriate, have been modernized, amended translations of the passages of Scripture included could, where necessary, have been substituted, and variety, flexibility and congregational participation could have been increased to an extent not practicable in an age of widespread illiteracy, yet without the basic character of the book being changed. The state prayers could have been adapted to a constitutional monarchy, and the occasional prayers and thanksgivings expanded to suit an industrialized age. As we all know, a different course was followed, resulting in an Alternative

Service Book instead of an updated Book of Common Prayer. However, since the Book of Common Prayer is still highly usable, and since it is intrinsically so much better than its alternative, the challenge that faces loyal Anglicans is to keep it in use, as a live option, during the ten years for which the other book is authorized, in the hope that by the end of that time better counsels will have begun to prevail.

Swallowing the ASB 1980

GEOFFREY SHEPHERD

The Alternative Service Book 1980 is selling well. What are we to make of an England in which a prayer book of all things has proved to be a favourite present for Christmas 1980? What resolutions will it have generated for 1981? Perhaps the combination of publishers was right in asserting that the issue of the new prayer book is the most important piece of publishing in the Church of England in the last three hundred years. It is a bold claim; but the fate of books after publication and sale is always something of a mystery. How many of the winter's purchases of the ASB will remain in English homes as inscribed keepsakes until the third or fourth generation? Or how soon will unread copies of the book creep into the Oxfam shops of country towns?

Success, as publishers and as churches know, is different from merit. The ASB has had an almost uniformly bad press. Most of the critics will have been laymen who have read the book, as of necessity, in their hearts and heads. Only a few interested clergymen who may have a sense of public prayer have found much satisfaction in the book, and most of their voices have expressed a petulance against objections rather than any positive approbation. There is no call here to conduct another cursory examination of the verbal deficiencies and infelicities of the book. They are manifest and multiple. Every page has its grief. All too often the text seems to have been designed deliberately to

Reprinted from the *Cambridge Review*, 27 February 1981.

flout an unfractured tradition, wantonly to bruise a sentimental heart. Yet the publishers are right. The ASB is an important book, and now certainly a presence in the land.

What is going to become of it; what is going to come out of it? During the next ten years or so, in many parish churches, services from this book, and only these services, are going to be heard, shared and seen; and only some of the services. It seems doubtful whether anybody yet, even the Liturgical Commission, has attended even in imagination all forms envisaged by the book. Presumably young clergymen of the next generation will be the people to become best acquainted with the book, as the Book of Common Prayer grows less familiar. Indeed they may be the only class of people to come to know the new book well. It is a big book, some 1,300 pages of it (including a new Psalter); initially it takes some hours even to get a sense of it. It is not so complicated as an old Roman breviary, but it still demands a steady eye and nimble fingers to follow any precise route through the assembled texts in all their variety. Here is God's plenty – if we may use a phrase which sponsors of the book may regard as part of the unintelligible language of 1662. So let us put it more acceptably: the ASB is a large, ingeniously and carefully constructed collection of documents, which in its organization and disposition of rubrics (on p. 46, for 985 read 983, and for 1050 read 1047) may remind one of the Notes and Tables accompanying an Income Tax assessment form. Thus even an ordinary page of service material displays silently a churchgoer's jargon. For instance a heading:

PENTECOST 14
(Trinity 13) Green

is followed in standardized form by Introductory Sentence, Collect, Psalms, Readings Year 1 (with reference to RSV, NEB, JB or TEV), Readings Year 2, Proper Preface, Postcommunion Sentence. Are these terms all familiar? The complexity of provision for a funeral service in sixty sections will require on vestry walls more than one flowchart of the type given under Section 47; but the complexity faithfully represents modern English secular administrative practice. Governmental legislation, trade union rule-books, university regulations, and now the ASB as an executive's manual, all display that capacity for elasticated codification which is a debilitating disease of our times. In this respect at least let nobody pretend that the ASB does not speak to our condition.

In the early centuries of Christianity in England, over which we should now draw a veil, each parish was required to provide itself with the books needed for the proper conduct of parish services. The ASB is certainly needed now for the proper conduct of our new services. But how can parishes, how many and how soon, acquire sufficient copies? Even special offers from publishers will not tempt the majority of parishes to find up to £1,000 for the purpose. In some parishes inertia and economy, we have no doubt, will reinforce a preference for the old Book of Common Prayer. In that ideal and unidentified real parish where full consultation takes place, liturgical practice will be determined by vicar and parochial church council; but no worshipful outsider will know what he is in for when he goes to church. What is more disturbing is that few PCCs and few vicars will have much idea of what they are intending in deciding on a particular sequence of liturgical items or of what they are excluding in settling for any selection. What is most likely is that many parishes, finding that variety is authorized, will continue to use the flimsy booklets of one of the earlier Series, or produce by amateur efforts favoured extracts of the ASB for local use. A liturgy conducted by pamphlet does not really fulfil the reformers' view or even the revisers' view that everything in the Church of England should be done decently and in due order. The real advantage of the ASB, with its scriptural readings and alternatives, will be foregone in practice, and it cannot, treated thus, expect to win much esteem. Does a good part of the future of Anglicanism, like much else in England now, as we are told, depend upon the state of local finances?

The real answer will depend much more directly upon the enthusiasm with which those who have received the new book this Christmas regard the promise and potential of the ASB – and maybe upon some of their New Year resolutions. Anglican faith and order now are open to many forms of change. One pressure legitimized by the ASB is centrifugal and drives towards congregationalism, whereby each effective parish will develop its own liturgical identity.

For the Church of England as a whole that would be a bad thing. But there are and were, apart from the Book of Common Prayer, strong inherent forces which draw the Church of England together and historically gave it that kind of exclusiveness that Nonconformity dislikes. And the ASB embodies some new attitudes which stand against or disarm congregationalism – in particular a liberal universalism and ecumenicism. Nobody nowadays will want to breathe a word against our Methodist brethren; some still see positive advantage in discreetly echoing Rome; nor should the cachet bestowed by an acquaintance with the Orthodox Church be unremarked; the Church of South India is now revealed as torchbearer. Only Dr Paisley seems unprovided for, and certainly the ASB is no book for him. The wrath of God is not much in evidence anywhere: the prescribed Psalms and readings have been counter-doctored accordingly. The royal headship of the Church is decidedly secondary in the new ecclesiastical order. The new calendar pays due reference to humanitarianism, feminism and modern reputations. The Jerusalem Bible of the Roman Church is an acceptable source of our readings; the daily lectionary is transferred bodily from Roman practice. Rite B has distinct possibilities for those who like to follow the fortunes of the new Roman Mass. Peace and unity and joy breathe over all. Would that changes in liturgies could bring about such good things!

In sum then the ASB nets the Church of England in a

polygon of unequal and disparate forces. In itself an ASB has no power to command. At most it has the status of approved authority which can only suggest and exemplify. Of course it is attached to no act of uniformity; nor could it be, for it seeks to enable variety. It purports also to be relevant to modern society – at least to a self-recognizing element in the multi-cultural society. It tries to give no offence and to be perfectly accommodating. It supports good causes and wants to be known as liberal. It does not want to nourish gloomy dark thoughts. Of course there is some evacuation of intensity as a result. The imaginings of destiny and history, the voice of prophecy, the horror of sin and death have to be kept under a mild control. It is perhaps no wonder that some sequences of the ASB sound more like 'cultural incantations' than divine praise and worship.

The Holy Communion services in the ASB occupy 98 pages with over 500 pages of necessary additional material (collects, epistles, gospels, etc.); in the Book of Common Prayer, in somewhat larger print, the Holy Communion takes 27 pages and the collects, epistles, gospels under 200 pages. Holy Communion has been the central Anglican service, in theory always, and certainly during the last hundred years in practice also. It is here in the treatment of the Holy Communion that we can best observe the aims and methods of the revisers.

None of the revisers was a theologian, although no doubt collectively they took theological advice as they saw fit. The revision was not conducted on theological principles; that is, they did not think to figure forth in a liturgy a consistent and coherent intellectual system of belief. When relativism rules, why indulge in a simple-minded pursuit of the unknowable? There is Truth of course, but it is a by-name of God: it can be invoked but need not be defined. So the revision is conducted on formal grounds. It is a business of assembling, extracting, and ordering appropriate pieces of public speaking in churches as recorded in documents of the past, and joining them together with short strips of modern prose. It is a practical activity of making a liturgy. Again, none of the revisers was a liturgiologist in the usual sense of the word. But then liturgical scholars have been very rare in England this century. No English university takes the subject seriously. Developed scholarship in liturgy requires facility in a dozen or so languages ancient and modern, a trained talent for minute philology, the ability to penetrate the specialist documents of distinct cultures, to identify unexpressed intentions and to understand strange processes of thought. Such heroic scholarship the revisers could not command. The ASB is the feebler for the lack.

But while serious liturgical study was neglected, there was what churchmen called a 'liturgical movement' stirring throughout the Western churches. In a sense it was a somewhat belated ecclesiastical response to social changes of the late nineteenth century: the growth of mass democracy, the rise of universal suffrage, universal education, with some of the cultural and aesthetic interests of post-Romanticism. Strictly it was a movement concerned less with liturgical forms than with the social context of worship, with liturgy as the 'Work of the People'. In open democracies one might indeed expect every worshipping community to produce its own forms of worship, and this is the spirit that can be sensed at its centrifugal work in the ASB. This is the spirit of liturgy which is to blow where it listeth. But even so the movement requires its guarantees. Normally in most societies of the past, in such a situation, one would invoke the practices of the forefathers and give some authority to a continuing tradition. But that path is not attractive to modern democratic societies. They can only go back to imagined origins, start again, follow a new course which must not repeat the past. In this situation the lack of serious study of historical liturgy becomes a positive disadvantage.

It is at this point that Hippolytus Romanus enters. In the index to *Anglican Worship Today: Guide to the ASB 1980* (edited by Colin Buchanan, Trevor Lloyd and Harold Miller), there is the same number of references in the text to

Hippolytus and Cranmer. There are twice as many references to these men individually as to any other writer. Cranmer we know, a saintly figure, archbishop, scholar, politician, prisoner, martyr; Hippolytus, bishop also, scholar, politician, prisoner, martyr, in his own time an anti-Pope, in our time perhaps an anti-Cranmer, but a shadow. The revisers' Hippolytus is largely the invention of Dom Gregory Dix, the learned and somewhat eccentric Anglican Benedictine whose *The Shape of the Liturgy* (1945) has been their prime guide in their treatment of the Holy Communion services. Dom Gregory Dix belonged to that generation of clever men in the 1930s and 1940s who preferred the sophistication of startling to any parade of basic loyalty – an attitude which puzzles and repels a later generation. But Dom Gregory in his time very much liked to tease Anglicans by displaying the inadequacies of their reverend reformers, particularly Cranmer; he was also interested in Hippolytus.

Hippolytus flourished in the first decades of the third century, before many questions of Christian doctrines were resolved. His intentions were orthodox enough, his opinions vehemently held but undeveloped. He wrote against the heresies of this time, and against contemporary Popes. When Callistus was elected Pope in 217, Hippolytus had himself consecrated anti-Pope. He was reconciled later with Pope Pontianus and with him was martyred. He was little remembered otherwise in the West. But in the Eastern world, known as Hippolytus the Roman, he was influential. He wrote in Greek, but only part of his work survives. A text, variously in Arabic, Coptic and Ethiopic, with some Latin fragments, indicates the existence of a lost work which, reconstituted from these diverse sources, is known as *The Apostolic Tradition*. In it Hippolytus treated of the orders of the Church, Christian initiation, fasting, the Eucharist, offerings, the rites of the Church and hours of prayers. Dom Gregory Dix in 1935 provided the best English edition of this reconstructed work and the most readily available. It became a fundamental text for his argument in *The Shape of the Liturgy*.

This book drew attention for the first time to the four-fold action requisite in the central so-called Eucharistic Prayer (from the Holy, Holy, Holy to the act of Communion): the four sections are the taking of the bread and wine by the celebrant, the thanksgiving, the breaking of the bread, and the distribution. Dix laid emphasis on actions, not on discourse and narrative. In all this exposition Hippolytus is useful. According to the reconstituted *Apostolic Tradition* the bishop monopolizes the liturgical function of thanksgiving, using such prayers as he thinks fit, and then leads into the eucharistic action which has acquired for Hippolytus at least a fixed form. And this Eucharistic Prayer is given in the *Apostolic Tradition*. If Hippolytus were as reactionary, aristocratic and backward-looking as his modern admirers like to find him, then it could be argued that the Prayer may well go back in form to what was in use at Rome much earlier. It thus would stand as the earliest Eucharistic Prayer. Hence its importance to modern revisers looking for origins.

Obviously the appeal of Hippolytus is considerable. He is a Roman standing for an early Roman tradition but outside the later tradition of the Roman Catholic Church. His influence in the East obviously makes him useful in seeking a prehistory for modern ecumenicism. His Eucharistic Prayer can be regarded as witness to the practice of the primitive Church yet suggests that it was used in a context of unprescribed, almost extempore ritual. The congregation participated apparently by a kind of self-projection into the performance. What better, more sympathetic guide could a modern reviser want? If there are missing links, if there are elaborate reconstructions, if his circumstances were unique, what should these things matter? These things are characteristic of modern archaeology. Why should not a piece of liturgical archaeology be as exciting, as scientific, as revolutionary in its implications as any other archaeological discovery, often so triumphantly proclaimed, so tardily written up?

To those less committed to the reorganization of the Prayer Book it may seem very strange indeed that the central service of the Church lovingly, passionately, faithfully prayed with and slowly modified, should have got it all wrong for over fifteen hundred years. 'Those who dwelt in a land of deep darkness, on them has light shined', viz. from the reconstructed page of a cantankerous Roman patrician scarcely remembered in the margins of written history. On the other hand, a modern person wondering at the muddle and confusion in thought and faith and practice in Rome at the beginning of the third century in Hippolytus' time, observing too the feebly structured thought of this primitive Eucharistic Prayer, might well think that the Church did well to develop a clearer Eucharist, and remember no more of Hippolytus than his honourable martyrdom. We are warned against idolizing Cranmer and his liturgy. Hippolytus with his undeveloped, unstable prayer looks a much flimsier prospect.

But the influence of Hippolytus is strong on all the eucharistic prayers in the ASB, and the different rites are organized round his prayer. The results are rather startling when all the rites are seen together in one book. The ordinary Anglican should realize what has happened. It may be suspected that, when years ago he encountered the different services of Series 1, 2 and 3 in use, he regarded them as modifications, elaborations of, or limited substitutions for, parts of the Communion service of the Book of Common Prayer. Rite A and Rite B indicate that they are nothing of the sort. They are different services, new inventions with different intentions. In this sense the new services in the ASB are not a replacement for the Holy Communion in the Book of Common Prayer. They offer something quite new.

These new services are meant to be the scripts for a regular public and corporate thanksgiving, primarily for the life and works of Christ. They are performances collectively undertaken by an ordained leader, with various other functionaries and an actively participating congregation of the faithful who stand around, who interrupt with various expressions of joy and praise.

An untrained layman of the Church of England can find it very difficult to actualize the general intention despite the preachments of clergymen on the Body of Christ. What models or analogies in common life could make the plot of the new services more intelligible? An appropriate mood of thankfulness might be sensed at a harvest festival perhaps, but performance is scarcely developed; or at a Remembrance Day ceremony at a war memorial, if thankfulness can triumph over sadness, with marching, wreath-laying, prayers, hymns, medals and bugles – here is public performance of the proper sort; or in a national act, for a royal jubilee say, where there is a day-long rite, from telegrams at breakfast time until the last firework fades at night. Are there better models that can help? Many Anglicans and many others may feel that somehow the performances are incommensurate with what is celebrated. Our culture has so deep an ingrained disbelief that public performance can adequately reflect real and inner values that it feels no need even to resent a performance; it can accept it smilingly as fun, put on the fancy dress, and play a role in high good humour. But everybody knows that enacted performances are not happenings in real life. Can Rites A and B link performance and perceived reality? Even some of those modern Christians who find fellowship in the Lord through motions of the spirit will find the extended formulas and the complex antique formalism of these rites inhibiting.

Underneath a modern desire for collective performance is a heap of illusions constantly spawning in the course of the thought and culture of the last two hundred years, some of which have grown into the wildest terrors of our times. The capacity for communal consciousness is not specifically Christian: the earliest Christians shared it with their pagan contemporaries. Our Anglo-Saxon forefathers centuries after the conversion found it dreadfully difficult to give themselves an individual Christian identity apart from the status given them by their own community. They knew the ecstasy of the *agape*: they called it 'hall-dream'. They did not need to be Christian to seek and find it. Their Church, which was somewhat more advanced in its schemes for society, had often to urge men to release themselves from the close, almost instinctive, bonds of community and kin. For a thousand years of Christianity it was apparently scarcely possible for a Christian, even a man in religion, to initiate and sustain personal private prayer. Hence the importance of what Sir Richard Southern has called the Anselmian revolution in the emergence of private devotion in the twelfth century. It was important because its fruits are permanent. Since the seventeenth century the privateness of personal religion has been accepted as the inalienable birthright of English-speaking people. Mere communal activities are felt to be superficial and deficient in power and commitment. Many people sense this even at their own weddings. But without a more or less complete obliteration of English culture, and indeed a physical destruction of most English speakers, followed by a total barbarization of human life, the old communal consciousness – taken for granted in the doings described in the Acts of the Apostles – is gone for ever and ever.

Dictators, and in a milder mode bureaucrats, like communal consciousness. And this century which has displayed in some areas of life a malignant itch for collectivism, has learned readily how to organize and manipulate false communal consciousness. There have been religious leaders and religious groups that cultivate it. There is nothing of this explicitly in the ASB. One could imagine, though, if one were to squeeze assiduously the scraps of Hippolytus, a creature of his time, an assumption of this kind would remain and could be savoured. And the Rites A and B of the ASB are, it must be admitted, constructed on something of a dilemma. This discrepancy between the principles of corporate responsibility and individual commitment is exposed rather cruelly in the long string of initiation services.

The Holy Communion service of the Book of Common

Prayer avoids these anomalies. It recognizes that the service is a special religious occasion which has to be carefully and personally prepared for. In scriptural fashion it consciously spiritualizes physical behaviour into verbal activity. It starts with the idea of the wayfaring Christian seeking a strengthening of his religious and moral strength and purpose. He goes to church with others of like mind and purpose. He comes diffidently and hopefully. He sets before himself there the common Christian standards of life by which he judges himself and finds himself lacking. He recognizes his role in the visible particular society in which he lives. He gives assent to the record of Scripture as stating historical, moral and spiritual truths. He makes his own personal statement of a common belief. He gives money publicly: he knows that money-getting and money-giving are fundamental activities in the life of the society in which he lives. He would listen to a sermon attentively and might expect it to re-inform the mind, stir the heart a little and strengthen the will.

But all this public common life in which he participates needs to be cleansed and renewed. In face of what he is to encounter in the Holy Communion he recognizes human inadequacy, human deficiency, human depravity. He knows some of his secret sins. He knows that some of his sins are secret even from himself. But it is because of these inadequacies, escapable and inescapable, that Christ came to men. How can the Christian be other than diffident as he comes to the Communion? He needs to be relieved of his sense of inadequacy and unworthiness. He can certainly do with comfortable words. In hope the heart leaps up, and consciously. The generosity of the promise given is assuring and humbling. Surely no words so satisfyingly and so expressively breathe a spirit of chastened hope and thankfulness as the Prayer of Humble Access, set in its developing context as it extends to the Prayer of Consecration with its mystery of re-enactment and culminates, as the tension is held in the acts of Communion.

This is not a celebration fit for the apostolic age perhaps, nor is it a Roman Mass, medieval, Tridentine or modern. It may not be what some modern clergymen look for, anxious whether their own role should be that of cheer-leader, or conductor of choruses, or executive president, or floor-manager or actor-manager. According to the Book of Common Prayer they should be rather ministers of grace; except when preaching, almost featureless. They know that what they do at the altar, though essential, is only a preparation for, and becomes less important than, what goes on in the hearts of faithful communicants including their own. It is after the Communion that communicants realize that what each has known is very similar to what all have known. There is a release into unanimity and praise. Then the people go home.

The 1662 Holy Communion ran such a course as has been traced. It successfully organized the central service for people who looked for a personal religion to spring naturally and powerfully out of their social life and common faith. Those who speak about the Anglican service, without polemic but out of experience, from the seventeenth century onwards even into the present century, testify that this is how it worked. Times change and requirements change. What is now felt to be lacking in the 1662 service is, one suspects, not a deficiency in religious content. Rather it is that people, clergymen particularly, no longer wish to accept the degree or the kind of community, the total visible parochial community within a larger but defined national community that earlier Anglicans assumed. If that is true the revisions are basically, but probably not consciously, political. In which case Hippolytus and his four-fold action is not particularly relevant to our needs.

What then is to be made of the ASB? To some friends of Anglicanism and to some enemies it will appear as a characteristically Anglican document – a set of compromises. Some difficulty may be experienced in deciding what it compromises with or about. With its enfeeblement of language, its liquefaction of doctrine, its social and eschatological blandness, its subtler foreign flavourings, its old fibrous residue of native stock, it has the character less of a compromise than of a jelly. It is a stabilization of current flux. It has a soft, stiff consistency: that describes exactly the general impression the ASB makes.

No one builds successfully on jelly. Nobody would expect that the ASB in itself will fetch people to church. It is unlikely to start a revival of religion; but it may very well signal a great change in the religious interests of this country. Its character indicates unease, its publication legitimizes the processes of change, its appearance displays the material and also the absence of other material with which change will work. But it may be some time before the tension in the jelly is sufficiently relaxed for the rich and varied nourishments properly to be served up and put to use.

But some developments seem likely as the ASB is adopted. The years will quickly eat at little bits of the book, at prayers and praises that seemed right enough in the 1960s and 1970s but are already beginning to sound quaint. And social institutions will change. Matins was convenient once for Sunday mornings. And Evensong for different reasons on Sunday night. Now the Family Communion has flourished for over twenty years, and has become a very respectable and conventional service to attend. It too will fade as a social institution. A massive revision of TV schedules or a change in sporting habits might prove too much for it.

More importantly, the Holy Communion as celebrated under Rite A or Rite B is likely to lose its centrality. Designed as performance it will lose its charm. In its present forms it cannot offer the intellectual or spiritual satisfactions which in the long term bring people to church. There is too little solid food. The hungry sheep will want to be fed. There will be extra-liturgical demands on substantive modifications to existing forms. It is happening already, as the *Church Times* recently reported.

Historically in Western Europe the emphasis in religious demand has swung between the Mass and the sermon. That devout upholder of justice, St Louis of France, given the choice, thought it better to hear a sermon than attend a Mass. His contemporary and rival, Henry III of England, no saint, much preferred a Mass. The natural history of worship seems to be marked by lengthy periodic swings. For all sorts of reasons, mostly unconnected with the arrival of the ASB, it can be assumed that a new age of preaching will return. We have passed through a period of total decline so that it is difficult to recall any age in English religious life since the twelfth century when the people of England were less edified by sermons than they have been in the mid-twentieth century. The situation cannot get worse; there are indeed signs that it might get better.

And this revival will be reinforced by pressures within the ASB rites if they are conscientiously followed. The Ministry of the Word occupies a prominent place in the new rites. Plainly it is intended to be preparatory and ancillary to the Ministry of the Sacrament. But as the inadequacy of these forms of the Ministry of the Sacrament becomes more obvious the Ministry of the Word will become more important and prominent. And the ASB itself affords encouragement for growth. The ASB contains a very large scriptural anthology. It has pages of lectionary references. Even to use the Bible properly within the prescribed rites will require practice, work and effort. Reading the Bible in public is not easy; and still more difficult is it to read effectively from the so-called Good News Bible – to make a vulgarized text carry a full public meaning. Bible readings will have to be rehearsed as carefully as choir anthems. A faithful and successful Ministry of the Word is likely to accumulate a momentum of interest and thought which may well invert the intended emphasis of Rites A and B. Instead of the Ministry of the Sacrament appearing as a dynamic outcome, it could be transformed into a generalizing conclusion to a more sacramental use of Scripture. Empty of a theology, afloat from traditional understanding, how could the Eucharist appear otherwise when an obscure ritual follows on after the open understood words of Scripture? Actions speak louder than words; but special words are still needed to tell us what supernatural actions say.

Should we wish the ASB well? I do not know. Certainly we might wish it were different and better. We should hesitate to wish it ill. But it is in the nature of things that jellies flop, and a flop in the revisers' English is probably a term for failure. Perhaps God mocks us all, gently. His service is perfect freedom and it is unlikely that that service is predefined by our alternatives.

Why Language Matters

DAVID COCKERELL

At a conference held to introduce the Ripon Diocesan clergy to the Alternative Service Book, Dr Jasper quite explicitly refused to discuss issues of language in relation to the Liturgical Commission's work; and I could see his point. Sniping over odd phrases is hardly conducive either to charity or to worship, and the quality of the 'numinous' which ASB is supposed to lack and the Book of Common Prayer to possess, is impossibly vague in definition, and probably exists more in the eye of the beholder than anywhere else. And anyway, is it not futile, and even rather blasphemous, for us to get stuck at the level of language, as though it were what really matters? Christian theologians who have concerned themselves with religious language, from St Thomas Aquinas onwards, have constantly reminded us that human language is a hopelessly and necessarily inadequate vehicle for the expression of divine reality: so to stick at the level of language is the most irreligious kind of missing the wood for the trees. This concern was expressed by Gerald Downing in a letter to the journal *Theology*:

> Dear God! is it really not obvious that the best (by whoever's criteria, however valued) we can do is pea-brained, loveless and drivelling unless God graces it; and then the worst we can do (even Cranmer, and *I* can't find much worse than that) may be a medium for the love of God.[1]

In a sense it simply does not matter what the language is like, because in the worship of God it is bound to be feeble, inadequate, unworthy. And it is at least silly to talk as though we could walk into church, unprayerful and unprepared, and expect the liturgy to do all the work for us. If we come before God worshipfully and prayerfully, we should find that the language simply doesn't matter, if only we work hard enough at our own faith to pray it.

I say all this as a self-corrective to an essay which from now on will be all about language. At the end of his life Aquinas had a vision through which he came to see all his great work as so much straw when compared to the greatness of the God towards whom it was directed. Those of us who discuss liturgy must retain a similar sort of perspective, lest we come to believe that it really matters. Furthermore, at a time of deep recession throughout the world and large-scale unemployment in our own country – to mention only one of our social and political problems – it is only the most blindly complacent and self-absorbed ecclesiastical organization which could afford the luxury of seeing liturgical revision as a dominant preoccupation for two of the most disturbed and disturbing decades of the century. That it has been so regarded is in itself of importance in reflecting on the way religious language has come to be used in the Churches in recent years. Here we have a significant indicator both of the Christian Church's changed position in our society, and of the nature of its response to that change. The incapacity of the Church in recent years to deal adequately with any issue except those internal to its own institutions, itself reflects a narrowing of the scope and meaning of religious language and experience, which becomes progressively less capable of being related in any significant manner to the wider world of secular concerns.

But before I examine further the implications of these considerations for the way language is used in liturgy, we must look very briefly at one or two more general issues relating to the nature of religious language.

Broadly speaking, we have taken over from philosophical empiricism, via science, the idea that language is only a tool, an instrument for communication. This means that words are only contingently related to the 'facts' or 'truths' ('ideas' in the traditional terminology of empiricism) which it is their business to communicate; and so a worn-out word, or set of words, can be thrown away like a rusted-up garden spade, and a shiny new model bought, while the non-linguistic 'truth' which it expresses remains undisturbed in the 'objective' world of facticity. The plausibility of this view, like much in the empiricist's scheme of things, lies in its common-sensicality: it seems obvious. But in fact scientific method has itself been the area where this view of language has recently come most forcibly to be questioned.

Contemporary philosophy of science is much concerned with the relationship between words and the phenomena which constitute the subject-matter of scientific investigation. Sophisticated scientific enterprise involves talk of theoretical entities which cannot be observed, and which seem to be almost entirely conceptual, so that the words which are used to describe them are heavily theory-laden. To cut a very long and complex story very short indeed,[2] this suggests to the philosopher of science that language plays a far more constructive role in the determination of scientific theory, and thus in shaping the possibilities of future scientific work, than a simpler sort of correspondence theory can allow. And, of course, similar considerations can be pressed against an instrumental view of language where it is found at work in theology.

An instrumentalist view of religious language suits well the theologian who wants to press an apologetic based on the idea that people who reject religion do so because they misunderstand (i.e. on the basis of a systematically misleading language) the nature of its claims. The traditional language of religion is misleading because it carries with it a metaphysic which is unacceptable to contemporary man; so we must jettison that language, and find another which will speak more meaningfully of the nature of religious truth to modern man. We find this kind of argument in Bishop John Robinson's *Honest to God*. For Robinson, the traditional ways of talking about God are 'symbolic language to represent and convey spiritual realities' (p. 11), so that the task of contemporary theology is to find a new set of 'symbols' which will better convey those 'spiritual realities' to modern man. What we have to do is 'to validate the idea of transcendence to modern man', to 'restate its reality' in other than those 'mythological terms which merely succeed in making nonsense of it to him'. And so, Robinson believes, we must take very seriously Paul Tillich's advice that 'you must forget everything traditional you have learned about God, perhaps even that word itself.'

This sort of programme can be criticized in a number of ways, but what is relevant here is the underlying assumption that, at the core of religious experience lie certain 'spiritual realities', to which the language which is used to 'represent and convey' them is related as a set of inter-substitutable symbols which can be changed, apparently by fiat, and without loss or change of meaning. The problem with this is that as soon as we try to say what these realities are, we use language, and to use language is to bring them under a more or less specific type of description (e.g. 'spiritual'). The idea that there can be undifferentiated 'realities' or 'experiences' is simply empty. Such a something-we-know-not-what cannot possibly bear the weight of being the experiential basis of religious (or any other kind of) belief. In fact, a reality can only be a reality, let alone a 'spiritual reality', where there is already in existence a language, a set of ideas and beliefs, in terms of which this is possible. For there to be 'the religious' or 'the spiritual', there must be available a language in which the religious or the spiritual can be spoken about.

This suggests that in religion, as in science, we are not concerned with static and unchanging 'truths' or 'realities' which it is the job of the language to 'represent and convey'. In each case there is development, there is change; in each case if there is not, there is decay, the progressive fossilization of an anachronism. But there is a great difference between the language which shifts subtly in order to reflect new emphases, new insights, facets of social and cultural change to which the religious believer must remain sensitive, and a self-conscious attempt to create a new language, as though that could be done by fiat decision, and in a social and cultural vacuum.

This is not to underestimate the importance of the pastoral concern underlying Robinson's programme. He recognized – and the enormous impact of his book is witness to this – that many people were having trouble with the traditional language of religious belief, and, implicitly, that this difficulty was bound up with a deeper problem as to how to make sense of the world which men and women ordinarily inhabit in terms of traditional Christian ideas. Behind the rather naive optimism of much of the 'secularization theology' of the 1960s, with its rhetoric of 'relevance', lay the problem, taken up from Bonhoeffer's writings in prison during World War II, that religious language seemed to have lost its ability to engage significantly with the wider world of common human experience: 'How do we speak in a secular way about God?', as Bonhoeffer put it. Increasingly since Bonhoeffer's death the world of moral, social, political, and scientific concern had divorced itself from religion, and since the 1960s that process has been accelerated by such factors as a continuing loss of public support for religion, reflected in declining church attendance, and immigration which has brought religious traditions such as Hinduism, Sikhism and Islam, into the centres of our cities. People today are less than ever able to see the language of Christianity as providing a self-authenticating framework for the interpretation of the world in which they live.

Confronted by such circumstances, it is all too easy to see how the Church can respond by becoming increasingly self-conscious, increasingly a self-contained and self-centred group which identifies itself in terms of the language and the practices which define its existence and which thereby distinguish it from other such groups. And so the central issue becomes that of a contrast between two ways of using and understanding religious language: on the one hand to express, and to keep alive the means of expressing, man's deepest common concerns, and, on the other, to create a barrier of theological intelligibility, to define and articulate the distinctive concerns and interests of the religious group.

The importance of this contrast, and its importance for liturgy, was made clear in a paper called 'Religious English', by Ian Robinson.[3] Robinson exploits a view of language which is quite different from the instrumentalist view which I have sought to criticize. He takes up the idea that what we are able to make of the world we live in, and our place within it, depends on the language which is available to us. We can make sense or nonsense of life; we can have a life which is full and rich or one which is grey and inhuman; but we cannot have the former without an appropriate language which keeps the possibility alive.

> 'Birth, and copulation, and death' is such an inadequate summary of human life, even without considering the things it omits, because in birth, copulation and death there is nothing specifically human.... The move from birth, copulation and death to initiation, marriage and burial is from an animal to a specifically human world. We may reduce the human realities represented by words like *marriage* and *burial* to nonsense; but without the possibilities they express there is no human life.[4]

The expression of such possibilities is a function of religious English: 'We are granted in such language the capacity to see our marriages as something more than the mating of beasts and our burials as more than waste-disposal; without this common human possession we would all die the death of dogs.' (pp. 47–8). Ian Robinson believes that the liturgical revisers have sold out, that they have robbed us of a 'possibility of living humanly' by substituting the flat and the second-rate for a genuine religious English which kept religion and with it the possibility of seriousness in life alive. Religious English is something that must grow and live in the hearts of men; it cannot be manufactured or produced to order.

The importance of Ian Robinson's paper for the present discussion lies in his insistence upon the complexity and depth of religious language, and on the fact that it ought to enable us to speak of *human* concerns, not just of 'religious' ones. Those who come seeking a christening, a marriage, or a funeral for a loved one, are implicitly asking for the 'possibility of living humanly': 'the move from birth, copulation and death to initiation, marriage and burial is from an animal to a specifically human world.' To send them away, or more subtly to exclude them by our use of language in liturgy, is to deny them that possibility.

I have tried to demonstrate, then, first that for there to be talk of the religious, there has to be available to us a religious language: religious ideas cannot be 'translated' without loss or change of meaning. And, further, if we are to be able to talk religiously about the problems and experiences of common human life, that language has to be such that we can significantly engage religious words with secular concerns. Only a kind of religious language which has the spontaneity and the robustness of that which reverberates through our consciousness and our culture can really do this. A self-consciously created form of language has all the artificiality of jargon, and, like all jargon, is primarily a device for excluding the outsider, the non-initiate, as powerfully and effectively as the secret codes and passwords by which small boys (and big ones) clan themselves into clubs and secret societies.

A topical and graphic illustration of the way in which language conditions the kind of life it is open to us to lead, the kind of understanding and self-understanding it is possible for us to have, is found in E. P. Thompson's influential essay *Protest and Survive*. Thompson rightly emphasizes the importance of language in conditioning our response to the threat posed by nuclear weapons.

> The deformation of culture commences within language itself. It makes possible a disjunction between the rationality and moral sensitivity of individual men and women and the effective political and military processes. A certain kind of 'realist' and 'technical' vocabulary effects a closure which seals out the imagination, and prevents the reason from following the most manifest sequence of cause and consequence. It habituates the mind to nuclear holocaust by reducing everything to a flat level of normality. By habituating us to certain expectations, it not only encourages resignation – it also beckons on the event.[5]

This is not the place to enter into a full debate of the issue of nuclear weapons, though what a series of letters in the *Guardian* called 'the deafening silence'[6] of the Churches in this matter is relevant to this discussion in a number of ways. What is certainly relevant here is the logical point implicit in Thompson's comments, that the more we grow accustomed to the ubiquity of scientific language, with its supposedly 'realist', 'objective' vocabulary, the more we condition ourselves to accept a world in which the deeper values and facets of human nature have no importance, or even no existence. We can reduce ourselves to automata and our environment to so much inert matter which we can then destroy, dispossess, use and abuse, with total impunity. Where the language of function and instrumentality is seen as exhaustive and definitive as an account of human existence, we create the conditions for our self-annihilation as human beings, so that our physical self-annihilation through nuclear holocaust becomes merely a logical consequence of the process we have begun.

This is why a biologist, John Durant, can write, in a discussion of Darwinism, that 'it may be that the creationists are worth listening to after all – not for their views on the origin of the species, which few scientists are likely to find particularly helpful, but for their insistence that the problem of the relationship between biology and human values be squarely confronted.'[7] That is to say, we do not have to accept that the stories in the opening pages of Genesis provide us with historical or quasi-scientific explanations of our origins as a species; but unless the values which these stories embody – set in the language of right, wrong, sin, evil, the values and responsibilities inherent in man's relationship with his social and natural environment – unless these categories are central to our understanding of man and his place in the world, then our self-destruction – if not through nuclear holocaust then through what Thompson calls the 'deformation of culture' – is inevitable.

The possibility of living a fully human life, one in which values, ideals, beliefs and the vision which comes through story, tradition and ritual can play their full part, is given to us in our language. Religious language can be part of this: it can go into what we make of our world, into shaping the possibilities of self-understanding that are available to us. The task of the theologian is then to explore how the world is described, what forms of description are appropriate to it and what part religious language has to play within such description. The result is a view of faith, and a language in which that faith can be articulated, which is robust, which can engage with the wider realities of life, which is experimental in the proper sense of that word: creative, practical and founded in experience. It can cope with uncertainty as well as with certainty, with doubt as well as with faith. It is not afraid of taking risks, and refuses to hide behind an inpenetrable wall of jargon or rhetoric. The alternative is a form of theological jargonese which can only serve to erect a barrier of intelligibility, to demarcate the boundaries of a 'pure' faith, based on belief in a God who is wholly transcendent, radically 'wholly other' and thoroughly removed from the world of secular concerns. Such a God cannot dirty his hands with the dusty stuff of science, politics or culture. Religion is totally *sui generis*, using its own peculiar language to express and articulate its own special concerns and subject-matter.[8]

My criticism of the Series 3 and ASB revisions is, then, fundamentally that they reinforce this latter way of using and understanding religious language, and thus instil in the consciousness of the Church a defective view of faith and a defective theology. This may seem an extreme claim to make of a set of liturgical documents which exemplify a remarkably high degree of theological self-consciousness, and whose theology is markedly self-confident and orthodox. But the function of a liturgy is not to be a theological manifesto; it is (amongst other things) to teach us, to show us, how to use the language and the beliefs of our faith creatively and constructively. This is not to be taken as an appeal for liturgical didacticism: indeed, one problem in the revised rites is precisely that they all too frequently lapse into the didactic. The process I have in mind works in a subtler way, through the unconscious assimilation of ideas and patterns of thought which then work spontaneously on how we think, react and respond to the world of other people and things in which we live. A sensitive and mature religious faith can only arise out of a process of subtle and complex interpenetration between religious words and secular concerns, a process in which each conditions and informs the other. Faith and experience are alike developing, growing things, not fixed bodies of data. Liturgy today should create a kind of religious language, and so a form of religious experience, which is robust enough to become part of this process; otherwise all it is doing is describing the peculiar concerns of a *sui generis* religious group. Wittgenstein wrote, 'A wheel that can be turned though nothing else moves with it, is not part of the mechanism.' The most disturbing aspect of the new Church of England rites is their failure to engage liturgy, and religious language, with the mechanism of human life as a whole. The language turns beautifully, self-confidently; but nothing else turns with it. It is not the language of life. Consequently these rites reflect the contraction of religious experience to the initiated, and of religious language to an in-group jargon. The language, and with it the beliefs it is used to express, is not used to give religious articulation to the common concerns of human life, but to create a barrier of theological intelligibility, a hard line of demarcation between the initiate, the 'insider', and the non-initiate, the 'outsider'.

I suggested early in this essay that this should not surprise us, given the situation in which the Church today finds itself. Our Church seems to have few theological resources, and sometimes little apparent will, to address itself to the wider issues of our age: indeed, it seems increasingly unable to deal with any issue which cannot be institutionalized into one of ecclesiastical polity. Thus, to take one example, the issue of women's rights is transformed into the question as to whether women should be ordained into the priesthood: a social and human problem is thereby converted into one which can be dealt with in terms of theological expertise and ecclesiastical politics. The challenge implicit in the *Guardian* headline quoted earlier calls for the development of a religious language, and a theology of Christian faith, which could more readily engage with the issues which confront us in the world today. The following are a brief sketch of a few of the components which such a theology would possess, not because I claim any originality for them, but because our contemporary revisers of liturgy seem to point us in a very different direction, and in so doing fail to give us the resources of theology or language for the authentic expression of a Christian faith for today.

1 Faith today must be seen as creative, developmental, experimental. It is a seeking, a striving forward, rather than a fixed-and-final stance based on the dogmatic assertion of certain theological 'truths'.

2 Such a faith does not go on in a hermetically sealed compartment of 'religious experience', walled in by its own special language, its own special interests and concerns. We have to live with, and to learn from, men and women of other faiths and none. Where the language we use is effectively exclusivist,

it tacitly denies that possibility, with disastrous consequences for the vitality and intellectual integrity of the Christian faith.

3 Religious language needs above all to have a quality of transparency. The curious idiom of the revised liturgies is not really contemporary English at all, but resides in a limbo world of theological newspeak, a language which, opaque and literalistic, almost entirely lacking any quality of poetry or of music, falsifies worship by reducing it to the didactic.

These stipulations may seem unsatisfactory and inadequate to those Christians who feel happier within the comfortable world of theological self-confidence which is conveyed through the revised liturgies. But to hide behind an impenetrable wall of dogmatic self-consciousness can only lead to a faith which is ever-increasingly distanced from the world of secular concern, which seeks to purchase invulnerability at the cost of intelligibility. Cut off from the flesh and blood of the world of men, emptied of secular content, the language and what it is used to say become a jargon, a code, a game, and eventually meaningless in the technical sense that the question of its truth or falsity cannot even be raised.

An authentic and contemporary religious language, in the sense in which I have defined it, does in fact exist, though, interestingly, in the work of writers whose stance vis-à-vis the traditional formulations and manifestations of Christianity is ambivalent. I want to end this essay on a more positive note by just mentioning two such writers.

The first is Sydney Carter, whose writing at its best exemplifies just the quality of wondering, of doubt, of exploration, which I have sought to describe. One of his collections of poems is in fact called *Nothing Fixed or Final*. Sydney Carter's songs and poems are personal, unself-conscious, they reverberate in the mind and the imagination. Sing 'Lord of the Dance' *anywhere*, to *any* age-group, and they'll know it. Carter's songs are based upon, and manage to capture the vitality of, real folk-song, not the pretentious and trivial ersatz of much 'contemporary religious music'. Indeed, the contrast between these two is instructively analogous to that between genuine religious language and the pastiche variety all too often produced by the liturgical revisers. The songs are also questioning, doubting, even at times cynical, and so strong meat for those who prefer the cosiness of charismatic choruses or the trite and old-fashioned trendiness of such as the Twentieth-Century Church Light Music Group. His songs are not intended to make us feel cosy or comfortable, and if we use them properly (i.e. not 'Lord of the Dance' prettified by trained choirs and organs), they will not. They have occasionally run into trouble with the self-styled upholders of orthodoxy; but then so did Jesus. They are, in short, authentically Christian.

> If you are a son of man
> Then you can be mistaken;
> You hang upon the cross of doubt
> And feel you are forsaken.
> And whether you will rise again
> Is more than you can tell –
> If you have been a son of man
> You've tasted this as well.[9]

As Colin Hodgetts says of Sydney Carter:

> The living, total experience is his concern. Not just words, but words and music; not just song, but song and dance; not one for the church and one for the square, but a dance which knows no such distinction, a dance which dances the dancer, a song which sings the singer, the dance and the song of life.[10]

My second example is the Welsh priest and poet R. S. Thomas. Thomas's writing is perhaps less immediately popular than Carter's, but he is an accessible writer, and he often speaks with the same voice as Carter, expressing the same doubts, the same questionings, the same uncertainty, and, at the heart of it all, the same faith. Thomas's writing, like Sydney Carter's, demands attention from anyone concerned with the search for an authentic kind of religious expression. But I am no literary critic, and I must let him speak for himself – and, in conclusion, for me.

> There
> is no body in the stained window
> of the sky now. Am I too late?
> Were they too late also, those
> first pilgrims? He is such a fast
> God, always before us and
> leaving as we arrive.
>
> There are those here
> not given to prayer, whose office
> is the blank sea that they say daily.
> What they listen to is not
> hymns but the slow chemistry of the soil
> that turns saints' bones to dust,
> dust to an irritant of the nostril.[11]

NOTES

1 *Theology* LXXXIII, (March 1980), p. 136.

2 The story is well told by Ian Hacking in *Why Does Language Matter to Philosophy?* (Cambridge University Press, 1975) esp. ch. 11.

3 'Religious English' in I. Robinson, *The Survival of English* (Cambridge University Press, 1973). An earlier, and fuller version of the paper appeared in *Cambridge Quarterly* vol. 2 (1966/7) no. 4. References here are to *The Survival of English*.

4 *Survival of English*, p. 47.

5 *Protest and Survive*, eds. E. P. Thompson and Dan Smith (Penguin Books, 1980) p. 51.

6 Correspondence in the *Guardian*, 13 November 1980 and subsequently.

7 The *Guardian*, 16 October 1980, p. 13.

8 cf. D. Cockerell, 'The Availability of God', *Theology* LXXXIII (July 1980), p. 249.

9 From 'Son of Man', in *Songs of Sydney Carter: In the Present Tense*, Book 3, (Galliard, 1969), reprinted by kind permission of Galliard Ltd.

10 *Exploring Worship* (Mowbray, 1980), p. 127.

11 From 'Pilgrimages' in *Frequencies* (Macmillan, 1978), reprinted by kind permission of Macmillan Press Ltd.

Biblical Translation

TOM PAULIN

Looking back at the recent lively, sometimes tragic, sometimes comic, controversy about the new version of the Church of England prayer book, it seems that a curious version of the Civil War has been fought all over again. The argument was between the Roundheads, who believed that religious language should be made clear, relevant and precise, and those Cavaliers who believed it should be sacramental, archaic and rather gamey. Although the traditionalists breathed at times that air of fusty meekness and wizened superiority that I associate with the worst aspects of the Church of England, their defeat is a sad one. The debate embraced and reflected the controversy about the New English Bible that has been sputtering for a number of years and I propose to examine a few of the words which won in this wider debate and compare them with the words they defeated.

In the Authorized Version of Job 26:7, for example, Job says of God 'He stretcheth out the north over the empty place, and hangeth the earth upon nothing.' In the New English Bible this becomes:

> God spreads the canopy of the sky over chaos
> and suspends earth in the void.

What is fascinating about this verse in the Authorized Version is that God 'stretcheth out the north'; God behaves as the God of the Old Testament is supposed to – with toughness and with no mercy. That word 'stretch' is a formidable and terrifying word, and I associate it with Lord Reith, that flowering and monumental Scottish Presbyterian who complained of feeling 'insufficiently stretched' during the years after he ceased to be Director-General of the BBC. So the God who 'stretcheth out the north over the empty place' is a very rigorous deity. However, the God who 'spreads the canopy of the sky over chaos' is a very different figure; I imagine him as a kind of Cecil Beaton, as a set designer, a trim and nimble chap with fairly exquisite taste. He spreads the sky as though it is a tent being erected for a wedding or a garden fete. Again, when he 'suspends earth in the void' those two verbs 'spreads' and 'suspends' make the earth seem light and flimsy, like a Chinese lantern. They lack the majestic terror of 'stretcheth' and 'hangs'. And though the modern, milder version may be recommended for its gentler, more forgiving idea of God, the Jacobean version is imaginatively much more powerful – that word 'north' is essential to its effect.

In the Book of Isaiah there is a verse which reads in the Authorized Version 'And the daughter of Zion is left as a cottage in a vineyard, as a lodge in a garden of cucumbers, as a besieged city.' (1:8). In the New English Bible this becomes:

> Only Zion is left,
> like a watchman's shelter in a vineyard,
> a shed in a field of cucumbers,
> a city well guarded.

The new version is a very respectable attempt, I think. The line 'Only Zion is left' is stark and simple, a tragic gesture. But we lose the personification of Zion as 'the daughter of Zion', and this means that we also lose the idea of the soul of the nation going to ground in a hidden cottage or lodge. In terms of resonance, however, the new version 'watchman's shelter' is more vivid – it suggests fire, vigilance, even cosiness with exposure to the night and the stars. However, the substitution of 'shed' for 'lodge' is diminishing; a shed in a field of cucumbers suggests the quaint ramshackle world of an allotment by a railway line.

Translation also is not simply a substitution of words, it has as much to do with cadence as with the individual words. What makes the New English Bible so generally dispiriting is that its translators have very muffled ears and do not understand that words must make a cadence to be beautiful. Which means that I belong with the high and gamey traditionalists, like Michael Foot, Dame Helen Gardner and all those others who regret the passing of the ancient words.

Bogus Contemporary

C. H. SISSON

It has long seemed to me that the Book of Common Prayer could do with a little editing. The exhortations, which are never used, in the Communion service might perhaps be relegated to an appendix; there might be some clearer indication of the date of Easter, than the Table to find Easter Day; the Golden Numbers – but no, surely they must be supposed to have charm, in a world which prides itself on its numeracy. Very little would be needed, to make the book easier for congregations to handle: for that matter, they have managed for upwards of three or four hundred years. However, the ecclesiastical authorities have now given us something better – or at any rate bigger. Here, in some 1,300 pages, is the result of a labour which has occupied 'first the Convocations and the House of Laity, and latterly the General Synod, for more than fifteen years'. It is with relief that one learns that this publication marks a pause in their 'programme of liturgical business'.

The book looks more like the product of a programme of liturgical business than the kind of simplification one might have hoped for. It is true that the date of Easter, up to the year 2025, can now be determined by a glance at a new table; there is a Table of Transference to amuse learned children during the sermon, and it is simpler than the Prayer Book exercise with Golden Numbers. But the pattern of the services themselves is of bewildering complexity. This book makes

Reprinted from the *Times Literary Supplement*, 14 November 1980.

too modest a claim, when it calls itself the Alternative Service Book. It is no mere alternative to the Book of Common Prayer, but contains within itself so many varied forms of service that it would be better called the Book of Alternatives. One gathers that those fifteen years of liturgical business did not end in anything that could be called unanimity, unless an exhausted agreement to differ can be called that. It is not that the ancient theological controversies are not muted. They are, although their aged heads pop up here and there. But what the variety of services primarily represents is a variety of tastes; there is certainly no objective principle which could determine the choice of one set of services rather than another. There are alternative blessings and alternative confessions. A bit of what you like does you good – that seems to be the underlying principle: what you like – within limits.

'Unity need no longer be seen to entail strict uniformity of practice', says the Preface. It can hardly be said that *strict* uniformity has been seen within living memory, and indeed the long years of indiscipline among the clergy are an important part of the background to the present disintegrative book. What is new now is that the notion of a standard of practice has in effect been abolished. So we have 'The Order for Holy Communion Rite A' and 'The Order for Holy Communion Rite B', but each of these proves, on examination, to offer a number of variants, to be adopted or not according to the devices and desires of clergy or congregations, or whoever is strong enough among them to get his way. Do you prefer the first, second, third or fourth eucharistic prayer? The first or the second intercession? And so on. Variety is the spice of life, they say; it is less certain that it should spice liturgy to the extent that no one but an expert in Alternative Services can really keep up with it, and that going into a church beyond his own parish boundary no one will know what he is going to find. Indeed, he will be lucky if he knows what he will find in his own parish.

All this is supposed to be good. It has, however, until

recently been a predominant part of Christian education for the churchgoer to hear familiar words until he knows many of them by heart. Not for me to say what may happen to souls, under the old dispensation or the new, but under the old, *minds* were actually filled with something. Not only were the words of Matins and Evensong, the Communion service, and the Psalter, so familiar as to be only just below the surface in the memories of ordinary Anglicans; the system provided for the public reading of the Bible in the Authorized Version. This education has, admittedly, long been slipping, with the decline in churchgoing and the virtual elimination – by the authorities – of Matins and Evensong as popular services; but the slipping cannot be taken as an argument for letting it slide altogether. The fruit of excessive variety will certainly be even greater ignorance, for let no one suppose that people will possess anything of the wealth of the Christian tradition unless they learn something first. Even the Lord's Prayer is now on sale in three versions – that of the Book of Common Prayer, which until recently every decently brought up child knew; that of Rite A *et passim* and that of Rite B *et passim*. The latter varies from the true English version only by tiny verbal changes so silly that no one but a pedant could have thought of making them at all – changes which, moreover, no one familiar with any range of English as it is spoken today could imagine would be clearer to anybody. So many people must have had a good idea during those laborious fifteen years, and so many people must have preferred their own good ideas to other people's, that there was no way of getting that much-to-be-desired pause in liturgical business except by concluding how right almost everybody was, and making a puzzle book of 1,300 pages.

The width of nefarious agreement over the text of the ASB has been made possible by the fact that the book itself was strictly unnecessary. There was no great theological issue at stake, no anxiety widely and deeply felt which the book in any manner resolved. The difference from the situation in

Cranmer's day, which is often invoked as a precedent and excuse, could not have been greater. Cranmer's books represented the resolution of agonizing differences; it is the lack of any comparable predicament at the origin of the new book which makes the latter so frivolous by comparison. Even the Prayer Book as proposed in 1928 was *about* something. Of course the ASB has behind it the Continental liturgical movement and the stream of domestic scholarship for which Gregory Dix's *The Shape of the Liturgy* may stand as an indicator. Dix's bitter pages against Cranmer have had their influence here, as well as those more illuminating parts of his work which have a bearing on the changes in the order of the liturgy now ambiguously promulgated. But, important as these scholarly developments are, they represent a shallow stream compared with the discontents which burst upon Europe in the Reformation. It is the chance confluence of this stream with the real current of the age – a self-assertive humanism the history of which runs from the more extreme Protestantism of the Reformation, through Locke and Voltaire to the current religion of democracy – which has swept the present book into being. To that extent the authors of the Preface are certainly right when they say that 'those who seek to know the mind of the Church of England in the last quarter of the twentieth century will find it in this book'.

But what a mind! It is distressing to those who have known and loved the Church of England, not only in Cranmer but in Hooker, Herbert, Vaughan, Jeremy Taylor, Swift, Berkeley, Butler, Law and many another, to find to what mouthpieces she is now reduced. It is not those great men of the Anglican tradition who are the mere stylists; it is not even the signatories of David Martin's notorious petition who hanker after that distinction. The authors of the ASB are the real literary gents. 'Composed in the very finest modern English', says the press release, 'this new service [*sic*] brings the form of Anglican worship right into the twentieth century'. Whoopee! In fact, there is hardly a page of straight twentieth-century prose in the whole volume. And as for the verses so coyly introduced into what used to be Evensong, they turn out to be by Robert Bridges:

> We see the evening light,
> Our wonted hymn outpouring.

You need to be something of a stylist to see that as more in tune with the twentieth century than Bishop Ken.

The pretence of modernity is fundamental to the ASB, and to apologias which have been so widely made for the new services. The practical thought in the mind of the more simple-minded parsons has been that there must be *some* reason why they could not keep their churches full, and that as everything really successful seemed to be *modern*, they had better try a bit of that themselves. That might not make church quite as acceptable as the telly, but they could try. The secret of many things, they had heard, was in good public relations. The Prayer Book and the Bible sounded so unfamiliar to those who were not familiar with them that it would be nice if things were said in such a way that everyone would think that they had heard them before, even though it was only because they had encountered just such language in the pages of the *Daily Telegraph* or some other 'quality' paper; so they started using translations of the Bible which sounded like that. (Only in limited circles is thinking yet advanced enough to look rather to the *Mirror* as a model).

Of course things did not work out exactly as had been hoped. One reason is that the ghosts of the Authorized Version and the Prayer Book were too powerful. It needs more than a prudential decision to speak of the things the Fathers of the sixteenth and seventeenth centuries spoke of, in a language which owes nothing to them. Echoes of the old speech sound through this new book, only the original rhythms have been nicked and chopped here and there and inept words introduced which do not carry conviction.

It may well be that the real difficulty about revising the Prayer Book at this time is that there is no contemporary theological language which really carries conviction. We have to have some patience in educating ourselves in our ancestor's language in order to know what they meant. I once heard a wretched child set up in church to read the story of the creation of Eve. The only comment one could make on the passage was that no one would believe a word of it. If such stories are not understood with the imagination they are not understood at all. The ordinary language of the twentieth century means by understanding something mainly mechanical and quantitative. Until this primary theological difficulty is faced, there can be no serious beginning of an attempt to restate the traditional matter of the Christian faith. And of course the restatement will be slow, partial, and hesitant – quite unlike the verse of Robert Bridges or the prose of Professor Frost.

It would seem all too simple a game to point to examples of sheer outrageous ineptitude in the language of the ASB, were it not that many people including, it would seem, most of the bishops and a large majority of the other members of Synod, have their perception of language so blunted that they simply do not know the living word, and the living cadence, from the dead. This should not surprise us because the living has to be new and anyone familiar with literary history knows that, since the date of the *Lyrical Ballads* at the latest, it has taken several decades for any new tone to win public acceptance. That is a phenomenon of the current phase of the language from which the writers of liturgies have no celestial exemption. One might say that the project of an alternative book was doomed from the start, given the many hands that were to meddle with it and the representative approvals which had to be sought at all stages. These difficulties could have been foreseen, but only by people of more literary perspicuousness than, apparently, those who actually had charge of the Church's affairs. At the risk of encountering readers who cannot see what is wrong with the new versions, I will give a few items from a schedule of comparisons which might go on for ever. Take Morning

Prayer. One of the 'sentences' reads 'In everything make your requests known to God in prayer and petition with thanksgiving' (*Philippians* 4:6). This is preferred to the Authorized Version's 'In every thing by prayer and supplication with thanksgiving let your requests be made known to God.' Perhaps only a trained palate would observe the difference here, and markedly prefer the older version. It is also rather hard to see what constitutes the 'modernity' of the later version. Second item: as to rhythm, the Confession drags along like a lump of dead meat; but those who do not see that cannot be made to see it. More will recognize the effrontery of preferring a version of the Venite which has 'In his hands are the depths of the earth: and the peaks of the mountains are his also' in place of 'In his hand are all the corners of the earth; and the strength of the hills is his also'. The reader who cannot understand the enormity of the substitution is fit only to be a member of Synod. In the Benedictus 'To shine on those who dwell in darkness and the shadow of death' (ASB) is not 'modern', but sham antique; and compare the rhythm with that of 'To give light to them that sit in darkness, and in the shadow of death' (Book of Common Prayer) which is every whit as intelligible. 'Bless the Lord all created things: sing his praise and exalt him for ever.' (ASB) 'Modern'? No, only mediocre sham religious. The earlier version which is being pushed aside for this, is breathtaking: 'O all ye Works of thc Lord, bless ye the Lord: praise him and magnify him for ever.' (Book of Common Prayer). As if in shame, the authors of the ASB reprint the Prayer Book versions of the Canticles in a sort of appendix to Morning and Evening Prayer. If they had that much shame, where was the courage which should have made them reject the inferior versions altogether?

The case of the Psalms is very odd indeed. The Psalter did not enjoy the benefit of 'repeated scrutiny by the General Synod', but, desperate to have something worse than Coverdale's (the Book of Common Prayer) version – as one easily might have – they hit on the English text published in

1976 by David L. Frost, John A. Emerton and Andrew A. Mackintosh. Good for them! But bad for the rest of us and an irreparable loss to any congregation that makes the changeover. 'Modern'? No. An insensitive pastiche. There are some good laughs for the student of the bogus contemporary. 'Praise him in the blast of the ram's horn,' sing our alternative Davids. 'Praise him in the sound of the trumpet,' answers old Coverdale from his tomb. Ah, Coverdale, we must tell him; at least we moderns know it *was* a ram's horn, and do not mix it up with any instrument we have actually heard in the twentieth century.

One can only hope that when the ASB at last falls heavily into the pews, the eyes of priests and congregation will be opened and they will see that this is not a Prayer Book made new for the twentieth century but a compendium of old hat including 500 pages of mutilated collects, sentences and readings from every version of the Bible except the best. They should laugh unsanctimoniously to see that the bishops have promoted themselves above the Queen, in the Church of England's first attempt since the Reformation to set itself apart from the polity in which it lives; and to notice the concurrence of innocent scholarship and political innuendo implied in the odd name of 'President' given to the priest at Holy Communion. I suggest that there should be a competition in every parish for the most striking pair of comparative phrases from the old book and the new. When the congregation has played this game for a week or two, they should hunt round to see where the churchwardens have hidden their real Prayer Books, and blow the dust off them.

'Unwillingly to School' – With the ASB

CHRIS O'NEILL

> A poet gives an image whereof the philosopher bestoweth but a wordish description which doth neither strike, pierce, nor possess the sight of the soul as much as an image doth...

Sir Philip Sidney compares the powers of the poet to touch the heart with the more cerebral appeal of the philosopher. His comparison prompts me to wonder whether the liturgical revisions of the Alternative Service Book are nearer to being 'wordish descriptions' than they are to being songs which 'strike, pierce [or] possess' the soul. I fear that there is little evidence of the poetic in the new services, and feel that the language of the new liturgy tends to be didactic and self-conscious in tone. Why is this undesirable? I would maintain that the most recent liturgical revisions are altering the proper function of liturgy, with the risk that the job will be botched in the eyes of all concerned.

My evaluation proceeds from two assumptions. First, the aim and function of liturgy is to point *beyond* itself so that the worshipper may be enabled *through* it to achieve communion with God. This communion with God may be achieved through materially symbolic or sacramental means, by the symbolic and evocative use of words, and even sometimes by the mechanical repetition of sounds (like the Hindu mantra) whereby the conscious mind's chatter is stilled or assuaged to enable the heart to take over and sing its songs to God. If we wish to teach or instruct the faithful, Christian tradition has always provided means of instruction: the sermon, Bible study and the confirmation class. If liturgy too becomes primarily didactic in tone, with what then shall we worship?

Secondly, religious language itself – especially that used in liturgy – is inextricably and properly both symbolic and poetic. Like all poetry, it needs to have beauty and quality if it is to be enduring or captivating. On the other hand, scientific language, which aims to be straightforwardly factual, can be flat and boring without loss of essential usefulness. The heart sings the songs it hears and it is the musical home that tends to produce the musical child; so also in our liturgical life. A child brought up where Mozart and Beethoven are in the air finds himself humming their tunes – in the same way that our dreams are often populated by the people and events of the preceding day. The heart, however, does not thrive on didacticism or bludgeoning, just as compulsory piano lessons rarely produce the sensitive musician; so also for the worshipper. The heart needs to be captivated and allured by things of beauty – the culture which is caught, not taught.

If what I have just argued is accepted, then two criticisms of the ASB's liturgical revisions follow. First, a didactic and simplistic use of words produces the effect of *self*-consciousness, which, by definition, focuses attention on the words themselves, so that the mind dwells on them and their authors, rather than passing *beyond* them to the Creator. This self-conscious tone indicates a betrayal of the proper aim of liturgy. Secondly, the language and concepts of the liturgy of the Book of Common Prayer, and indeed the biblical and patristic texts on which it was based, belong to an ancient and mentally distant world, far removed from the secular twentieth century. Any attempt to render their words *alone* into modern English creates the same bald, self-conscious and didactic tone that would be achieved by paraphrasing Shakespeare or Donne. Husk and kernel are not easily separated, and the attempt is as perilous as trying to clothe your grandmother in hot pants, with results often as graceless.

Antique concepts survive in the ASB text with a rather uneasy metaphorical status. In earlier centuries the populace at large may have spoken of angels and archangels without scruple, blush or second thought. Indeed, it is a standing joke among modern philosophers that their medieval counterparts discussed seriously how many angels could balance on a pin head. Yet there, clothed now only in their scanty twentieth-century English, the same beings stand on pages 131, 133, 136 and 139 of the ASB apparently totally unabashed. The high priestly function of Christ is comprehensible when you know the Jewish background, but the office itself ceased many hundred years ago. The retention of this image in an ancient and poetic text is required by the principles of textual integrity, but in a thorough-going twentieth-century text its use betrays an incongruous antiquarianism.

The apparent didacticism, the superimposition of modern language on ancient concepts and the singular lack of poetry deprive the worshipper of songs worth singing. As a substitute he is offered the liturgico-classroom, with a teacher provided by the Liturgical Commission. The man in the pew thought he had come, not to be taught, but to worship. He is given instead lesson material which is a self-conscious and superficial paraphrase of an ancient text, in the language of the Tax Office memorandum 'which doth neither strike, pierce, nor possess the soul...'.

Music and Church Worship

ANN BOND

As a professional musician and organist of a large parish church I thought it would be most useful if, instead of echoing the points made by other writers about doctrine and language in the new liturgies, I aimed to give a factual picture of the implications of the Alternative Service Book for the music in our services, and to look briefly at the whole place of music in parish church worship.

Before I do this, however, I should say a few special words about music in the cathedrals. Many people, alarmed by what is happening, assume that the new liturgies pose serious threats to traditional cathedral music. In fairness, this is not the case. In fact cathedral choirs are generally enjoying a considerable boom, and the traditional music is flourishing. Even 'progressive' clergy seem to recognize, however grudgingly, that there is a place for 'centres of excellence' in worship – places where the finest in music can be offered up on behalf of those less skilled. This is often referred to as the 'power-house' theory – i.e. we can all visit our cathedrals occasionally to recharge our spiritual batteries. What a tribute, even if back-handed, to the numinous power of the traditional musical worship and the great texts which inspire it!

It is true that some cathedrals are using the new ASB rites for their Sung Eucharist. This need not affect the traditional music, however, since cathedral choirs operate independently of the congregation, and the rubric which allows 'well-known'

Reprinted, with minor alterations, from *Faith and Worship*, Summer 1980.

settings of the old words can be invoked to cover *all* the traditional English Communion settings, plus Latin ones as well. It is not unusual to hear Palestrina, Byrd or Schubert masses sung in a Rite A context, the only difference being that the sung Credo is omitted. Keeping up Choral Evensong as a sung daily Office is also almost bound to involve the traditional music: quite apart from the fact that it is unthinkable to jettison the glories of Weelkes or Sumsion, practical considerations are strong. It would take years to build up a repertory of new settings of the responses and canticles sufficient for a complete cycle of daily cathedral services, even if composers were attracted by such barbarisms as 'Lord, now you let your servant go'! If there were to be an 'Achilles' heel' of traditional cathedral music, it might possibly be the Psalms since the new ASB 'Collins Psalter' is pointed to fit traditional Anglican chant and therefore offers, in theory, an instant alternative. However, cathedral organists, having by definition grown up with the Psalms as choirboys, are mostly staunch champions of the splendid language and rhythms of Miles Coverdale. They may well recall that the 1662 revision of the liturgy avoided altering the Psalms out of deference to the singers, and do the same themselves today. In any case they are, as a body, educated and articulate people, not easily coerced or frightened by talk of 'irrelevance' or a few obscurities in the old version.

Thc numinous power of cathedral music needs no emphasis: ever since Milton, countless people have testified to the power of its ineffable beauty to 'bring all heaven before mine eyes'. During the past century the influence of the Oxford Movement spurred many parish churches to emulate the cathedral style of service – worship enhanced by an offering of the finest possible music – and some notable local traditions were built up. Such parish churches are now however relatively few in number: elsewhere, a greater measure of congregational participation has long been the order of the day, and the extent to which the music is capable of real inspiration depends very much on the talents – or limitations

– of the local choirmaster and organist. I do not mean 'how *complex* is the music?' but 'how *fittingly* is it done?' Can the organist choose the right sort of music, has he a natural feel for the drama and flow of the service, and – crucial quality – can he infuse vitality into non-professional musicians?

A gifted and dedicated person can make music flourish in the most unpromising places. There is, however, always a dearth of such people in parish church music, and it is hardly surprising that poorly-paid amateurs are not always able to drag liturgical music out of the doldrums – this calls for a lot of skill. But low standards of traditional music unfortunately offer yet another pretext for restless clergy to introduce the new liturgies: there is a widespread (though mistaken) belief that this will inject new life into congregational singing, since the ASB Eucharist in particular is heavily biased in favour of congregational 'do-it-yourself', and its more informal tone consorts easily with a shallow, lowest-common-denominator type of music. And so, in too many parishes, the worst happens. Let us now look at the musical implications of some of the ASB services in detail.

The Communion. Congregations intending to sing their ASB Communion are, in practice, limited to new musical settings, since most priests are adamant about people having 'the right words' in front of them. This conflicts with the rubric about the permitted use of older settings. (If the Liturgical Commission had been sincere about that rubric, they would have printed the 1662 words alongside in the little green Series 3 books during the experimental period). Merbecke and Shaw, two of the most familiar settings of the Ordinary have, in fact, been adapted to the terse new words, but few musicians regard this as either artistic or practical – the new versions don't flow, and memories of the old musical phrases keep tripping one up. (The adaptation of Martin Shaw's version has now been withdrawn, at the request of his widow.) Some parishes have produced compositions of their own, and there are about twenty published settings of the new words, some (like Hurford's) meant for a competent choir plus a people's part, others weakly meandering or blatantly 'pop' in style. All suffer, naturally, from the banality of the words, which weights the scales heavily against composers. The opening of the Gloria is a particularly frequent casualty, the words being quite unable to call forth anything but pathetic dactyls or skittish triple rhythms.

One should note that there are many problems of musical flow and continuity in the new liturgies, since (as in *opéra comique*) there are so many transitions from speech to music, each of which has to be engineered by little organ preambles. The problem is aggravated by the practice of the laity reading the Gospel and the consequent disuse of intoning. Intoning has no equal for audibility, dignity, and ease of flow, and its passing should be a matter for much concern. Sung responses before and after a said Gospel are both awkward and illogical! Other musical deficiencies of the new rite include the tucking-away of the Agnus Dei as a communion motet: the optional Kyrie/Gloria: and the absence of a sung Creed – surely a lost focal point. In many churches, indeed, the music of the Ordinary is now very thin upon the ground, in spite of the new bits and pieces (e.g. the Acclamations, one of the few likeable features of the new rite).

Matins and Evensong. Parish churches have much to lose here. Practically all the traditional music is invalidated if the ASB is followed literally. In fact, all that remains is traditional Anglican chant, which can still be used for the ASB 'Collins Psalter' and the new versions of the canticles. The new responses are so different that old settings cannot be adapted. The same goes for the Litany. The choir can, of course, do a traditional anthem – but will it fit into the new 'low-key' atmosphere? Will there, indeed, still be a choir? (Many clergy oppose 'elitism' of any kind).

I have not so far mentioned hymns, although these constitute a large part of what the congregation sings. There is, of course, no direct threat to the traditional hymns from the adoption of the ASB: but readers will be aware of the proliferation of new-style hymn-books ('Living Lord' and so on), and experience shows that once the *tone* of the services is altered by the adoption of the new liturgies, the way is wide open for informal hymns. In fact, it can also work the other way round – a few commercial-type hymns are duplicated and used in normal services for a few weeks to 'soften the congregation up' for a proposed change of liturgy. It is all justified by fine-sounding reasons, chiefly that of attracting the young. (My experience tells me it does not keep them: many, bored by such hymns at school, yearn for more sustaining fare.)

This matter of the *tone* of the service is crucial. Do we want 'transcendent' worship (the lifting of ourselves up to God's glory, the offering of our best, though conscious of our own great unworthiness) or 'immanent' (God as found in the familiar and everyday)? Do we want awareness of salvation or social consciousness; beauty and awe or musical matiness? These are, of course, over-simplifications – and in any case true *religion* should involve both transcendence and immanence. There is no reason to infer, however, as many clergy do, that therefore *worship* must involve both too: this confusion of mind leads to endless trouble. How can one identify oneself sincerely with a lowest common denominator offered as 'worthship'? All PCC members – which I trust means all Prayer Book Society members – need to have thought carefully about immanence and transcendence, formality and informality in worship: these concepts are vital tools in discussion when the vicar brings up controversial proposals. They should realize, for instance, that by no stretch of the imagination can the guitar be regarded as a transcendent instrument – whereas the organ, in all but grossly incompetent hands, can, both intrinsically and by force of association. (One could well make out a lengthy theological justification in the medieval style for this view!)

Our church music either elevates us or ties us down to everyday things. It can be carefully rehearsed or shoddily spontaneous. Most important, the two approaches do not mix. Many vicars, anxious to please or placate, advocate amazing mixtures of the formal and informal within a single service – a bit of Merbecke, a 'pop' hymn or two, a Gelineau psalm. This usually offends more people than it satisfies, and *musicians oppose it whole-heartedly,* since the techniques of the different types cannot agree. A robed choir singing a revivalist hymn is a cultural nonsense: and the disciplines of formal choir-work – diction, tone, deportment – are ludicrous when applied to the informal. A decision to include informal hymns or 'popular' mass-settings could, logically, call the very existence of the robed choir in question. Furthermore, the organist will be placed in an agonizing dilemma, since his musical integrity is at stake. PCCs should be warned.

Transcendent worship, then, involves standards, and at least an attempt at perfection – our best is still unworthy of God. My own considerable experience, however, is that the adoption of the new liturgies invites – nay, urges – musical standards to fall, in the belief that everything in worship must be accessible to all. Hard-and-fast solutions are not easily suggested, since so much depends on local conditions: but I have said enough to make it clear that there is a great need of local leadership and an informed laity. The Royal School of Church Music, while not committed exclusively to the old liturgy, can offer a great deal of help to those wishing to perform it worthily with limited resources. And those seeking guidance on the principles of music in worship would do well to read the relevant chapter in C. H. Phillips' *The Singing Church*, recently reissued as a paperback by Mowbrays. The present liturgical aberrations would have been inconceivable to Phillips, but he presents a magnificent argument in favour of the transcendent – which yet charitably and humbly recognizes that all men are at different stages along the road which leads (in heaven) to perfect worship.

A Goodly Heritage

G. G. WILLIS

By the time that the present Book of Common Prayer, which came into use on St Bartholomew's Day, 24 August 1662, was in preparation, the Church of England had used a liturgy in English for over a century. This liturgy had by then established a recognizable liturgical type, standing on middle ground between the Latin rites of the Roman Catholics and the informalities of the Puritans, which left almost everything to the discretion of the minister. The Book of Common Prayer was not a novelty: it was a careful revision of an existing rite; it represented an improvement in the direction of Catholic and traditional liturgy. The aim of the English divines of the seventeenth century, beginning with Richard Hooker at the end of the sixteenth, was not one of innovation, but of restoration, and their moderation proved to be the main cause of the stability of the English rite in the three hundred years which have followed. The cautious and scholarly revision of 1662 presents a stark contrast with the radical and indeed reckless revision which has been pursued for the fifteen years from 1965, a work based on no principle but that of novelty.

The title of the Acts of Parliament which have authorized the Prayer Book from 1549 onwards has been 'Act for the Uniformity of Common Prayer', and until the Prayer Book (Alternative and Other Services) Measure, 1965, uniformity was a principal and characteristic quality of English worship; from Berwick-on-Tweed to Sennen you could be reasonably sure of finding the same service on the same day in every church, great or humble. This principle has in recent years been sacrificed to individualism and eccentricity, to novelty and variety, and innumerable choices of rite, of Scripture readings, of intercessions and even of eucharistic canons, are permitted by law. There are no fewer than seven orders of the Holy Communion, all of them with internal options and choices, and the variety of worship is immensely greater than the variety of medieval use between one diocese and another, of which the Preface to the 1549 Prayer Book complains. These differences were small variants of the Roman rite; our present variants are often fundamental differences not only of liturgical structure, but of doctrine. The aim set forth in 1549 'that henceforth there shall be but one use for the whole realm' had its advantages in the sixteenth, seventeenth and eighteenth centuries when the population was stable, and many worshipped in the same church all their lives. But we are more mobile, and therefore uniformity of worship is much more desirable. Yet we have abandoned uniformity. There are those in the present age who positively seek instability. It has been described as an age of revolution, and indeed people often seem to be turning round until they are dizzy. Yet in religion, which is concerned with immutable things and with God who is the same yesterday, today and for ever, men have always had a longing for stability. In St John's Revelation the picture of the final bliss of heaven is of a state where there shall no longer be any sea (the symbol of restless change) but a city which has foundations, whose builder and maker is God; a walled city is the symbol of security and stability. Uniformity in liturgy is therefore a stabilizing influence, and it unites us to our past.

On the practical plane it makes devotion much easier. Hitherto we have been able to go to church, knowing exactly what would be said. If great variety is permitted, we are wondering which options the officiant will choose, and if the church is large or the minister careless and inaudible, we find ourselves straining to hear what is happening, or wondering whether we are supposed to stand, sit or kneel. All of this is distracting and inimical to devotion. It also gives scope for the individualism and even the fads of the minister. In the seventeenth century this was one of the most frequent complaints against Puritan ministers, and when the laity had endured it for about fifteen years under the Great Rebellion, they were heartily glad to get back to the treasures of their beloved Book of Common Prayer. They could now hope to hear the Scripture lessons appointed by the Church, not those chosen by the minister, who could very easily exercise his discretion so as to exclude any doctrine of which he disapproved or in which he was not interested, just as in the *ad libitum* intercessions of modern times the political and social opinions of the minister are often only too apparent. Uniformity protects the laity from such dangers as these.

Much of the criticism directed against revised services is concerned with language. Indeed the degeneration in the language is the most noticeable change in the services, and the change which most easily distresses the ordinary folk. New styles of language mean instability and unfamiliarity, both of which are opposed to devotion. But the attack of traditionalists should not be directed exclusively against deficiencies of language, important as these are. It is important to expose the deficiencies of doctrine which new services display. In the Church of England such doctrinal inadequacies are very serious, and perhaps insufficient attention has been paid to them. Yet in the long run they are corrupting. They produce Christians who have a one-sided, distorted view of the Christian faith. Anglicanism is a definite type of Christianity, well-balanced, founded upon Scripture and tradition and reason, and therefore unsympathetic to beliefs which are unscriptural or unreasonable or untraditional. Such a faith is nurtured by the Book of Common Prayer, while modern experiments tend to lack balance and moderation. This may be due to the fact that modern services have not been devised by scholars steeped in liturgical history and in the writings of the early Fathers and the Primitive Church, but by busy amateurs, such as those who amend liturgical drafts from the back benches of the General Synod.

The divines of the seventeenth century did not emasculate Christian truth to accommodate it with the spirit of the age, and therefore they produced stability, which has lasted over three hundred years. The twentieth century, being an extremely self-satisfied age, thinks it can do better than any of its predecessors; in this it is mistaken, except perhaps in the mechanical sciences. In the Reformation period in the sixteenth and seventeenth centuries the Church of England, unlike Continental Protestants, did not pursue a popular fad but tried to set itself in the broad and balanced tradition of the early Fathers, and it therefore succeeded in preserving some age-long traditions, such as the Sacred Ministry of Bishops, Priests and Deacons which elsewhere had been lost.

Nobody has ever claimed that the Prayer Book of 1662 is perfect, but it is not difficult to see it is a great deal better than any of the substitutes or alternatives which have recently been proposed and certainly it succeeds, better than they do, in preserving the balance between opposing schools of thought in the Church of England. It is indeed a goodly heritage, and it would have been a disastrous mistake to have prohibited its use, as some dioceses wished to do in 1974.

When Prayer goes Pop

BERYL BAINBRIDGE

The Alternative Service Book for 1980, not to be confused with the Bedside Book, or some treatise on an extension of the Army, Navy and Air Force, is to be published tomorrow. The Dean of York, Chairman of the Liturgical Commission, insists that it is not meant to supplant the old Book of Common Prayer, merely to be laid beside it. Nobody will be compelled to use it, though that is rather like finding a brand new car at the door when the old one in the garage is still in working order. One imagines that the Church Commission is praying that the new vehicle won't be left rotting at the kerb; it would surely be a waste of effort and investment. It is not the first time that the contents of the Prayer Book have been revised, revamped and updated, nor, if the Church Commission has its way, will it be the last. They are already talking of the ASB for 1990.

No exact date can be given to any entire Western system of offices earlier than the time of St Benedict. At this period, though the Churches of Rome and Milan, of France and Spain differed from one another in many particulars, all had adopted Lauds, Vespers, Compline and Matins. Augustine, arrived in Kent, introduced a form of liturgy based on Roman ritual, with ordinary daily offices derived from Southern France. By the eleventh century this usage, modified and adapted, was collected in the Breviary, so called because Pope Gregory had shortened the existing ritual. In

Reprinted from the *Sunday Telegraph*, 16 November 1980.

the fourteenth century, altered once more, it was known as the Prymer. Rejigged, it later began to be called the Prayer Book.

In 1641 an attempt was made to lessen the hostility of the Puritans towards it by introducing other changes. Talk of change continued until motions were entertained in the House of Commons which showed that no alteration in ritual would pacify opponents who sought the ruin of the Church and who were rapidly increasing in power. The idea of making concessions was laid aside as useless.

Three years later an Ordinance of Parliament took away the Prayer Book and substituted 'The Directory for the Public Worship of God in Three Kingdoms'. To use the old Prayer Book in a place of worship or in the home was punishable by a fine of five pounds for the first offence, ten for the second and for a third a term of one year's imprisonment. The voice of the Church of England was silenced, and Presbyterianism, after trying to bring a spiritual despotism into every parish and household, was in its turn obliged to yield to Independency. In the words of an observer of the time: 'There ensued a state of distraction and impiety...the natural tendency of which was to divide men into two classes, one anxious to find terms of agreement in order that religion might not be easily extinguished, and the other indifferent as to whether any form of religion remained.' Nothing has changed, except that the numbers of people indifferent to religion now totally outnumber those who believe. Those rollicking centuries of saints and martyrs, of reformers and innovators, have gone for ever. Nobody is fighting to retain this or that form of worship, and it is not psychology or the Welfare State alone that can be blamed for it. The Church should have realized that evil might be explained out of existence, and that once the common man was no longer in danger of starving to death his reliance on God would understandably weaken.

The Church shouldn't worry about the size of the flock. It should wait, unchanged, on the sidelines. It is not the language or the ritual contained in the Book of Common Prayer, and used for the past 400 years, that has caused the decline of the Church of England, nor will the ASB for 1980, or 1990 for that matter, achieve a spiritual revival. Indeed, in mistakenly thinking that what is needed is a more easily understood form of worship, the Church Commission may effectively shut the doors of the Church for ever. In any century there were but a few who were religious in the true sense. The bulk of humanity trailed behind, ignorant, superstitious and fearful. A belief in God requires an act of faith, and the sustaining of such an implausible proposition requires that the language and ritual of prayer, of baptism and burial and Communion, should be both mystical and difficult.

The Church Commission should have learnt the lesson of the Roman Catholic Church, which in electing poor misguided John as Pope, began the process that swept away the Tridentine Mass and dealt itself a death-blow from which it will never recover.

Galileo, in proving the truth of the Copernican system, threatened to shift heaven out of reach of the people. Life on earth being brutish and short, it was necessary that they should have somewhere better to go when they left it, and preferably it should be straight up. God was waiting directly overhead and infinite space was inconvenient. I am not suggesting that the Church Commission should ape the Inquisition, but it might be better if it went backwards instead of forwards. If the Church would stop mucking about with the Prayer Book and cease to worry about popularity, its time might come again. It would be a pity if the people, caught in a wave of nostalgia for the past, turned and found the Church no longer recognizably ancient.

Anticipating the publication of the ASB for 1990, I offer a revision of the revision of the Burial Prayer on page 321 of the ASB for 1980.

The Old Fella is very nice and it takes a long time
For him to blow his top. Like a Dad is nice to his Kids,

so is the Old Fella nice to them kids that are Scared to hell of him. He knows what we're up to. He Remembers we're just specks of dust. We're a bit on the Frail side. When it gets windy, like a flower in the Market we get chucked in the bin. But the Old Fella Goes on being nice, and he'll be alright with those Bastards that follow after.

Like Nation, Like Church, Like Book

BRUCE REED

An important sociological dimension to the debate on the Alternative Service Book is made clear by the question: 'What kind of Church produces that kind of book?'

Comparison with the Book of Common Prayer sharpens up the point at issue. Internal evidence in the Book of Common Prayer (1549 Preface) shows its purpose was to unify the Church of England liturgy by replacing the diversity of diocesan rites with one national use. A major cohesive factor was the declaration that the sovereign was the Head of the Church. Subsequent revisions to the Book of Common Prayer in 1560 and 1662, after its rejection by Mary I and the Commonwealth respectively, reasserted both its primacy in worship and the headship of the sovereign.

In contributing to the Book of Common Prayer, the compilers were seeking to reconcile their theology with the politics of the day. As representative Englishmen they followed the precept 'to keep the mean between two extremes' (1662 Preface) in identifying the boundaries, the order and the authority of the Church, and relating those to the nation. The Church as reflected in the Book of Common Prayer was elitist, and one whose fortunes were tied to the State. The ordinary people were never consulted; they were expected to follow and be obedient. The book itself reflected an authority and power both in the structure and language of its rites and ceremonies in divine worship. Rather than speak down to the people in their dialect, it sought to raise them to its own level of felicity in worshipping God. The fact that over the centuries large sections of the public refused to conform to this model was unfortunate; the Church said that the opportunity was there for them to make use of if they wished.

Today such elitism would shriek of oppression and loss of individual freedom; hence the wish of some to rebel against the Book of Common Prayer. But their anger may be due to a different perception of society. The concern to safeguard individual values may be over-emphasized because the protester is unaware of other values which have been lost in the meantime: values deriving from the corporate aspect of society. The Book of Common Prayer is the embodiment of such corporate values. As Head of the Church, the sovereign was also the representative citizen, so to pray for 'our Sovereign Lady Queen Elizabeth' is to pray for oneself and for one's fellow citizens. The burden involved in sustaining this corporate identity is well expressed by Shakespeare, a younger contemporary of the original compilers of the Book of Common Prayer, in *Henry V* where before the battle of Agincourt, Henry proclaims:

> Every subject's duty is the King's; but every subject's soul is his own.
>
> ....
>
> Upon the King! Let us our lives, our souls,
> Our debts, our careful wives,
> Our children and our sins lay on the King!
> We must bear all. O hard condition. (IV, i)

The various attempts made by the Church since 1662 to revise the Book of Common Prayer have failed not because of their theological or ecclesiastical deficiencies, but principally because they were felt as interfering with the corporate relations between the populace and its symbolic head.

The ASB reflects a totally different set of values. It is the final product of dedicated study, extended experiments, debate and prayer by both clergy and laity, and the result of careful negotiations between Church and Parliament. The ASB mirrors a Church which sees itself threatened more by external forces than by internal differences and rivalries. The many alternative rites and forms of prayer which are authorized indicate that the Church of England is prepared to allow diversity and gives space to groups of church members to plot their own theological path through the multiple choices on offer.

But in celebrating diversity, the concept of the unity presented in the ASB is suspect. By selecting different forms, theological truth can be interpreted and legitimated by parties who now have no need to work at their differences with each other. Instead of each of the diverse parts seeking to embody and to represent the whole Church of England, however inadequately, the parts can only represent themselves and their particular version of the universal Church. This church situation is paralleled on the political scene, where an emphasis is growing that elected representatives can only represent decisions of their own party and not the interests of the whole electorate, however they voted.

In producing the ASB, the current leaders of the Church of England have therefore *de facto* given up what they would consider is its 'pretence' of being the national Church. For them the reality is that the Church has reverted structurally to its place in the nation before Henry VIII. It has become a series of islands in a national sea of indifference, secularism and other expressions of faith, Christian and non-Christian. Any criticism of the ASB appears to provoke its advocates to voice their anti-establishment opinions.

If the Church of England exists only to further its own private objectives then changes in worship are rightly left to the authority of its leaders. But if the Church exists to serve the human needs of the society in which it functions, then any alterations in the conduct of its affairs will have wider significance and need to be taken into account. Take a recent incident to illustrate this possibility: we suggest that those who voted in the House of Commons and the Lords in order to put pressure on clergy to ensure the use of the Book of Common Prayer were less concerned about the language of the liturgy than about loyalty, loyalty to the nation. They were trying to prop up a Church as though it could still signify authority and historical influence, and thus be a force in integrating a crumbling national life. The wide divergence of interests of those who voted together is itself evidence of the wish for integration. They stood for those other citizens who need to see the Church of England as a symbol upon which they can project their hopes, their loves and their fears and their hatred, whether or not they ever darken its doors, alive or dead. For them the Church of England is *their* Church, and not the possession of the Church Commissioners.

The ASB is thus the indicator of a malaise present within the established Church. This malaise is also characteristic of our national life, of which the social unrest in Brixton, Bristol or Belfast are manifestations, namely the continual and restless tension between parties formed around strong personal and cultural beliefs. Far from being an instrument to transform the spiritual life of our society, the ASB is affirming its deficiencies.

The remedy is complex, but it lies in the understanding of corporateness, where any one part stands for the whole. Thus does St Paul describe the Church as the Body of Christ (1 Cor. 12). The ASB is deflecting the Church of England from engaging in that corporate task. The Book of Common Prayer has been found wanting, but at least it embodies a concept of corporate society which those who compiled it believed the Church needed to sustain for the health, well-being and freedom of the people it serves.

Parisn, Church and Prayer Book

W. H. VANSTONE

Beneath the placid surface of the most ordinary parish, there is always a hidden ferment – the private and personal ferment of birth and death, of sickness and recovery, of marriage and estrangement, of a job lost and a job found, of growing friendships and ruptured friendships, of the horizons of personal lives contracting or expanding, growing darker or growing lighter. The longer a priest ministers in a parish the more he becomes aware of the detail and depths of this endless ferment. The more he becomes aware, too, of its effect in giving to the church community a rather fluid or fluctuating outline, in blurring or softening the distinction between worshippers and parishioners, between those who are 'inside' the Church and those who are 'outside'. A particular vicar may hold in private or expound in public criteria which imply a clear and hard line between those of his parishioners who are in the Church and those who are outside, but in the course of time he becomes increasingly aware that this line is constantly being crossed in both directions. Another vicar may feel it improper to make such a sharp distinction among his parishioners, but he cannot be unaware for long of constant variations of interest and allegiance, of the response of one person to the Church's mission becoming more eager and that of another more cool.

Public events such as a mission, a campaign or the arrival of a new vicar may bring a flurry of change in the relationship between a number of parishioners and the active centre of the Church's life. But the principal and continuing source of change and movement lies in the ferment of private and personal life. It is for particular and personal reasons, on account of particular things which have happened to them personally, that most people move inwards or outwards in relation to the Church. And here lies one of the major problems faced by the clergy: while recognizing the force of such particular and personal reasons, they must try to create in their place, or at least underpin them by, general and universal convictions.

A mother is in hospital, and members of her family come unwontedly to church. One respects their motive; one wants them to feel that 'they have come to the right place' and that what happens in church is relevant to their concern. So the vicar is inclined to mention the mother and her illness specifically and by name. But it would be unfortunate if the family were to conclude from this that the mother had a place in the prayer of the Church simply because she was their mother or because she was a particularly good mother or because she was particularly ill. It would also be unfortunate if another family, coming unexpectedly to church for the same kind of private reason, should hear many specific references but none to their own particular concern, and should thereby conclude that the Church's prayer was only for 'insiders' or only for those well-known to the vicar. It would be unfortunate too if a groping, inquiring person, searching for he knows not what, should encounter on coming to church a highly specified form of worship – prayer for very particular people and causes, a very specific 'intention' at the Eucharist, a sermon rigidly confined to a particular and narrow topic.

If a parish church is to provide adequately for the ferment of private and personal life in the parish, it must provide in its worship both 'a place' and 'a space' for each person who comes to worship. One has one's place to the extent that one is individually known and that one's particular needs and aspirations are recognized and met; one has one's space to the extent that one retains one's privacy and is addressed and treated in worship simply as a creature in the presence of the Creator or a child of God in the Father's house. Clearly it is no easy task to make proper provision in worship for both place and space, but it could reasonably be argued that modern forms of worship provide primarily for one's place, older forms primarily for one's space.

There are occasions in the history of a parish when the provision of *place* is of paramount importance. A church may be so nearly dead, or so tightly 'possessed' by a small group of worshippers, that the generality of parishioners would be inclined to say, almost in so many words, 'there is no place for us there'. A new vicar coming to such a church may rightly feel that it is up to him in the first instance to initiate a new and better relationship between worshippers and parishioners. For the time being, he may feel, he himself must so control the worship that the stranger or infrequent attender is 'made to feel at home'; that his presence is recognized and his particular concern referred to; that his unfamiliarity with worship is assisted by instructions and explanations; that, before long, he is offered some special part or function in the act of worship. Contemporary forms of worship, especially at the Eucharist, offer to the vicar unprecedented opportunity for such control. Facing the congregation across the altar, he sees all that is going on, and all who are present are aware that he sees them. It is he who composes or supervises the specific content of intercessory prayer; his instructions and explanations, being set in the context of modern liturgical language, do not obtrude or seem out of place; by custom if not by law, he distributes to whom he will such functions as reading the Epistle, leading the intercessions and administering the chalice. The dominance of the priest, normally the vicar, in modern forms of eucharistic worship is extremely striking, and it can, in certain phases of a church's life, be valuable in assuring a place of worship for the uninstructed, the newcomer and the parishioner with a particular and private motive for being present.

But the characteristics of modern worship which give the individual worshipper his place tend also to restrict or usurp his space. Intercession which refers to particular and known concerns must inevitably leave less time and room for the very private anxiety or yearning, for the need or hope too personal to be expressed in public or too indistinct to be articulated at all, for the confusion, doubt and wonder which, so far from being occasional intruders into the mind of the worshipper, may form a large part of its normal constitution. Only a rather generalized form of prayer can allow space and freedom for the multiplicity of thoughts and aspirations of those who share in it. Similarly it is only a certain comprehensiveness in the words and themes of worship that can allow space for the growth of the individual's understanding and concern from the particular preoccupation which first brought him to church to a wider vision of what is involved in the relationship between God and man.

One's space in worship tends to be restricted by particularization. It tends also to be invaded or usurped by personalization. It is not everyone who is 'made to feel at home' by the well-meant instructions of the all-seeing celebrant at the modern Eucharist or the equally well-meant greetings, handshakes or embraces of fellow worshippers; those who are, by instinct or conviction, rather private persons may well feel that this kind of personal attention smacks less of Christian charity than of transatlantic manners. Space is preserved only by a measure of restraint, and this is true physically and emotionally as well as intellectually and spiritually. That worship should provide, or at least permit, a certain 'distance' between worshipper and worshipper may be as necessary as that it should suggest a certain distance between man and God and imply a certain distance between the limited and particular concern through which an individual may come to church and the 'ultimate concern', to use Tillich's phrase, which the church represents and proclaims.

A parish, as we suggested at the beginning, is always in ferment, always a place of movement. There are times in the history of some parishes when the church becomes so isolated from the generality of parishioners that it becomes a dead centre rather than a still centre in the fermenting life of the district. At such times the paramount need is to restore to parishioners 'their place' in the church; to establish the relevance of church worship to particular and personal concerns; to ensure that newcomers and occasional worshippers do not feel 'out of place' or 'in the wrong place'. At such times of restoration modern forms and manners of worship may be helpful – especially since they offer to the parish priest, who is likely to be the initiator and principal agent of restoration, an extremely dominant position in the ordering and control of worship.

But there are other times – longer times, normal times – when the ferment of parochial life is already being felt, to a greater or less degree, within the church; when it is already coming within the walls of the church; when people are coming to church for particular and personal reasons, because certain things have happened to them, because it is a certain season of the year, because something has brought it home to them that they ought to come. That they ought to be, on such occasions, 'in their place' is not really a matter of doubt: the need is that, having taken their place, they should also find and feel a certain sense of space. The need is that, when in their place, they should experience a dimension larger than that of the particular need or occasion which brought them to their place; that they should find room in worship for the thought too private to be spoken or the feeling too obscure to be articulated; that they should feel free from the hidden pressure or manipulation of too marked attention or too immediate involvement; that they should find their privacy left intact save only for what they themselves wish to disclose or choose to share.

The language, the substance and the manner of Prayer Book worship tend to allow space to the worshipper. This is not, of course, to say that no conceivable alternative could be equally 'spacious': but no spacious alternative at present exists. In the alternative forms of worship available in the Church of England at the present time the dominant tendency is to provide a place for each at the expense of space for each. Why this should be the case is not altogether clear. It may have something to do with the incidence of a phase of greater mobility in society, a phase in which many are uprooted, insecure and unrecognized, 'in search of an identity', in search of a place. That the Church should attempt to provide such a place is entirely proper, but if one's place is to be a place of worship it requires space around it – space which suggests the true dimension of what one is and does in worship. It is the absence of space in modern forms and manners of worship which makes them unsuitable for long-term use in any church which is in real and living contact with the ferment of its parish.

The Issue of the American Prayer Book

DOROTHY MILLS PARKER

The Prayer Book issue is surely one of the most controversial and divisive matters in which the Episcopal Church has ever been involved. It has caused widespread unhappiness and confusion, serious membership loss and polarization, and has been a factor in the growing schism in the American Church.

At the 1978 worldwide Lambeth Conference of Anglican Bishops in Canterbury, great stress was laid on diversity in unity, and the necessity for respecting and safeguarding opposing positions and rights if that unity is to be maintained. The main focus of this stated consensus was on the issue of the ordination of women. But surely it must also be applied to this other crucial issue which has so divided and fragmented the Episcopal Church.

Lambeth 1948 stated that 'the Book of Common Prayer has been and is so strong a bond of unity that great care must be taken to ensure that revision of the Prayer Book shall be in accordance with the doctrine and liturgical worship of the Anglican Communion.' But by Lambeth 1978 the liturgies of the various member Churches used successfully in the daily worship of the Conference could claim only a common pattern rather than common prayer. If all

Extracts from Dorothy Mills Parker's *The Prayer Book Issue* (Society for the Preservation of the Book of Common Prayer).

this diversity can be sanctioned in Anglican worship, surely the basic traditional liturgy that is our common heritage and treasure should be included as an official option in perpetuity, in all provinces of the Anglican Communion. That is the main stance of this paper and of the organization and individual support that have made its publication possible. A great deal has been said officially, in praise and support of the Proposed Book of Common Prayer, but there has been little real opportunity for rebuttal on the same scope and level.

First of all, the objections to it do not stem from the alleged opposition to all change, but from the desire for constructive rather than destructive revision and the safeguarding and conserving of those things that are changeless and eternal, and vital to the faith, order and life of Anglicanism. In such a presentation I speak for countless faithful and devoted church people who are deeply disturbed and concerned about present trends in the Episcopal Church, in liturgical revision and other areas, and who are not being heard or heeded. Whatever our respective positions in this time of so much division in the Church, all are agreed that traditional Episcopalians must band together and make a stand before it is too late.

Worship has been defined by Evelyn Underhill, in her comprehensive work so entitled, as 'the response of the creature to the Eternal', and the liturgy as 'the ordained form within which the whole Church performs its praise of God... whose prevailing note has been and must be adoration rather than edification.' It has also been described as

> the dedication to the Most High of all that is best in what the eye can see, the ear hear, the voice say or sing, the mind conceive, and the hand execute – the sanctification of colour, sound, and sense, of skill and intellect, imagination and devotion. Thus it is that worship calls for art, and that art so often finds its noblest use in worship.

All Anglican Prayer Books up to now have been living testimonials to this, from that first English Prayer Book of 1549. This was written not in street language but in a heightened vernacular, the noblest language of its day, which accounts for its timelessness. The objective was not to reduce worship to a level immediately understood by all, but to raise people up to a higher level – to inspire, chasten, ennoble, and sanctify them – and above all, to glorify God. The line from the Cantate Domino says it well: 'O worship the Lord in the beauty of holiness; let the whole earth stand in awe of Him.'

The whole matter of current liturgical revision has been misrepresented as a widespread demand for a contemporary liturgy against the objections of ageing, diehard conservatives opposed to any change, which simply is not so. There was no such demand from church people, and the Proposed Book is not a revision but largely a new creation.

Some of the strongest protests have come from those outside the Episcopal Church – from outraged editors and writers in the big dailies to a polemic in none other than the *Wall Street Journal*. One such critic, columnist James Kilpatrick, spoke for the multitudes both within and without:

> The book of Common Prayer, like the King James Bible, is not the exclusive property of Anglicans...but the common inheritance of all literate men. And when a committee of earnest butchers...good clerics but bad poets...begins to hack away at it, critics from every denomination...deserve to be heard.
>
> Suppose an activist group of impatient modernists descended upon the National Cathedral...destroyed the buttresses...pulled down the intricately carved stones...discarded the rose windows...and covered the floor with linoleum...and that they acted throughout from the very best intention.... Cries of outrage would come from persons of every faith or of no faith at all... Episcopalians are not about to wreck their cathedral,

> but are seriously bent on vandalism of another sort. In an act of cultural destruction they appear to be determined to remodel one of the great works of English literature, the Book of Common Prayer. In this wretched work...they have yanked the poetry apart...sought out the lines that sang and destroyed them.... Most of the beautiful, familiar passages have been savagely, recklessly attacked.... These are not the minor emendations in the respectable pattern of 1895 and 1928. This was the work of a wrecking ball, smashing its way to perdition.... The Book of Common Prayer, like the Cathedral, is an organic whole. In seeking to tear it down and put a jerry-built text in its place, the revisers have done those things they ought not to have done. If this is not a sin against God, it is most surely a sin against mankind.

The new rites supposedly appeal to the young and to the underprivileged, who allegedly cannot appreciate Elizabethan English. But listen to these two letters, among many received:

> I am 25 and have been revolted and saddened by the shoddy changes in our Church. In my first years at college the liturgy contributed greatly to keeping my sense of values in a radical world. It was a known in a world of unknowns, a standard in a world of greys. There I found my strength, only to be disinherited by the trial liturgies – tasteless, bland and intellectually condescending. The drive to make religion 'relevant' is not only distressing but shortsighted, when tied to the oblivion of current usage after it is no longer current. I resent being told that the updating of the liturgy is for the young people of today. This implies that we are so shallow, and our understanding so limited, our sense of aesthetics so small, that we must be talked to in 'simplified' language or lured into church by a religious hootenanny. Many of us feel disinherited, copped-out-on, by somebody's idea of the needs of youth. I'll tell

> you what youth needs – stability! A centre to hold onto in a world where nothing is sure, not even the Church. God to me is not a pal or a buddy or a superstar, but the inexpressible Jahweh, the limitless Power, who is evident in the praise and penance, the timeless worship of the Book of Common Prayer.

The second says much the same, in fewer words: 'I am young, black, and from what some might call a deprived background, drawn to the Episcopal Church by its liturgy. But when it scraps the old Prayer Book...I'll be looking for another church.'

The Church is not exempt from the law of change. But if it goes too far in its accommodation to the secular world, it may fall victim to forces beyond its control, to the Zeitgeist – the spirit of the times – and it is in this context that the Prayer Book issue must be examined and understood. The revisers may have thought they were responding to a cry from the outside, but whether or not they realized it, the substance of that cry was to phase the Episcopal Church out of existence. 'For that which drew and retained most people – the maintenance of their faith through the intelligent recitation of a supreme literary and spiritual liturgy – is gone past recalling.' So says another critic.

The Anglican Book of Common Prayer has bound together all branches of the worldwide sixty-five-million-member Anglican Communion, people of every race and background. It had enabled High Church and Low, Anglo-Catholic and Evangelical, liberal and conservative, rich and poor, intellectual and illiterate, to worship together within one body that has been the wonder of Christendom. But with each province of the Anglican Church now creating its own version, common prayer, the cement that bound us together, will soon disappear, and once gone, cannot be retrieved. The book which has united Anglicans the world over has now become the very instrument of disunity and division. Prayer Book revision should have been the concerted task of the whole Anglican communion rather than of its separate provinces. And its best scholars, literary as well as liturgical, should have been employed, just as in the creation of the King James Bible. In the new rites the distinctive Anglican essence is gone.

The Latin rite in England consisted of various forms or 'uses', of which the most famous was the Sarum or Salisbury use. That first English Prayer Book of 1549 replaced a liturgy so complex as to be nearly unintelligible. As the Preface of the new book explained, there had been 'more business to find out what should be read than to read it when it was found out.' The same could now be said of the Proposed Book, and in that sense it is regressive rather than progressive.

In providing a liturgy both simple and uniform, Cranmer translated the Latin into English and adapted the several uses into one common rite – concise, succinct, inclusive. Minor changes were made in the 1552 revision, and though the English Church came briefly under papal submission again with Mary Tudor, it stabilized for good under Elizabeth, and it was her 1559 Prayer Book, differing but little from the first two, that was brought to Jamestown in 1607.

The revisers insist we must have a liturgy that is more understandable. Yet I have never heard any complaints about the old Prayer Book on that score. All sorts of people have made its language their own, to their great enrichment. They may not have understood the exact meaning of every word. Who does? Many modern literary luminaries are far more obscure. The fact is that countless people have been drawn to the Episcopal Church because of its Prayer Book, and countless people of all ages are now leaving it because of the drastic changes.

For the new book is a radical departure from its predecessors, and the changes within it far outnumber the combined changes of all previous revisions. The Rite 2 Eucharist is far closer to the COCU rite than to the 1928 Prayer Book. (COCU is the Consultation on Church Union, a group of some dozen Churches, of which the Episcopal Church is one, whose goal is a projected monolithic pan-Protestant union in which our Church as we have known it will disappear.)

The charge of idolatry has long been levelled at Prayer Book churchmen. It is not idolatry of a book, but loyalty and devotion to the faith it represents. Such a charge, by those who rush to embrace every innovation, is unreasonable indeed. Many parishes today, now that the proposed book is in use, do not even have the option of the traditional Rite 1. Some zealots removed the old books when the trial rites first began, and many people, during all this time, have been unable to worship, marry or be buried to the old formalities. This is not loving pastoral concern, but real cruelty. I wonder if those rectors who imposed it and those bishops who supported them have any regard for the traumatic effect this has had on those in their care.

Two other factors should be mentioned here: the huge expense of revision and the acute membership loss that drastic revision has helped to cause. The high costs of revision and ultimate replacement of prayer books (altar, pew, and individual) have been played down and all but suppressed. The revision process began in 1950, with the issuing of the first Prayer Book Studies, but really got under way in 1962. The first trial service, the now discredited Liturgy of the Lord's Supper, appeared in 1967. Services for Trial Use (the Green Book), in 1970, was followed by Authorized Services (the striped, so-called Zebra Book) and its offspring, known as Son of Zebra. With the 1976 paperback blue Draft Book and the hardback Proposed Book, this makes six separate editions, not counting the various Prayer Book Studies. Do you have any idea of the cost of all this, plus eventual complete replacement of the old with the new?

The editor of one of our Church publications made a survey (based on official records from national Church headquarters and General Convention proceedings, and on printers' estimates) of the costs from 1962 to 1979. Here are the figures. The revision process itself, $695,000. The successive editions and studies, not including the Draft Book and the Proposed Book, $2,089,765. Sum of these two, $2,785,665. Printers' estimates, at 1975 costs and membership figures, come to $790,601 for clergy copies, $31,748,070 for communicants (not including unconfirmed baptized members), $1,331,110 for all parishes, missions and cathedrals: a total of $33,839,799 for replacements. Add the first figure for a grand total of some thirty-six and a half million dollars, a conservative estimate and not allowing for inflation. By now it is probably considerably more.

Church officials have tended to discredit this survey, drawn from their own records, and to rationalize the costs, citing previous revisions and normal replacement of worn books. But those costs are as minimal, in comparison, as the previous revisions themselves. Add to the cost the tremendous waste of the five previous editions of trial services, now obsolete and unusable, and the countless 1928 Prayer Books now being discarded, many of them gifts and memorials. How can such a cost possibly be justified, with all the hunger, poverty, and unbelief in the world today? How can Church leaders ask us to support the current ninety-six-million-dollar Venture in Mission project, in view of such profligacy? Especially when the revision was not asked for, has met with violent opposition, and has been a prime cause of the appalling membership loss?

According to *The Episcopalian* our membership reached a high (3,429,153 baptized persons) in 1967, but has been declining ever since, with a sharp drop in 1969, for a total loss of over a half million (571,640) through 1975. The *Yearbook of American and Canadian Churches* records this as the sharpest drop, percentage-wise, of any mainline denomination. With escalating losses it is now estimated at close on a million – about a third of our membership – over the last decade. At this rate of attrition, there will not be much left of the Episcopal Church by the end of the next two decades. And with the formation of the Anglican Church in North America, where people are assured of the traditional liturgy, the exodus continues. All the loss cannot be attributed to the Prayer Book issue, but this is a very real factor, and the decline is concurrent with the years of liturgical revision.

A recent Gallup survey showed six million Americans in transcendental meditation, five million in yoga, three million in the charismatic movement, two million in Eastern religions. Church leaders seem strangely oblivious to this growing emphasis on mysticism and prayer, which is an indictment of their inattention to spiritual values in their over-emphasis on social activism and relevancy. They also seem unaware or uncaring of the basic reason for these developments – that the new liturgies have lost the numinous and transcendent, and Church people are being forced to seek these qualities elsewhere.

It was too generally assumed that it could not happen: that most Episcopalians could not really want to scrap the old Prayer Book. By and large they do not, but proponents of the proposed book made certain that delegates to diocesan conventions were committed to it. And these delegates elected the Deputies to General Convention who voted in the new book.

Generally, church people did not realize what was at stake. The Society for the Preservation of the Book of Common Prayer (SPBCP) was not sufficiently well organized. The SPBCP offered the services of one of its founders, Dr Harold Weatherby, Professor of English Literature and a liturgical scholar. His 'Open letter to the SLC' was ignored, and when, later, he was proposed through all the proper procedures to fill a vacancy on the Commission, he was rejected.

The draft book was not yet in congregational use. Many Deputies had only slight knowledge of its contents and the myriad amendments added at convention, though they were overwhelmed by SLC propaganda. Most who spoke at two open hearings were for the book's rejection, but these were not voting deputies.

The Presiding Bishop was ignored when he counselled

against hasty adoption of the new book. Neither Bishop Allin, who made five separate pleas for the 1928 Prayer Book as a perpetual option, nor the Archbishop of Canterbury, who asked for the old to be used along with the new, made any impression. Besides, the two full days set aside for Prayer Book discussion were shortened into a single (Saturday!) afternoon. And trivial amendments reduced the time for substantial debate from one hour to only twenty-three minutes. Vociferous supporters of the new book made it plain that no opposition to it would be listened to. Thus the new book was accepted on pain of a short, sharp guillotine and the general outcome attributed to the action of the Holy Spirit.

Any claim that the new book is the product of democracy is questionable, for the average churchgoer has had no part in it and no traditionalist liturgical scholar or genuine authority on English composition has been asked for his opinion by the liturgical commission. Even so, those who supported the book could not agree on its final form as the arguing of the bishops over Confirmation showed. In short, the proposed book was not ready for acceptance. But no further revision could be made. It had to be voted on exactly as it stood, incomplete and a source of contention. Many will see this as the worst of all possible results since it provided for a book which is totally unacceptable to traditionalists and a cause of disagreement and disarray even among its hasty supporters. The final act was the referral of the optional use of the 1928 Prayer Book to a commission to be appointed by the Presiding Bishop. This has now been done, and there the matter rests.

This brings us almost up to date. The Draft Book was incorporated into the Proposed Book, published in hardback and authorized for use. It is to be used, studied and evaluated in comparison with the 1928 Prayer Book. But to relegate the 1928 Prayer Book to disuse obviously goes against the whole process of comparison. The Presiding Bishop's suggestion that the 1928 Prayer Book should remain a perpetual alternative is pastoral and practical sense. If the Proposed Book is as great as its supporters claim, then it will prevail and the old book will fall into disuse. Moreover, the new book is now the official liturgy, and permission is necessary to use the 1928 book.

The official rationale behind the Proposed Book has been that the Church owes it to the unchurched to speak to them in language they can understand. But many potential converts are deterred by the new rite. Besides, the Church has a deep obligation to those who have served it faithfully for a lifetime. These are the traditional supporters who are now as strangers in their own Church, much confused and greatly distressed.

Despite all the post-Minneapolis talk of reconciliation and respect for individual conscience, there has been little general evidence of it. Supporters of the old Prayer Book are regarded as subversives, obstructionists, potential schismatics or as so antiquated they can be ignored until death removes them. And all because of loyalty to those things to which universal allegiance was heretofore required of all. To all too many, reconciliation seems to mean capitulation.

A general plebiscite on the issue, on the local and national level, though repeatedly asked for, has never been granted. This can only be for fear of the outcome. Indeed the American Gallup poll, conducted by Dr George Gallup, showed traditionalists in the majority. Attacks on its credibility were made which later reappeared in virtual carbon copies when English Gallup produced the same result. Before Minneapolis, request for space in one diocesan paper when the Draft Book was being examined, was turned down on the grounds that both sides were being covered. But with minor exceptions, the evaluations that appeared were completely laudatory. Request for post-Convention space for a minority report was likewise refused. A resolution by a Washington parish, calling for a diocesan poll of the parishes on their liturgical preference, was finally accepted 'unfavourably' by the Resolutions Committee, and voted down, 151 to 101, at diocesan convention, to much applause. Resolutions for retention of the 1928 Prayer Book have met with similar treatment in other dioceses.

While some bishops have been lenient, others have made Rite 2 the norm in their cathedrals, with any Prayer Book service relegated to the early hours. In some churches, at least one late choral service is specified for the traditional; in others there is constant change from one rite to another, with no set pattern, creating endless confusion and insecurity. And in all too many, all traditional rites, including Rite 1, have in effect been proscribed. Moreover in almost all the seminaries new clergy are inducted solely with the new ways.

The most drastic step of all has been the widespread removal of the 1928 Prayer Book from the pews. In many cases it has disappeared overnight, with no warning or explanation save that the bishop ordered it. While at least some diocesans have made it clear that their authorization of the new book for use and its placement in the churches was not a directive for the removal of the old one, all too many rectors favouring the new rites seem to have passed the buck to the bishop in this respect. Many strongly resent any criticism of the new book, perhaps because it gives them licence to do almost anything, and are determined to dispose of the old books before any demand for their return or their retention can be launched. They also seem to have little regard for the effect their removal has had on the congregation.

Two quotations from other sources may be used in summary. The Revd William Ralston, a parish priest, says,

> This was not a continuation of the orderly process of careful revision, but a drastic break with it, a regression to the parochialism of the Middle Ages, which Cranmer had corrected. The new book is a vast compendium of liturgical options, variations, and confusing directions.... A new pattern is already emerging: Rite 2, with

contemporary translations or paraphrases of scripture and quotations from Martin Luther King, Bonhoeffer and others; lots of people doing different things, and much conversation and overt expressions of peace, joy, celebration, and love. For some, this is a viable way to worship, but for most Anglicans it is not. Instead of a set form to which clergy and people were mutually responsible, the congregation is now at the mercy and tastes of the rector, who is protected by the inherent good manners of most Episcopal lay people.

In his book, *A Certain World*, the late W. H. Auden joins the chorus:

> The Episcopal Church...seems to have gone stark, raving mad....And why? The Roman Catholics have had to start from scratch, and as any of them with a feeling for language will admit, they have made a cacophonous horror of the mass. Whereas we had the extraordinary good fortune in that our Prayer Book was composed at exactly the right historical moment. The English language had already become more or less what it is today...but the ecclesiastics of the 16th century still possessed a feeling for the ritual and ceremonious which today we have almost entirely lost.

In conclusion, we have lost, along with the beauty, commonality and theological integrity, our Anglican essence, our order, much of our catholicity, our missionary zeal, our greatest source of unity and nearly a third of our membership. There has been no great upsurge of renewal and growth, and the local gains claimed by supporters of the new rites have been far outweighed by the appalling overall losses.

An Australian Prayer Book

BARRY SPURR

The worshipper in an Anglican church in Australia today is most likely to be found with *An Australian Prayer Book* (1978) in his hands. This compendium, occasionally decorated with line drawings of Australian wildflowers (its frontispiece, the 'spike wattle', should not be taken as an indication of an Anglo-Catholic bias) is allegedly intended 'for use together with the Book of Common Prayer, 1662', but has already superseded it in many parishes at most services. The most striking characteristic of the new book may be summarized in these words from the book it is replacing 'Concerning the Service of the Church':

> the manifold changings of the Service, was the cause, that to turn the book only was so hard and intricate a matter, that many times there was more business to find out what should be read, than to read it when it was found out.

An Australian Prayer Book (hereafter *AAPB*) astonishes for the complexity of its arrangement, the multiplicity of its alternatives (from markedly different forms of one service, through three yearly cycles of readings – incorporating in themselves a variety of texts – to alternative collects) and, therefore, for the extraordinariness of its claim, in the introduction to a liturgical smorgasbord, that it is designed to 'strengthen the unity' of the Church. It is a well-established Anglican principle that the manner of worship need not be the same everywhere, but that is a different matter from guaranteeing that it should vary in each parish.

AAPB is a testament to disunity. It expresses the agreement of its authors to disagree about everything they possibly can. In this way it is a typical product of the Australian Church – a Communion embracing the extremes of conservative evangelicalism and Anglo-Catholic papalism – pretending to act in concert but producing cacophony. Such variety is not the spice of religion and *AAPB*, in spite of its claims to the contrary, will exacerbate the national problem rather than alleviate it.

To characterize more precisely the disunity reflected here it is important to appreciate that the Anglican Church in Australia may be defined by Matthew Arnold's description of his 'crowned Philistine', Henry VIII: one possessed by 'the craving for forbidden fruit and the craving for legality'. The satisfaction of these mutually exclusive appetites in the provision of what are called 'radical' and 'conservative' alternatives is the leading motif of *AAPB*. When you encounter a radical alternative you can be sure that the Anglo-Catholics (from, for example, the Archdioceses of Brisbane and Adelaide) have won the day, while the craving for legality of the evangelicals (led by the Archbishop of Sydney, and Primate, Sir Marcus Loane) must have triumphed when we read, for instance, that 'the Ordinal was prepared in both radical and conservative revisions, but canonical and legal requirements showed that it was not possible to include the radical version in this Book'. Obviously neither side would budge on the Eucharist, so conservative and radical forms of the 'sacrament of unity' exist side by side and are celebrated in parishes which are neighbours in geography only. Theologically, *AAPB* officially sanctions the erection of a barrier of alpine proportions between antipodean Genevas and Romes.

However, it will not surprise liturgical observers in these days to discover that the good intentions expressed in its preface are entirely overthrown by the evidence of its text.

Anyone who has sifted through the documents of Vatican II, noting the elgant confidence with which the very wonderful benefits of liturgical renewal are anticipated there, and then has recourse to the daunting reality of parish worship will be no stranger to the gulf which yawns between theory and practice in contemporary church life. Observe the bathos of the translations out of Latin into the vulgar tongue; the apotheosis of parochialism (in intercessions) and idiosyncrasy (in the indulgence of ritual whims and fancies), and the architectural iconoclasm and psychological naivety of westward celebration with freestanding altars. This innovation has gone ahead both in Rome and Anglicanism in spite of incontrovertible proof from liturgical scholars of both Communions (such as Fr Bouyer and Professor Macquarrie) that it has no authority whatsoever:

> what is to be deplored is the insistence that celebration toward the people is proper, primitive and original. The tradition that Christians pray toward the east, in expectation of the coming of Christ, is much more clearly established than any idea that the eucharist should be celebrated around a table.[1]

All of these changes were designed to revive church life. *Aggiornamento*, however, has quickened the decline of congregations and vocations worldwide, and damaged the liturgy almost beyond repair. The dreams of the 1960s have turned into a nightmare today.

AAPB reflects the international situation: it is a theological patchwork and a linguistic potpourri. In the First Order (Evangelical) of the Holy Communion little violence has been inflicted upon 1662, beyond the alteration of a few phrases and a tinkering with the occasional word, such as the unnecessary replacing of 'property' with 'nature' in the Prayer of Humble Access. Everybody, in this scientific age, knows that the 'property' of some thing or being defines it, and would use that very word; whereas 'nature' is a specifically human or animal characteristic (as in 'a good-natured woman') and especially inappropriate in reference to God in this prayer which is designed to establish a disjunction between the Almighty and unworthy humankind, so that the benefits of Communion might be more fully appreciated. Then there is the inevitable victory of 'you' over 'thou' and its derivatives, as in the aesthetically repugnant 'hallowed be your name', where it has been assumed that congregations incapable of giving themselves up to the dated 'thou' (I would call it 'timeless' and argue for its retention), will be *au fait* with the archaic 'hallowed' – for which the Shorter Oxford is unable to cite an extra-ecclesiastical use beyond the seventeenth century.

Such occasional unjustifiable and gauche alterations in vocabulary in the First Order are relatively small things. For of equal importance to vocabulary in the creation of beauty and dignity in liturgical language is the rhythm in which words are cast: the First Order, by retaining the cadence of Cranmer, is infinitely superior in this way to the radical (i.e. Catholic) Second Order. If words of prayer are to be remembered and treasured, yielding up their profundity through repetition and familiarity, then they will need not only to be accurate, but resonant and rhythmical. Perhaps most Anglicans today would prefer the theology of the Second Order, but to be given what is merely necessary in religion is never enough, for as God dispenses (so John Donne reminds us in *Sermon II*) 'that which is convenient too', so our liturgies must not only feed us to the satisfaction of our doctrinal appetites but 'feed us with marrow and with fatness' to the elevation of our spirits. The Second Order of *AAPB* so keenly pursues a doctrinal precision – the craving for forbidden fruit in the face of the Evangelical craving for legality – as to neglect the cultivation of its beautiful expression. The language is bathetic, except in those moments when an overdeliberate attempt has been made by prosaic minds to cultivate verse-like speech, when the result is a parody of liturgical utterance.

An example of this ineptness is discovered in the Sanctus

Holy, Holy, Holy Lord, God of power and might.

This is the sing-song idiom of the nursery school. The rhythmical violence done to the Latin and Tudor models has produced an anthem as resonant with holiness as the multiplication table. There is an undeniable beat also (would that we could ignore it!) in the opening lines of the Gloria

> Glory to God in the highest
> and peace to his people on earth

This metre is immediately reminiscent of the embarrassing drivel of the *In Memoriam* column, to which it is perfectly suited:

> When God went gathering roses
> For his beautiful garden of rest,
> He stopped and plucked you my darling
> For he only takes the best.

Then, in the matter of vocabulary, there is the superannuation of the Cranmerian collect. In some instances, *AAPB* retains fragments of the original, as in its version of the collect for St Mark:

> Almighty God, we thank you for the gospel of your Son Jesus Christ committed to us by the hand of your evangelist Saint Mark: grant that we may not be carried away with every changing wind of teaching, but may be firmly established in the truth of your word.

Attempts to improve on perfection invariably lead to emasculation. In this linguistic vandalism, the finest moment in the original, the violently percussive phrase 'every blast of vain doctrine', is subjected to a characterless feminizing, with its jingling 'ing' rhyme – 'every changing wind of teaching' – which lulls the senses like an insipid breeze, producing an effect quite opposite to that turbulence of heresy which, thematically, it is meant to convey. Completely forgotten, of course, is the perfect balance in the original between that dark, threatening image and the attenuated serenity of 'the truth of thy Holy Gospel' – the still voice after the whirlwind.

Next, in the collect for St Matthew, a vague, jargonistic euphemism – 'his place of business' (linguistically congruent with that contemporary officialese that speaks of your home as your 'abode') replaces the precise description of Matthew's worldly profession in the original: 'the receipt of custom'. The iconoclasts then develop a narrow precision when applying Matthew's secular example to our material condition: 'set us free from all greed and selfish love of money.' The original modulated meaningfully from Matthew's personal worldliness to the general malady – 'the inordinate love of riches' – which certainly includes greed and the selfish love of money. Avoiding the narrow conception of a mere idolatry of cash by suggesting something more gross and fearsome in 'riches' – the traditional translation of the Aramaic 'Mammon', who is customarily associated not only with the god of wealth (Plutus) but with the more terrifying and larger sinfulness of the deity of the underworld (Pluto) – the original expands meaningfully from the individual to the general. The modern version, by failing to fix the individual precisely, has nothing to expand from, and, by limiting the scope of the general, has nowhere to go.

The difference in this case, and in numerous examples of the modification of Cranmer in *AAPB*, amounts to the difference between poetry and prose. This disjunction may be illustrated as well by quotations from modern translations of the Bible, in comparison with their King James prototypes, as from the liturgy. To 'have borne the burden and heat of the day' (Matt. 20:12) for example, has been reduced in the New English Bible to 'sweated long in the blazing sun'. The modern version has reproduced only a prosaic interpretation of the original, stripping it of the metaphoric implication of the oppression of the spirit under which time-bound man groans. The 'burden and heat of the day', its tedium and discomfort, suggests a heaviness and anxiety beyond the limits of taxing work in a heatwave. The Greek *baros*, which it translates, means 'weight', and on each of its four appearances in Scripture, all in the New Testament, it is its metaphoric use which is intended; as in Galatians 6:2: 'Bear ye one another's burdens, and so fulfil the law of Christ.' By eschewing the poetic phrase, this dimension of meaning and, thus, the spiritual implication of the condition described, are lost.

In the collect for St Luke in *AAPB*, the poetic elaboration of the metaphor of the physician in the original – 'by the wholesome medicines of the doctrine delivered by him' – is abandoned, and we are left, flatly, with 'his teaching'. An incapacity for metaphor has always been a mark of the prosaic mind.

Finally, in collects which have no model to destroy, the authors' complete lack of verbal skills is starkly revealed. Here, chosen quite at random, is the petition for the 'ninth ordinary Sunday':

> Father,
> your love never fails.
> Hear our call.
> Keep us from danger
> and provide for all our needs.

Could it be that this brutal, staccato ejaculation, almost comical in its mean and sullen phrases, was in the mind of the Bishop of Rockhampton (as he then was) when he wrote, in the Preface to *AAPB*, of a liturgical language ' "alive" for our times'? In what possible sense of the word is this prayer 'alive'? It seems to me to be utterly still-born, lacking any vital spark, inert semantically, static rhythmically, impoverished imaginatively, referentially platitudinous. Take even the blandest of Cranmer's collects, that for Rogation Sunday, for instance:

> O Lord, from whom all good things do come: Grant to us thy humble servants, that by thy holy inspiration we may think those things that be good, and by thy merciful guiding may perform the same.

To elevate the simplicity of the petition the balance is established thematically and stylistically between the image of God as the source of 'all good things' and the desire of the petitioner to 'think those things that be good': an echo in language enacts what the prayer would achieve in faith.

Yet the Bishop of Rockhampton invokes the example of Cranmer in the context of the activities of the Australian Liturgical Commission! Cranmer is described by Hilaire Belloc as a 'jeweller in prose', who

> gave to the Church of England a treasure by the aesthetic effect of which *more than by anything else* her spirit has remained alive and she has attached to herself the hearts of men.[2] (my emphasis)

As Cranmer translated out of Latin into the best and clearest English of his day, so the Australian Liturgical Commission, it is triumphantly proclaimed, has accomplished the same feat.

This invocation of Cranmer destroys any confidence we might have entertained in the literary and historical intelligence and imagination of the Commission. And if they, as liturgiologists, have not these attributes, what can they do? For any undergraduate in English and History could tell the Bishop of Rockhampton that his position and Cranmer's are as different linguistically and culturally as they are historically. Certainly Cranmer used the best and clearest English of his day (as Stella Brook has shown thoroughly and fascinatingly in *The Language of the Book of Common*

Prayer), but that was a language uniquely propitious for the lively expression of transcendental yearnings and truths: it was the language of a theocentric age. Moreover, Cranmer's was a time in the development of English – the unique time – when written and spoken language enjoyed a vital community. And Cranmer, Ridley, Coverdale and the translators of the Bible had sensibilities propitious for the task before them.

So while the Bishop of Rockhampton would have us believe that Cranmer's achievement was one of translation, that was, in fact, the least of his abilities. For Cranmer knew what to translate with regard to vocabulary and in rhythm. Like Shakespeare (who gladly borrowed from him; see, for example, *I Henry IV*, I, ii, 170ff.) he was sensitive to the appropriateness of the 'relaxed style' of idiomatic English, but alert, also, to the necessity for the elevation of diction at moments of high mystery or grave profundity. His creative achievement transmuted the dry bones of theology into the milk of faith.

Secondly, in the matter of the understanding (or misunderstanding) of the history of the period in which Cranmer wrote, it is assumed by modern, sentimentally egalitarian liturgiologists, that when the reformers referred to a language 'understanded of the people' (Article XXIV), they meant that they were seeking a liturgical speech that was easy for everyone to understand. That Cranmer was writing for the numerous unlettered folk, or those of rudimentary education in the congregation, as well for that elite which, at any time, is capable of understanding, is not borne out either by the character of his liturgical writing or by what we know of the disposition of his faith. For as the language manifestly presupposes a literate and cultivated auditory, so the temperament of a man who could speak so disdainfully of the 'rude and ignorant common people' (in a letter to Henry) must not be harnessed to the democratic car. In *Paradise Regained*, Milton has 'our Saviour' remark

> and what the people but a herd confus'd,
> a miscellaneous rabble, who extoll
> Things vulgar (III, 49–51)

and Gordon Campbell comments 'the undemocratic remarks of Milton's Christ would have seemed quite unexceptionable to Milton's seventeenth century readers.'[3] It is a modern fabrication to interpret 'understanded of the people' as 'understanded of all the people'. And those levellers in the grip of this democratic emotion, such as the Bishop of Rockhampton (who is anxious to establish *AAPB* as 'a people's book, not just a Commission's production', as if that would be a poor thing, like the Authorized Version, perhaps, which was produced by a committee), have no business to impose their twentieth-century cranks on figures from distant and very differently disposed societies who would not appreciate the imposition. You may not like the facts of religious life in the sixteenth and seventeenth centuries, you may find the personalities of a Cranmer or a Henry abominable, but nothing is to be gained from misrepresenting them to suit your purposes.

It might further be urged that those who are ignorant of literary and historical circumstances (from which liturgy springs, as surely as it does from theological convictions) should not presume to engage in liturgical composition and apology until they have acquired that knowledge. And once possessing it, they might find themselves less confident in their activities, and learn to appreciate the refusal of such men of our time as W. H. Auden and T. S. Eliot, devout in faith, learned in history, distinguished practitioners in the art of poetry, to be drawn into the business of liturgical reform, being pessimistic about the propitiousness of contemporary language and the persuasion of modern culture for such an undertaking.

Further, in acknowledging that Cranmer wrote a contemporary English, one has to be careful not to imply that he was prompted by the contemporaneity, for its own sake, rather than by his brilliant perception of the unique perfection of English at that time and, hence, its suitability for his task. But the Bishop of Rockhampton would enrol Cranmer as a supporter of the contemporary idiom in liturgy *per se*. But does it really need to be pointed out that contemporaneity is worthless if your present speech is inadequate to the task of expressing what men feel and do in worship? Such contemporaneity of utterance is worse than useless, for by its association with the here-and-now it is likely to obstruct devotion to eternal things, rather than encourage it. It is not nearly enough for the Bishop of Rockhampton to assert, as if it were a self-evident truth, that we 'need to bring language and style into contemporary idiom'. Such mindless idolatry of the present is no less heinous than that of the past (of which opponents of modern liturgical language are customarily accused). And even if it could be demonstrated that contemporaneity in worship is a virtue in itself, and even if we could concoct a liturgy which would be comprehensible to everybody (their different ages, temperaments, intellects, socio-economic backgrounds notwithstanding) and thus embrace the chimera of a liturgical language 'clear for the people of our day', '"alive" for our times', what about the people of tomorrow, or the next day?

Noël Coward told us years ago that we live in 'a changing world'; our language certainly is constantly evolving, constantly deteriorating, and if our religion is to provide a strength and stay in this mutable and mortal condition, then it needs to embody, and be expressive of, changelessness. You can no more live in a perpetual state of revolution in liturgy than you can in life; to seek to establish immediate 'clarity' for today relegates you to anachronism and obfuscation tomorrow. And what is clear for some at any time will always be a mystery to others; yet who would say that the faith of millions over the centuries for whom the Mass and Cranmer's liturgy failed the test of clarity Sunday by Sunday, but stirred them to devotion, was less than perfect in comparison to that of those confident persons who claim to have discovered, in 1978, a liturgical speech that is 'clear' and 'alive'? In any case, it is vanity to believe that clarity of expression will necessarily be achieved by contemporaneity of language: a timeless mystery, dimly perceived, will be more tellingly set forth in a language, in music, in ritual actions, when there is little that is reminiscent of our daily lives, but much that is suggestive of a higher plane of existence. How susceptible to clarity of expression in liturgical language is the Christian faith? How clearly can you express the Anglican belief in the Real Presence of Christ at the Eucharist without stripping the belief of that elusiveness which is its life? Clarity, it seems to me, is the least of the attributes of liturgical writing.

The Bishop of Rockhampton, not content with having scandalously misrepresented the achievement of Thomas Cranmer and having played fast and loose with the meaning of words, calls in his closing remarks upon the authority of a modern Australian prelate, the first Chairman of the Liturgical Commission, Bishop Arthur. He writes: 'All have recognised the force of a sentence Bishop Arthur wrote in his preface to *Australia 73*, "A form of words is only a means to an act of worship".' But how can this be true, when even the author of the statement, in correspondence with me in 1974, told me that he regretted it? And certainly it is a regrettable remark. For since the dawn of civilization, whether we like it or not, men have sought to verbalize and vocalize their feelings about God and their concern about their relationship with Him, in private meditation and public worship. Nothing less than the history of mankind has shown that words are indispensable to worship (the conspicuous minority status of Quakers, with their so-called 'sacrament of silence', supports this view). And even if you know in your heart that you have failed in the quest for a suitable mode of address to God, it is pointless to assert, as the Bishop of Rockhampton does, revealing what he imagines to be a trump card, that words are dispensable. How ironic it is that one who sits so lightly to words as the Bishop of Rockhampton, who is able to find something compelling in the statement that 'words are only a means to an act of worship', should represent the Australian Liturgical Commission in introducing this gargantuan assembly of liturgical verbiage! Once again, the facts fly in the face of the theorizing.

The Church in Australia, and the Western Church as a whole, is bedecked, like the emperor in the fable, in new clothes for which fantastic claims are being made. Everybody wants to believe in them, for the Church always needs to articulate decently and beautifully what is thoughtful and sensitive in men – the words of their lips and the meditations of their hearts – and present these soberly and adoringly to her Founder whose Bride she is. But there has been more than one honest and perceptive witness in the diminishing crowd of the faithful to date who has remarked that she is going about, like the foolish, hoodwinked emperor, undressed and unadorned. Predictably, a hue and cry was raised by his subjects; so the voice of protest is growing amongst Christian people. Those in authority ignore it at the peril of the Church.

NOTES

1 George Every, *The Mass* (1978), p. 164.
2 Hilaire Belloc, *Cranmer* (1931), p. 258.
3 John Milton, *Paradise Regained*, ed. Gordon Campbell (Dent Dutton, 1980), p. xxvi.

The Primate and the Prayer Book

DOROTHY MILLS PARKER

Parker Your Grace, I am happy to see you again. I covered the 1978 Lambeth Conference and also your enthronement.

Runcie I know you did.

Parker I'd be grateful for your comments about the new Anglican liturgies. With each province now developing its own contemporary rite, will the Anglican Communion not lose the strongest focus for unity afforded by the traditional Book of Common Prayer, which with minor local variations, was shared by all branches of the Anglican Church?

Runcie That is a very good question, because Anglicanism does centre on a style of worship. In the sixteenth century, we didn't pledge ourselves to a religion of the Book and the Book only; what we did do was provide for common worship for the people, so that Anglicans might know the will of God and be given strength to do it by reason of spiritual nourishment through common prayer.

This is absolutely central, and it has been a matter of concern to me as to whether this would be lost in the efforts to update the Prayer Book all over the world. But at this meeting of Anglican Primates this week, we have used each day the liturgy from a different province, and the basic style and structure do seem to enable us to worship together

A personal interview granted by the Archbishop of Canterbury to Dorothy Mills Parker during the Primates' Meeting in Washington. Reprinted from *The Living Church*, 31 May 1981.

with essential variations albeit a less dominant English style.

So I am encouraged to think that the Anglican style of worship, now a common pattern of updated Prayer Books, still holds us together, and may also enable us to worship more easily with other Christian traditions who similarly have updated their own liturgies.

Parker How do you think the new compares with the old?

Runcie I think that in the English-speaking world (now probably a minority), the epic language and the marvellous resonances of the Anglican liturgy are in danger of being lost, and I'm very sorry about this, for although fundamental changes in reordering the liturgy were necessary, so drastic an updating of language was not desirable.

What the new rites lack, *and this is very serious*, are the kind of phrases which nourish people's souls. I've often visited anxious people in hospitals and have been able to share with them, from the old Book, words like 'He shall not be afraid of any evil tidings, whose mind is stayed on Thee.' *This is very important.*

Parker Do you think the new Alternative Service Book will cause as much pain and division in England as the new Prayer Book has caused in the American Church?

Runcie It has, of course, caused some pain in England... But you see, in England there is a difference. The new contemporary rites are only an *alternative option* to the traditional 1662 Book of Common Prayer, which remains the official liturgy, so there is a choice. The traditional Prayer Book *is used and will continue to be used.* There is the danger, of course, that those congregations which have seized onto the ASB will not use the old book. I know there are areas, particularly in the inner cities, where 1662 is not used at all.

Parker Is it still used for the main services in most English cathedrals?

Runcie I think about half in half, for the main services. I think in *all* cathedrals there should be at the very least one Sunday celebration according to the 1662 Prayer Book. At Canterbury the early service, which I often celebrate, is always 1662.

I think if we can keep the traditional Prayer Book in services that are more personally devotional and corporately strengthening, in our cathedrals and main centres of worship, we shall continue to be enriched by its glorious language. I have therefore pledged myself to maintain its use, as far as I can, in my own province, and to commend its continued use in other parts of the English-speaking world, though I, of course, have authority only for England.

Parker I think, Your Grace, that what is generally feared over here, as in England and elsewhere, is that the old rites, which have been so universally cherished by young as well as old, and by people in every walk of life, will although officially allowed, gradually die through disuse and be lost and forgotten. Do you think this will happen?

Runcie Not if I can help it!

Parker That is an impressive list of people who signed the petitions in England calling for the restoration of the 1662 Prayer Book to the central place of worship in English churches.

Runcie It is.

Parker Do you think they will be overridden?

Runcie Again, not if I can help it. I don't share the opinion of those who are inclined to sneer at the cultural lobby, on the grounds that many who signed it are not regular church-goers, and shouldn't be allowed to influence decisions about our liturgy. That, to me, is un-Anglican, for Anglicanism has always attempted to include rather than exclude, and although some of these people may seldom go to church, they should not be despised, for they find, in the marriage service and the burial office, for instance, a contact with God which should not be cut off. I expect to receive some of the proponents of these petitions after my return, and perhaps be able to give them some reassurance.

Parker Thank you, Your Grace, for giving me your time and thoughts. I am sure this will be very informative to our church people in America, to whom the issue of liturgical reform in the Anglican Communion is of continuing interest and concern.

Prayer and Mammon

MARGOT LAWRENCE

How much pressure is there, tacit or otherwise, on bishops and clergy actively to push the Alternative Service Book? Certainly there is a strong impression in some quarters that this is happening. Some dioceses, for instance, are having special cathedral services to inaugurate (and help pay for) the new book.

One diocesan news letter urges all parishes to switch to ASB despite its cost: 'Where there is a will, a way will be found.' 'There seems,' said one traditionalist, 'to be no one responsible for arranging that at least one church in each area should still make the old Prayer Book available.'

There is also a feeling that some parochial church councils, whose agreement to ASB is required by law, are being conned into a position they might not adopt if aware of all the facts. One Prayer Book Society member was told by the vicar: 'The PCC have voted to go over exclusively to the new book after Christmas.'

'I don't believe the PCC can do that legally,' this parishioner commented. 'They can support the new book, but they have no powers to ban the old.' Yet PCCs are being subtly pressurized to do just this. Why?

Most of the argument over the new forms of service centres on tradition and language. The Book of Common Prayer, its adherents claim, is hallowed by centuries of usage and its phraseology expresses profound truths

Reprinted, with additions, from the *Daily Telegraph*, 5 January 1981.

supremely well. Not so, say the revisionists, the ASB is more in tune with modern thought, and we must move with the times.

Personally, I agree the language of the new book *is* more in tune with modern thought, and that is exactly why we still need the Book of Common Prayer. Modern thought is often sloppy and imprecise, and so is the ASB. To give just two examples, there is, first, the General Confession in the Holy Communion service. In the new book, it calls on us to declare, with trendy humanism, that 'we have sinned against You and against our fellow men.' But surely *sin* can, by definition, only be against God? The commission of it may sometimes harm our fellow men, but that is another matter. The new version is bad theology. Again, the new version of the Nicene Creed asks us to declare what 'we believe', not what 'I believe'. How on earth can I answer for what the man or woman in the next pew believes, or they for me? Asking us to do so, merely blurs the question of what I, me, myself, believe. Perhaps it was meant to do so.

As the arguments polarized, one point was consistently overlooked or ignored – the new book is potentially big business. A considerable investment has been made in it, and many people, not least the Church, stand to gain financially from sales. This is not to say that some arguments for the new services may not be valid. It *is* to say that those asked to choose the new services should understand that a financial contract is being pushed as much as a spiritual one.

The Book of Common Prayer is not in copyright. Special enactments have always prevented unauthorized printers from reproducing it, but the book, like Shakespeare, *Paradise Lost*, *Pilgrim's Progress* and other works prior to the Copyright Acts, is not subject to them.

But the new ASB *is* copyright. 'The Church in its wisdom has ordained to retain the copyright, and is receiving a royalty from us on copies,' says A. J. Holder, managing director of Eyre and Spottiswoode, who print the Book of Common Prayer and tendered successfully for printing ASB.

The copyright fee, a Church House spokesman said, is currently the standard commercial one of 10 per cent., i.e. 35p or 40p per book, depending on the edition: £400,000 to the Church's income if one million copies sell, and a direct levy on anyone buying the new book. (No one knows yet what will be done with the money once publication costs are recouped.) Parishes opting to bypass the new volumes and run off photocopies of the services still have (rightly) to pay copyright and get permission.

It would be naive to suppose the Church insensible of what might, with no punning intention, be termed a vested interest in promoting 'the greatest publishing event in the Church of England for over 300 years,' to quote a *Church Times* correspondent.

The Eyre family, now Eyre and Spottiswoode, have held the Royal warrant to print the Prayer Book and the Authorized Version of the Bible since 1769. Oxford and Cambridge University Presses do so *cum privilegio* by their charters. A fourth firm, William Collins and Son, is allowed to print the books 'by licence'.

The university presses, like Eyres, got contracts to print the new ASB, but Collins did not, while four new firms have been brought into the scene – Mowbrays, William Clowes, the Society for Promoting Christian Knowledge and Hodders.

What has happened in the parallel world of Bible publishing is instructive. New versions are not just big business, they are colossal. The AV is still handled solely by the original four, and sales are steady if unspectacular. But when Collins, with the Bible Society, produced the Good News Bible in 1976, it sold two million copies in two years. In 1978 Hodders brought out their New International Version, with comparable results. The publication of new versions of holy writ (eight since the war) has become, in recent years, one huge monopoly-busting exercise for profit.

New versions are saleable – the figures prove it. But (like almost everything promoted commercially) they are of their nature transient, and that is good for business too. Second-hand bookshops and parish jumble sales indicate new versions discarded with monotonous regularity, but no one ever throws out an Authorized Version.

The question now is, could something similar happen to the Church's services? At first sight, this might seem ridiculous. Whether we like ASB or not, it has Synod's seal of approval and can't be tampered with by anyone with investment money, as the Bible has been.

Or could it? For consider. What is bang up to date today will one day seem quite out of date. When the novelty of ASB has worn off, is it cynical to predict fresh updating, an Alternative Alternative? Indeed, when he launched the new book, the Bishop of Durham happily predicted that it would be subject to revision probably before the end of the century. Fifty years hence, when copyright expires and anyone can print the ASB without permission or fee, is it conceivable that new in-copyright forms might be useful to keep standards pure and cash flowing?

The temptation, I would think, would be strong. But I forgot – the compilers tried to ditch 'Lead us not into temptation' for 'Do not bring us to the time of trial', surely a more commercially orientated plea.

Replacing the Prayer Book by newer forms is rather like demolishing a Tudor mansion to raise a tower block. There may be good reasons for, or against, but what so often sways the argument conclusively is that some people make a good thing out of redeveloping, whereas no one gets rich by preserving something old. And the concrete blocks don't last too long either.

Sociology and the Questionable Truth

ROGER HOMAN

Sociological method is often misunderstood. Those who practise it do not necessarily claim to be disinterested in the reality they investigate nor do they reckon that their labours provide them with a comprehensive insight of the universe. In accordance with scientific method as practised in other fields, the sociologist normally proceeds with reference to properly framed hypotheses which he may expect either to confirm or to refute. These hypotheses are often developed in relation to his political, ethical and cultural motivations, so that students of women in society and of educational opportunity are invariably concerned to demonstrate the degrees of disadvantage affecting women and the children of the working class respectively. Conversely, some kinds of inquiry are not undertaken because of the misuse to which their results could be put: an example here is the omission of certain questions about ethnic minorities from the 1981 general census in Britain.

Much the same is true in medicine: the heart surgeon and cancer researcher are not expected to be indifferent to the preservation of human life and a prior moral commitment does not invalidate their discoveries. What matters is rather that they will not be so committed to prior hopes or expectations as to misconstrue the results they obtain. It is in this sense that sociological method may be said to be scientific or 'hard': in its ideal form, the personality of the investigator and the methods he deploys are rendered unobtrusive in the acquisition of data, so that in any inquiry investigators with contrary views or expectations would obtain similar results.

Further, the sociologist must know his limitations. His conceptual categories and methods of inquiry provide no purchase, for example, upon the Being of God. They do enable him, however, to investigate the phenomenon of belief and the social behaviour surrounding it. Dr Eric Kemp, Bishop of Chichester, rightly invokes a caution by Jackson in the preface to Boulard's *An Introduction to Religious Sociology*:

> There are aspects of the Church's life which sociology cannot penetrate. The Church is more than a social, historical institution: it is the Body of Christ. This ambiguity of the Church's nature sets certain limits upon religious sociology.[1]

Dr Kemp's definition of the reality as meta-sociological inclines him to a cautious view of scientific evidence:

> Sociological surveys...need to be regarded very critically and the assumptions behind them carefully examined. The ordinary person who has not the means to do that is well advised to take them always with a pinch of salt.[2]

It is remarkable that Dr Kemp does not counsel the faithful to take with a pinch of salt anything that is dispensed to them in the form of theology. Just as the realistic sociologist recognizes that he has no special competence to speak about the nature of God, so the theologian must respect the limitations of his own insights of social behaviour. Indeed, there are some very eminent theologians who have shown this kind of self-awareness. Karl Rahner, for example, is sensitive that the official doctrinal authorities of the Church indulge in 'epistemological imperialism' when they venture into sociological speculation:

> The first step to be taken is the recognition in all honesty that we do not know the situation in which we ourselves stand in terms of sociology and human ideas.[3]

Likewise, Hans Küng is willing to recognize that theology no longer has 'any elitist privileged access to the truth' and that churchmen are 'vitally dependent on the natural sciences if they are vitally to conduct their task'.[4]

As a consequence of the epistemological proximity of sociological insight and common sense, however, non-professionals often stray into sociological territory. A particular risk is involved when the trespassers are clergy, because historically a special kind of authority has attended their pronouncements. So while Archdeacon Eyre in the *Guardian* (9 October 1980) dismissed the Chichester survey as 'tendentious' and Dr Kemp prescribed his pinch of salt, their own quasi-scientific assertions in favour of modern liturgies were liable to command an unwarranted deference. For example, Richard Eyre rejected the outcome of a survey to which 103 of the 105 parishes in his archdeaconry had responded by preferring the testimony of the most unrepresentative constituency imaginable:

> Those whose congregational life has been invigorated and knit together on the basis of the alternative liturgies will know how much and how little value to attach to this survey. (*Guardian*, 9 October 1980)

Had they read the survey, they might also have discovered how rare a breed they constituted.

It has been principally to refute fraudulent and unscientific claims made on behalf of the modern services that sociological methods have been deployed in the course of the Prayer Book campaign. We were mindful that the advocates of alternatives were retailing their personal impressions in the guise of hard truths: they were already playing the game of sociological evidence but without keeping to the rules. Partial and incomplete evidence was being readily adduced to discredit the case for retention of the traditional forms.

The petitions of the 600 laid before the General Synod in November 1979 included the signatures of artists and musicians, politicians, writers, scholars, lawyers and actors.[5] The responses to these petitions included two kinds of recurrent assertion verifiable if at all by sociological method. First, the petitioners were denounced as an elite group of cognoscenti and literati; the ordinary man in the pew, it was supposed, preferred modern language. According to the Revd Michael Saward, the ordinary people of Ealing were finding Prayer Book services 'absolutely beyond their comprehension' and were staying away whereas Prayer Book supporters 'all seemed to live at "The Old Manor, Gushington-in-the-Puddle" or some such address' (*Church Times*, 29 February 1980). Second, the complaint was made that many of the signatories were not churchgoers. You cannot win on this one: had the petition been restricted to regular worshippers, the rejoinder would have been that the people who mattered were those on the fringes who should be attracted in.

Such were the themes of the correspondence columns of *The Times* and *Church Times* in November and December 1979. It was consequently decided to instruct the Gallup Organization to put these claims to the test, and this was made possible by a research grant obtained by Professor Martin at the London School of Economics. The purpose of the Gallup Poll was to measure preferences for traditional and modern forms of service and versions of the Bible in various age groups and according to regularity of worship. It is axiomatic in questionnaire design that questions should be so framed as to avoid inclining the interviewee to a particular kind of response. As an obvious example, we could not ask 'Which do you prefer, the good old Prayer Book or this ghastly modern stuff?' We would have obtained worthless results thereby and would have jeopardized the professional reputation of Professor Martin and the respect and business in opinion polling enjoyed by Gallup. Questions were designed by a team of sociologists that included Professor Martin, Professor Richard Fenn of the University of Maine and myself, and were screened by Mr Gordon Heald, Assistant Director of the Gallup organization. Notwithstanding, when the results were published, Mr Derek Pattinson, Secretary General of the General Synod, thought we might have been oblivious of basic principles: he advised, 'In any form of survey the nature of the answers is so often determined by the questions' (*Church Times*, 13 June 1980) and doubted whether any questions devised by David Martin, a professor of sociology, 'could have the openness and objectivity that was desirable' (*Church Times*, 20 June 1980).

The questions used were always simple and open, for example:

Do you prefer the traditional Lord's Prayer or a modernized version?

From which version of the Bible do you prefer lessons to be read in church?

Authorized Version
A modern language
Other
Don't know

What kind of service do you prefer for a wedding – the traditional or a modern language alternative?

It is difficult to see how these questions were other than open and fair, and the critics of the Gallup poll attempted to discredit it in general rather than demonstrate its specific faults. Indeed, Mr Pattinson made his critical press statement before he had seen the questions.

The results of similar polls conducted in the USA and West Germany indicated a high level of support for traditional forms and it was with some confidence that the Gallup organization was commissioned to assess support in Great Britain. In the event, the results of the British survey showed how inaccurate had been the claims of the modernizers. Far from being the luxury of the privileged classes, it was found that greater support for traditional forms came from the lower socio-economic groups than the higher: for example, only 66 per cent of Anglican respondents in the highest social group preferred wedding services in the traditional form whereas 77 per cent of the lowest group expressed such a preference. In all questions, respondents in the south of England were rather less fond of the traditional forms than respondents in the midlands. Notwithstanding, Canon Townshend of Norwich suggested that Prayer Book support was coming 'from south of the Thames, in the "mink and mattins" belt' (*Times*, 14 June 1980). As was expected, the elderly were more traditionalist than the young but even in the youngest age group (16–24 years) 72 per cent preferred the traditional Lord's Prayer, 65 per cent wanted the traditional wedding rite and 55 per cent preferred lessons to be read in the Authorized Version. The compelling evidence of this nationwide poll is that 'mink' is *not* a correlate of 'mattins'.

The questions were only asked of those 1,178 respondents who declared themselves as Church of England and these were further assessed by regularity of attendance. The agenda which Gallup addressed had been established by the claims and objections made by the modernizers in the wake of the petitions of the 600. But still they did not believe: from Crowthorne in Berkshire, Wolverton in Warwickshire and Thornham Parva in Suffolk, incumbents boldly contradicted Gallup with particular evidence of parochial experience (*Church Times*, 20 June 1980).

Another range of assertions was made in the discussion of Gallup. It was noticed that regular worshippers were more tolerant of innovations than infrequent attenders. This phenomenon might have been expected: there would naturally be a higher rate of falling away among the disaffected and a greater adaptation among those who persisted. If so, it was hypothesized, a general survey would reveal an association of liturgical innovation and decline in membership. In the spring of 1980 I obtained from the Chichester diocesan office membership statistics for each of the 105 parishes in the Archdeaconry of Chichester and enquired by telephoning incumbents or church officers the form of service used at the main act of Sunday worship: responses on the latter inquiry were obtained from 103 parishes. The comparison of figures for 1975 and 1980 showed that parishes using the Book of Commmon Prayer throughout the period had sustained a mean growth rate of 3.7 per cent whereas those maintaining Series 3 had suffered a mean decline of 3.6 per cent: the rate of decline suffered by parishes adopting Series 3 for the first time was a mean 14.9 per cent.[6]

Once again, the advocates of modern forms were eager to discredit the survey. Two of the incumbents I had interviewed wrote to the *Bognor Regis Observer* (17 October 1980) saying they had never heard of me. Because of my known preference for Cranmer, Archdeacon Eyre dismissed the survey as 'tendentious' and he also found fault in my obtaining information from the diocesan office:

> If Dr Homan did not speak to incumbents the thing is unreliable and not to be taken seriously. It was an irresponsible piece of work. (*Church Times*, 10 October 1980).

He wrote to the *Guardian* (9 October 1980) to complain that I had not contacted the Rural Dean of Brighton: this was a curious objection since I have attended the main act of Sunday worship at Brighton parish church every week except holidays since 1963 and hardly needed to ask my own vicar what form of service we used.

These being the principal recent contributions of sociology to the Prayer Book campaign, we may observe certain consistent features:

1 Sociological method has only been deployed to check claims that were scientific in principle but inadequately researched in practice.

2 However scientific the collection of data and however extensive the sample, individuals persist in pretending to confound sociological evidence with personal testimony from localized experience.

3 Our critics give us little credit for understanding the methods we use. The sociological analysis of liturgical change is like the playing of professional football: there are always those on the terraces who think you are oblivious of first principles.

NOTES

1 F. Boulard, *An Introduction to Religious Sociology: Pioneer Work in France* (London, 1960), p. xi.

2 E. Kemp, 'Sociological surveys', *Chichester Diocesan News* (November 1980), p. 2.

3 K. Rahner, *Theological Investigations 14: Ecclesiology, Questions in the Church, The Church in the World* (London, 1976), p. 105.

4 H. Küng, *On Being a Christian* (London, 1977), p. 87.

5 D. Martin (ed.) *PN Review 13: Crisis for Cranmer and King James* (Manchester, 1979).

6 R. Homan, 'Church membership and the liturgy', *Faith and Worship* no. 9 (1980), p. 22.

Letters to the Editor

DEREK BREWER

Two articles by Professor David Martin and later on the petition on the Book of Common Prayer to the General Synod (5 November 1979), with concurrent publication in *Poetry Nation Review*, provoked a spate of letters to the serious newspapers. I collected the letters from 21 December 1978 (*Daily Telegraph*) to the 14 June 1980 (*The Times*), including those in the *Guardian* and the *Church Times*, and gave a brief account of their numbers in a letter published in *The Times*, 21 June 1980.

> The letters begin on 21 December 1978 in the *Daily Telegraph* following the publication of two articles by Professor David Martin on the 18 and 19 December 1978, and the latest letters counted are from your issue of the 14 June 1980. The grand totals include a few cases of more than one letter written by the same person, and some letters which are equivocal, but I have allocated them all to one side or other as best as I can. The numbers of letters are: from clergy in favour of the new liturgy, 48; from clergy against, 18; from laypeople in favour 17; against, 68.
>
> Counting heads is no substitute for rational discussion. These numbers are small and crude; furthermore the respective newspapers may themselves have published unrepresentative numbers of letters. You yourself, Sir, declined in December 1979 to publish a letter from me and 5 others all opposed to the new liturgy, and

> that one letter would have had some effect on the numbers I have counted. Bearing in mind these and other qualifications, one may still emphasize the feebleness of lay support for the new liturgy (17 against 68). Clerical support for the change, though strong, is not quite so overwhelming (48 against 18).
>
> The present situation is thus very different from that of the early sixteenth century which is sometimes quoted as a parallel. At that period there was a well-attested widespread passionate desire of many amongst all classes of the English people to have the Bible and liturgy in English. There is no corresponding desire for radical change among the vast majority of literate laypeople now.
>
> Our situation is also very different from the successive sixteenth-century revisions of the English texts. In the sixteenth century there was a strong effort to preserve as much continuity with previous versions as possible.

Although I have kept no tally of letters since then, there is no reason to suppose any difference in the balance of opinion, which entirely supports that found in Professor Martin's Gallup poll. Furthermore, the reviews of the Alternative Service Book later published were largely hostile. There is no doubt of the general dislike of the new services felt by most of those laymen capable of and willing to express their opinions in letters. What is even more interesting is the quality of argument used to defend Series 3 and its congeners (now conveniently to be referred to as the ASB). The present essay lists and examines those arguments.

The 600 and more petitioners were described by Mr Alec Hill as 'actors and others – who, I guess, are not regular churchgoers' and by Mr Andrew Deuchar as 'an odd assortment of politicians, actors, servicemen and atheists', 'a small group of people who by virtue of their position in secular life are able to gain widespread publicity in the media' (*Church Times*, 16 November 1979). Apart from the misrepresentation of a highly miscellaneous list (though the petition did include such people) it is a curious array of those whom the Church is presumed to wish to have nothing to do with: actors, who if they cannot 'communicate' (a favourite word in its secular sense with the clergy) are 'nothing worth'; politicians, who must lead and advise our public life; servicemen, who confront death to protect us; atheists, whom it would be desirable to convert. If *they* all object to being bitten by ASB, then it would seem worthwhile to pay attention to their complaints.

The Revd P. J. Winstone accused some of the petitioners of hypocrisy because they did not attend church (*Guardian* 10 November 1979); Viscount Cranborne was accused by the Revd R. A. Babington of 'somewhat hysterical anti-clericalism' (*Telegraph*, 19 January 1979); Canon Ken Brown recommended the General Synod to tell this group of 'assorted well-known people' 'politely, but very firmly, to mind their own business' (*Guardian*, 9 November 1979). When the findings of the Gallup poll about liturgical preferences were published, Canon H. L. H. Townshend wanted to know how many of the 'C of E people questioned came from south of the Thames, in the "mink and mattins" belt' (*Times*, 14 June 1980). The Revd Michael Saward remarked on the applause his own speech received at the General Synod despite the fact that he had been described as intemperate and outrageous by 'superior persons'. He referred to the articles in *PN Review* 13: 'the fangs are reeking with the blood of the Series 3 hunt. Let me add a selection of quotations, so that all may contrast my fairly moderate attack with the presumably "Christian attitudes" of the wolf-pack.' He listed some of the strong words of critical condemnation that have been used by so many and various people about Series 3, and after some further paragraphs about the 1662 services being absolutely beyond the comprehension of his own congregation in Ealing, remarked that, 'It was the "innocent sheep" who responded with personal abuse, and they all seemed to live at "The Old Manor, Gushington-in-the Puddle" or some such address. That, in itself, may not be insignificant' (*Church Times*, 29 February 1980).

This is to confuse criticism of Series 3 with personal abuse, and defence of Series 3 with personal abuse. What is most significant in the attitudes expressed here is the profound hostility to education, social responsibility and general culture, together with the assumption that the petitioners are rich, likely to be members of an hereditary gentry, live in villages south of the Thames, and have no business with the Church. It would indeed be most interesting to have a sociological analysis of the petitioners. Speaking as one of them, an academic who is the first generation in his family to have received secondary-school education, or regularly to go to church, I suspect that the clergy would be surprised at the number of such scholarship boys. We treasure the tradition which we have, often with difficulty, found for ourselves. And though such names as Lord Glenamara rightly sound very grand, its bearer may be more familiar as Mr Edward Short, no scion of an ancient and noble house, but for many years the distinguished Labour MP for Newcastle-upon-Tyne Central. It is true that as a politician and a war-time serviceman he falls into two categories which may be regarded with contempt by supporters of ASB. As a former headmaster, a graduate and an educated man, he may incur even further distrust.

The stereotype invented by the defenders of ASB may be dismissed as having little relevance to the petitioners. For all I know, anyone who conforms to the stereotype may well have no interest in the Church. The attribution of such a stereotype to those who value the traditional liturgy raises some profound questions. Hostility to the rich and well-educated is in part a genuine Christian tradition. As St Paul remarks to the Corinthians, 'not many wise after the flesh, not many mighty, not many noble, are called, but God chose the foolish things of the world, that he might put to shame them that are wise' (1 Cor. 1:26–7). It is curious that none of those who were angered by the petition invoked this text.

Yet they were wise to refrain. Paul was writing in a very different context. Moreover, like so many Christian paradoxes, it continues to apply even when it has made the reversal from wisdom to folly. Those who, like the members of the General Synod, might well wish to apply to themselves the same text (more appropriately and flatly phrased in the New English Bible) and agree that few of them 'are men of wisdom, by any human standard; few are powerful or highly born', yet as soon as they assert for themselves the power to decide the mysteries of God for this age, they become, if not men of wisdom, at least powerful in our affairs, and themselves susceptible, if they believe they are right, to the same paradox.

This, however, leads to one of the main points of substance in the arguments advanced against the Book of Common Prayer and in favour of ASB. It is advanced negatively in various degrees by those who say that 'Cranmer', or '1662', is now incomprehensible. The Revd Saward's congregation has already been referred to as finding it totally so. He nevertheless puzzlingly adds that 'an educated and able man' in his congregation described the use of the 1662 service as 'a gimmick'. It sounds, not surprisingly, as if the 'educated and able man' thought that the service might be used to bring people into church, since a gimmick is presumably an attraction, but the Revd Saward seems to repudiate such an aim, if it involves using the traditional service.

The Revd Pete Pridham wrote in response to an earlier letter from a layman, that three things put him off organized religion: 'The incomprehensible language of Cranmer's Prayer Book. The arrogance of those who would try to impose their own predilections in worship upon others. Ignorant lay-people who resent clergy (and others) having a hot line to God' (*Telegraph*, 8 January 1979). The indefensible cliché of incomprehensibility contains a real point, but clearly deserves a more subtle presentation. The attack on 'arrogance' comes strangely from a party which has been consistently shown to represent a minority of the Church of England, albeit a majority of the clergy, and has consistently imposed its own predilections in worship on others. The claim of the clergy and unspecified 'others', presumably not 'ignorant lay-people', to have a hot line to God comes equally strangely from those who find arrogance in others. The Revd Simon Parkinson, who considers Cranmer as rootless (!) compared with ASB, thought Professor Martin's articles of 18 and 19 December 1978 in the *Daily Telegraph* were mischievous, and that the paper should not have published them (*Telegraph*, 21 December 1978). So much for the desirability of full informed discussion by lay-people, and the likelihood of their wishes being taken into account.

More positively, there is a real problem about the language of the Book of Common Prayer. The Revd J. E. Burrows remarked that 'While modernization will not convert the young, it is doubtful if they will be converted without it' (*Telegraph*, 21 December 1978). Mr Gurney MacInnes (*Telegraph*, 28 December 1978) wrote that the liturgy should be in ordinary everyday language as understood by the people, as did the Revd Peter S. Ballantyne, (*Telegraph*, 30 December 1978) and Mr Stephen J. Trott (*Church Times*, 30 November 1979). Canon George Brett wrote that 'The Book of Common Prayer is (*sic*) designed for the use of the Common People, and not, as your correspondents seem to imply, exclusively for intellectuals, or even for the Conservative Party at Prayer. The purpose of worship is to help us to get through to God, not to preserve culture, language or even our national heritage.' The Book of Common Prayer and Bible have failed to appeal to the masses, 'Therefore an alternative must be found'. When Canon Brett asked his Mothers' Union in about 1975 whether they preferred 1662 or Series 3 these representatives of 'the masses' unhesitatingly said 'Series 3' because 'We understand what we are talking about [it's more meaningful] and we are able to participate more (*Times*, 19 November 1979). (It is to be presumed that the phrase in square brackets is Canon Brett's own gloss.) This introduces a related concept, that liturgy should be functional (Revd M. Saward, *Times*, 17 November 1979, who questioned in elaborate imagery whether the Church of England should be a 'jewelled corpse' or 'a living pilgrim', a 'lifeboat' or itself a 'leaky old tub seeking safe harbour'). Another image used for both the Book of Common Prayer and the Bible is 'a tool for the job' (Canon David H. Bishop, *Times*, 14 June 1980, Revd D. R. J. Penney and Revd V. C. Hatherley, *Church Times*, 23 November 1979). Canon Bishop thought that the language of liturgy ought *not* to be, as a *Times* leader had said it should, 'dignified, solemn, resonant, universal, hieratic and unfashionable'. Liturgy should be 'understandable, celebratory and contemporary'. The irrelevance of beauty, of the country's national heritage, and the wrongness of preserving 'a questionable aesthetic' (Canon Bishop again) are points that occur directly or indirectly in several letters. Cranmer, it was claimed, quite erroneously, was himself a wrecker (Mr C. R. Busby, *Telegraph*, 4 January 1979), and used the everyday language of his time (Canon Ken Brown, *Guardian*, 9 November 1979). The general level of understanding of the nature of the problem was, however, illustrated by Canon Ken Brown, who invited contemporary scholars to use Cranmer's English, and ended the main part of his letter, 'Yea, verily', and by parodies of biblical style by the Revd Ronald Treasure – who concludes, very aptly, 'Thine, in confusion of language' (*Guardian* 10 November 1979) – and the Revd Eric Thacker (*Times*, 24 November 1979). One might also note the self-defeating argument that God does not mind how he is addressed (Revd R. A. Babington, *Telegraph*, 2 January 1979).

The failure to understand that language has many different purposes and registers, that not everything of value can be conveyed in everyday language, that there are problems of meaning in language beyond one-to-one correspondences, that not all meanings may be available at every period of language and that beauty is an aspect of meaning rather than a dangerous distraction from it, is very striking. The defenders' ideal of language is as a 'tool' of instant appeal to 'the masses'. They want only the language of advertising, as if they were selling soap. Why should it be assumed that religious truth should be immediately communicable to those who have not prepared themselves to attend to it? No one assumes that about science or history or literature. Why is it assumed that poetry or beauty have no relation to meaning when anybody who has given any thought to the matter knows the opposite to be the case? We know there is an educational crisis. The domination, in the educational thought of the last thirty years, of the ideals of expressiveness and spontaneity, with reduced emphasis on information, system and accuracy, has left many of the young unequipped to deal even with the ordinary language of ordinary life; hence the great fuss about the new '16+'. Some letters refer to this crisis; but should we, because of a perhaps temporary educational crisis, therefore consciously exchange a good for an inferior article? No one for one moment thinks that we ought to abandon our scientific inheritance because fewer children are nowadays taught arithmetic properly.

But liturgy of course is not science, any more than it is literature or drama. What it shares with all these human activities, and which so few of the revisers seem to understand, is that it also is in its very essence a self-justifying activity, an act of worship indeed, an end in itself, fully human, purely gratuitous, not a means, not, as our graceful modern language has it, a 'tool'. This is too complicated a proposition to do more than assert here, but it is basic to an understanding of the nature of liturgical language, of the importance of repetition with variation, of rhythmical power, beauty, stability, of the relationship with other aspects of the spiritual life, national culture, personal religion. Liturgy is communal faith verbally and historically objectified, not an advertisement, nor an instrument of conversion.

Why should it be so readily assumed that the clergy have no responsibility for the national culture? Are our minds and feelings in all their historical complexity not part of their care? They recognize social responsibilities. We hear much from some clergymen about how we should encourage the national religions and beliefs of other cultures, even to the extent of subsidizing their guerrillas. Why is it only English national culture that is so bad, or so irrelevant? How can religion be conceived of independent of its setting? And how can its setting be understood without reference to its history? A community that denies its own history loses its identity, as we see happening rapidly to the Church of England. At no period in its history since the Anglo-Saxons has the Church of England been of so little significance to the nation at large. When the Church does not care about the nation, the nation ceases to care about the Church. Moreover, our historical national inheritance includes one of the world's great literatures, and, like it or not (and many critics nowadays do not like it), that literature is profoundly Christian. Of course the passage of time changes concepts and language, and in the end everything perishes, but no normal person suggests that we should deny ourselves food and drink today because sooner or later one day each of us must die. The Church of England should be grateful that, unlike most churches, it has inherited a great liturgy which is religiously valuable *because* it is beautiful and meaningful, not in spite of it. There may be a place for the language and ethos of advertising in the Church; that place is not the liturgy.

Some further points need consideration. The question of theological change was raised in some letters. The most extravagant claim was in a brief article, not a letter, by Canon Ian Dunlop in the *Church Times*, 30 November 1979, who appeared to regard by implication practically the whole of the Book of Common Prayer as theologically unacceptable, though subsequently he denied this (*Church Times*, 14 December 1979). Canon Paul Wansey remarked that the new service is an Easter Celebration of the Risen Lord (*Telegraph*, 10 November 1979), whereas the 1662 service is a Good

Friday service for the personal devotion and redemption of those present. It seems odd that personal devotion and redemption should no longer be thought necessary. Canon Dalby considered that 1662's 'theology is rather narrow, with its almost exclusive emphasis on the Cross, and little mention of Creation or of the Resurrection' (*Guardian*, 8 November 1979). Canon Bishop asserted that profound changes had been made in the new liturgy, though he did not specify them (*Times*, 14 June 1980), and in the same issue the Revd C. G. Sykes remarked that the Book of Common Prayer 'reflects the now all too obvious theological misunderstandings and the strife of the centuries which saw it come to birth.' The difference of theology is also emphasized by Mr Stephen J. Trott (*Church Times*, 30 November 1979).

This is a serious matter which deserves fuller discussion. What *are* the major theological changes? Where can we find them set out? Is it really the case that we now know that personal devotion and redemption and the Cross are less important? Are we really meant to pass by the Cross as we hasten, without personal devotion and redemption, to the Resurrection? Is the doctrine of the Resurrection, in any other than a complex symbolic significance, to be regarded as now the central doctrine of the Church of England? An interesting light was thrown on this by a gathering of East Anglian clergymen about March 1981. They came unanimously to the conclusion that it would be 'better to be Red than dead'. Their interest in the national inheritance extended to the assertion that this country should on no account attempt to defend itself. Presumably one would not want to be resurrected into a nuclear waste! Paul said he preached Christ crucified, but Paul was undoubtedly wrong, by our lights, about many things; perhaps he was wrong in this. The new theology puts all in doubt. The Revd Martin Linskill wrote, 'The revisions, whose linguistic results we no doubt all deplore, were encouraged by no one for literary but for theological, liturgical and pastoral reasons central to the Church's life: that the Word of the Lord should once more bite...' (*Times*, 22 November 1979). How deplorable linguistic results can also 'bite' is not clear. Moreover, not all proponents of the ASB agree, since Revd Michael Saward finds in the ASB 'the powerful gospel of a crucified Saviour' (*Times*, 17 November 1979). However, he seems alone in this, and as he is one of the very few even among the defenders of the new services who finds them 'beautiful', he may also be unrepresentative in this and other matters.

Another theological point was raised. Mr Hayman Johnson remarked that the eucharistic doctrine of 1662 was unacceptable to many of 'catholic opinion in the Church of England', whereas Series 2 has produced a valuable change by sacrifices on both sides. He also valued more spontaneity and found that 'the linguistic perfection and excellence of 1662 made some people ill at ease' (*Telegraph*, 28 December 1978). The Revd Paul Warren found that Series 3 stood up well to constant repetition, and 'is clear and easy to follow, recognizably similar to the Roman Catholic and Methodist Eucharist, with plenty of opportunity for congregational participation, and expressing a balanced theology' (*Guardian*, 8 November 1979). These points were repeated by the Deans of Worcester and St Paul's in a joint letter, balancing 'the admitted defects' of the ASB against clearer structure, congregational participation, and 'its sensitivity to the traditions of worship of other Christians' (*Times*, 14 June 1980). Canon George Austin, however, argued as 'a Catholic within the Anglican tradition' that he was defeated by the four possible Eucharistic Prayers and the 'menu of alternatives and permissible additions or omissions' (*Times*, 6 December 1979). Whether indeed Roman Catholics and Methodists are equally satisfied by the Church of England's simultaneous approach to both I do not know. Why the Church of England should approach them, rather than they the Church of England, is also not clear, though it may be that such approaches have been made. For those of us in the Church of England who have no urge to transfer our allegiance either to the Roman

Catholics or to the Methodists, but are perfectly content to regard them also as Christians, going on in another way not notably more successful or attractive than our own, the question is not particularly important. There seems no obvious reason, fashion apart, for us to sacrifice our own characteristics in order to imitate them, any more than they should sacrifice theirs to imitate us.

There is much more that could be said on the wider questions raised by these letters, and I have made no attempt to list the points made in the many letters attacking the new services. The series of letters in the various newspapers give rise to many reflections. When one looks at the justifications advanced for the revision (apart from the mere assertions that some congregations like them very much) one cannot be very cheerful. Unless we stir ourselves it seems all too likely that just as the Book of Common Prayer marked the full emergence of the Church of England, so the ASB will mark its disappearance. The feebleness and lack of urgency of expression, the facile and evasive optimism of its theology, the bewildering multiplicity of its practices, will encourage the proliferation of Churches that are minor sects of local quietist groups, constituency parties run by enthusiasts. They will be populist in intended appeal, tiny in actual membership, autocratic in practice, hostile to the traditional virtues, hospitable to passing fashions and with about as much significance for the majority of English people as any other local group.

Parliament and the Language of Prayer

In 1974 Parliament divested itself of legislative responsibility for the doctrine and public worship of the Church of England – almost but not quite. It made permanent an earlier grant of temporary powers by which the Church, through its own procedures, could authorize forms of service other than those prescribed in the Book of Common Prayer of 1662. There were two reservations. Any new services had to fulfil the condition that they were neither contrary to, nor indicative of departure from, the doctrine of the Church of England in any essential matter. Lest Parliament, or anybody else, should be given the scarcely possible task of adjudicating on what is or is not conformable to the doctrine of the Church of England, it was enacted that whatever received the final approval of the General Synod should be deemed to have fulfilled that condition. The other reservation was that the forms of service contained in the Book of Common Prayer should continue to be available for use in the Church of England. Available for use does not mean in use, as has become painfully apparent.

According to the present rules the incumbent and the parochial church council together make their selection from the lengthening à la carte menu of authorized forms of service. Ecclesiastical democracy has some of the same limitations as trades union democracy: the shop stewards

Reprinted from *The Times*, 8 April 1981 (editorial).

and those who attend meetings decide things with a freedom that bears little proportion to the typicality of their opinions. By a conspiracy of enthusiasts, as some think, or by default, as seems more likely, the Prayer Book is falling into desuetude. And very many members of the Church of England are very unhappy about it.

Today attempts will be made in both Houses of Parliament to get a Prayer Book Protection Bill off the launching pad. The Bill would introduce a modest amendment to the effect that 20 people on a church electoral roll may together require the incumbent to see that on at least one Sunday a month the principal morning service is taken from the Prayer Book. Its adoption would mean that part at any rate of the old liturgy was not merely available for use but available for attendance, which is what really counts.

If Parliament were to be seriously tempted to take the measure up it would undoubtedly precipitate a disestablishment crisis. The Church of England's sensitivity on the subject has been evident over the matter of the London mitre. That is only a pinprick compared to resumption by Parliament of an ambition to regulate the worship of the Church of England. But if it would be imprudent of Parliament to espouse the Bill, it would be just as imprudent of the bishops and the synodical apparatus of the Church to brush it out of the way.

There is a wide and profound unhappiness about the relegation of the historic liturgy of the Church of England. It is fed by many tributaries. For some, it seems the wanton abandonment of a priceless endowment, as if the Church were to demolish its cathedrals to take to civic centres. For some, the language of the Prayer Book is the language of prayer, expressive of doctrinal and devotional meaning precisely because it is fixed, customary, timeless, apart from everyday use, and resonant of the piety of past generations. For some, loss of the liturgy means loss of the sense of history, loss of one of the dimensions of faith. For some, particularly the elderly who were nourished by the public worship of the Church, not to be able to find the familiar and to them sacred forms is a sharp and cruel penalty.

None of this is to decry the merits, conveniences and appropriateness of the various alternative services the Church of England has evolved; or to deny that many much prefer them. But unless the Church takes more seriously the commission it received in 1974 and keeps the Book of Common Prayer *in* use as well as *for* use, it will carelessly abuse many loyal sons and daughters and deprive the next generations of acquaintance with an uncommon efflorescence of Christianity: a dignified, settled, devout and valid liturgy.

Prayer Book Protection Bill: Parliamentary Debate

On 8 April 1981 the Prayer Book Protection Bill was proposed in the House of Commons by Viscount Cranborne (Dorset, South):

I beg to move, that leave be given to bring in a Bill to provide for parishioners in any parish to require certain forms of service to be used in the parish.

It is a sad occasion when any hon. Member should feel impelled to seek leave to introduce a Bill such as this. The Book of Common Prayer is one of the glories of English literature. I am gratified to find that so many of my right hon. and hon. Friends and Opposition Members have seen fit to give me their support because the Book of Common Prayer and the forms of service contained therein have permeated the English language. They have enriched it and formed the basis of part of the tradition of England. That language was produced many centuries ago. It has matched man's highest aspirations. Those religious aspirations have separated man from the animal kingdom.

Until recently, the Book of Common Prayer was available to all people who wished to use it. Many hon. Members have acknowledged the beauty of the Book of Common Prayer. They have expressed the hope that its language and form of service would not be lost and would not remain

Extracts from *Hansard*, 8 April 1981, col. 959–60 and 613–64.

unavailable to those who wished to use it in their worship in the Church of England. I would go so far as to quote my hon. Friend the Member for Wokingham (Mr van Straubenzee) in a typically distinguished speech which he made in the debates in December 1974, when the House considered the worship and doctrine measure. He said:

> I believe in all conscience, as one who would regard it as retrograde beyond measure if this book disappeared from the services of the Church, that those like me would have a power to our elbow which the law does not currently provide if the measure were passed. (*Official Report*, 4 December 1974; vol. 882, col. 1691)

I have heard a strong rumour that after I have spoken my hon. Friend the Member for Wokingham will seek to catch your eye, Mr Speaker, in order to oppose this motion. I look forward to his speech. I know that he will address the House with his customary scholarship and eloquence, and that he fully supports the beauties and glories of the Book of Common Prayer.

However, I feel a trifle sorry for my hon. Friend because he will be supporting a point of view which, in retrospect, has managed to achieve the slow murder of the Book of Common Prayer since the passing of the 1974 measure. Far be it for me to anticipate what my hon. Friend will say. He will make his speech in his own good time. However, I suspect that when he speaks he will deploy certain arguments, and I shall hazard a guess as to what at least one of them will be.

My hon. Friend will say that I am meddling in matters of great constitutional importance. He will say that as a result of the 1974 measure a concordat was, in effect, put into operation between Parliament and the Synod of the Church of England which clearly provided that the initiative in legislative matters governing the Church should come from the Synod and not from the House. I do not deny for a second that that has been the effect of the 1974 measure. I would not seek to argue with my hon. Friend if that is the main basis of his argument. But that concordat was made on two clear conditions, and it is one of those to which I draw the attention of the House.

I can do no better than to quote a great luminary of the Church of England, the former Archbishop of Canterbury. At the time of the debates on the worship and doctrine measure, he stated in another place:

> Again, it is not a Measure for abolishing the Book of Common Prayer. As I shall presently show, it gives to the Book of Common Prayer a secure place which could be altered only by the action of Parliament itself. (*Official Report*, *House of Lords*, 14 November 1974; vol. 354, col. 868)

The Archbishop of Canterbury was supported in this House by the then hon. Member for Kingswood, Mr Terry Walker, who stated:

> If the Synod should ever wish to alter this so that the 1662 book, or some services in it, were to be abolished, the Church would have to come to Parliament with another measure and thus, the Book of Common Prayer is given a secure place in the future of our worship.

My contention is simply that it is not Parliament which is in danger of breaching the concordat; the Church has breached it. I pay tribute to my hon. Friend the Member for Gloucestershire, South (Mr Cope). He is an ornament to the Government Whips' Office. We on the Government Benches have come to value his prescience. In the same debate he stated:

> In spite of the safeguards referred to by a number of hon. Members, I believe that it will make permanent

> the decline, to put it no stronger, of the Book of Common Prayer. (*Official Report*, 4 December 1974; vol. 882, col. 1571–1649)

I fear that my hon. Friend's forebodings were correct.

What has happened – and there is evidence of this in the colossal amount of correspondence that I have received during the regrettable publicity prior to my application this afternoon – is that more and more people throughout the country find it impossible to attend a service in which the Book of Common Prayer is used. The clerics of the Church of England have brought about the beginnings of the slow strangulation of one of the greatest glories that this country enjoys. If the House needs an example, I have it on good authority that in the majority of theological colleges in the provinces of Canterbury and York the 1662 Prayer Book, or, indeed, the 1928 Prayer Book, are not in use at all.... There is a new generation of Church of England priests who do not know of the Prayer Book and who are, therefore, all too happy to override the evident rights of parochial church councils, as my hon. Friend the Member for Wokingham pointed out in 1974, to decide whether to use the 1662 liturgy or alternative services.

My proposed Bill is moderate. It will merely ensure that, if 20 people in a parish so petition an incumbent, that incumbent should hold one service a month – the principal service of the morning – according to the rite of 1662. I hope that the House will support me in ensuring that the 1662 Prayer Book can be enjoyed by everyone who wishes to do so, instead of its being consigned to the muniment rooms, where only scholars and the cognoscenti may appreciate it.

House of Lords Debate on the first reading (8 April 1981): extract from Lord Sudeley's speech:

There is always a suspicion of the undertow of a commercial

influence which can corrupt religion like anything else. Points about money I suspect will always cut more ice in your Lordships' House than points about the imagery of prayer or religious doctrine, and one must ask what cash-conscious parish would buy the Book of Common Prayer if it gets a 20 per cent discount on the purchase of the Alternative Service Book, or even some pamphlets which cost under £1 each.

Then, we know about the colossal sums to be obtained from the publication of religious texts through the massive sales of new versions of the Bible, and while the Prayer Book is not copyright the Alternative Service Book is and it attracts a copyright fee of 10 per cent, that is to say 35p or 40p a copy. So if 1 million copies are sold this means about £400,000 to the Church. In this connection, it is important to remember that the Alternative Services are still in process of experimentation and when you have a commodity – it can be a new liturgy or anything else – the more transient the commodity is the more money there is to be made out of it.

Then, the young clergy, in particular, promote the new services owing to their lack of exposure to the Prayer Book at theological colleges. For this reason, if the Bill passes its Second Reading I should like to table an amendment that the Prayer Book should be required for worship at theological colleges. Present evidence for the absence of the Prayer Book from theological colleges is very disturbing. One bishop has questioned the priests ordained in his diocese since 1974 over what had gone on at the theological colleges where they received their training, and he found that, though the Prayer Book may have appeared as an item in various courses of worship and liturgy, there was no systematic instruction in it. And the position over worship was even worse. Among the diet of Series 2 and 3 use of the Prayer Book varied from occasional or optional to never at all.

More evidence has been adduced by Professor Martin in the latest issue of the Prayer Book Society's journal, *Faith and Worship*, in which he says that wherever he has preached Evensong at theological colleges he has never heard the Prayer Book, and Professor Martin adds that at Westcott House, which is perhaps the foremost theological college, they do not have the Prayer Book at all, or indeed have anything else except Series 3. It is very much to be hoped that Professor Martin can be persuaded to collate all the evidence he has collected on the absence of the Prayer Book from theological colleges in the form of a full printed report which can be presented to Parliament or Synod for debate.

Further argument for more protection for the Prayer Book now becomes clear, if we consider that if the present trend of liturgical manner continues, it will induce some ministers to forget or even [not] to know the Prayer Book and so no choice will be left between the Prayer Book and the Alternative Services. The circumstances in which the Prayer Book may be forgotten are easy to envisage when whole areas of the country are becoming left with no proper provision between the Prayer Book and Alternative Services; and as to the Prayer Book becoming quite unknown to the younger generation, while under the Worship and Doctrine Measure the parochial church council can override the vicar for the three main services on Sunday, it is quite wrong that when it comes to the occasional services of baptism, confirmation and marriage and burial, the laity are left with no rights against the clergy whatsoever. How should the confirmands who have no need to be instructed in the Prayer Book have any idea what it is?

The cumulative drift towards the new services is not assisted by the failure of the BBC to observe the same impartiality in the broadcasting of services which they give in allocating time to the points of view of the two main political parties. Holy Communion and Matins according to the Prayer Book are hardly ever broadcast, and at Christmas all services were broadcast from the Alternative Service Book. Incidentally, in further illustration of the bias of the BBC, I might mention that on the Radio 4 programme on 5 April, entitled 'Sunday', where this programme was concerned with this particular Bill, can I ask what innuendo was intended when the commentator did not say that the Prayer Book Society has shown that most of the laity preferred the Prayer Book; he said instead that the Prayer Book Society is said to have shown something of that kind. Furthermore, the wrong question was put in front of my first answer. I did not say that the Prayer Book was preferred by the intelligentsia as against the lower reaches of society. In this context I was referring not to the Prayer Book but to the Alternative Service Book.

Part of the conclusion of the Lord Chancellor's speech:

I cannot end this speech without a personal tribute to Cranmer's book. I do not call it the book of 1662. It is stamped on every page with the genius of Cranmer, from start to finish. He was a liturgiologist of the greatest genius, as, for instance, is recognized in the somewhat hostile criticism of him in the book on *The Shape of the Liturgy* by the late Dom Gregory Dix. His language was magical. His sense of dramatic structure was superb. To give only one example, the forms of the General Confession in the Communion service are infinitely superior to those used in the alternative book.

He had the wisdom to keep the cadences of the 15th-century language in the Lord's Prayer and the Creed. I once heard an episcopal service in Gaelic. I knew when the Lord's Prayer was being pronounced, because I knew its own cadences, and it can be sung to the same music. Whether one says 'Our Father which art in Heaven' or '*Pater noster qui es in coelis*' one knows that it is the Lord's Prayer, wherever it is said.

I am sorry that it has been found desirable to change it... But it may also be true, for aught I know, that some of the supporters of the new book adopt somewhat superior attitudes to those who do not happen to agree with them. In particular, it may be that there has developed a new breed of ecclesiastical laymen; if so, I am not among them.

Extract from Lord Glenamara's speech:

The Synod has launched an Alternative Service Book. I do not complain in any way about that. I have no objection to it. I noted what was said in the Synod when the book was introduced. Indeed, there are safeguards in the Worship and Doctrine Measure of 1974. But the problem to which the noble Lord's Bill is addressed, is that the Book of Common Prayer is never used in a great many churches – I have made very careful inquiries about this – while in others it has been relegated to the status of an antiquity which is brought out, rather grudgingly, occasionally and used for the odd service at a very inconvenient time. I have experience of this myself. So the safeguards in the Worship and Doctrine Measure and the assurances at its launching are, to say the least, not working as we expected.

A generation of young people is growing up in this country to whom the Book of Common Prayer will be completely unfamiliar. I think that is a real tragedy. There is evidence, to which the Bishop of Durham has referred – professionally assembled evidence – that what is happening is against the wishes of the majority of churchgoers. But the process of substitution – and I am afraid that that really is what is happening – goes on relentlessly throughout the country. I think 'relentlessly' is the right word. I am told that the process is fuelled by the enthusiasm of the bishops, who twist the arms of the incumbents, as only bishops know how, and any incumbent who holds out is too often regarded as an old-fashioned fuddy-duddy.

Speech by Lord Dacre of Glanton:

My Lords, in these few remarks I wish to make only a few, as I see it, cardinal points. First, it is of course said that the State, by previous enactments, has allowed the Church, in religious matters, a certain amount of autonomy and that the balance thus achieved should not now be disturbed. But autonomy is not independence. Parliament has not surrendered its sovereignty. The authority which grants autonomy grants it within limits, explicit or implied, and if those limits are transgressed, it can – perhaps must – intervene to regulate, redefine or even withdraw such autonomy.

If the Church Establishment wants independence, it wants disestablishment.... The Church cannot logically demand, as some of its leaders in their recent public pronouncement seem to demand, the absolute freedom of independence combined with all the advantages of establishment. In this particular case I submit that the Church authorities are seeking to break and have, in fact, already broken the express terms of the autonomy conditionally granted to them. They are seeking to change what has been called the lifeblood of the Church. Had they stated openly that this was their intention, would Parliament have granted them that autonomy? I do not think so. But they have adopted what is known as 'salami tactics', and now it is they who are effectively disturbing the agreed balance between Church and State; and Parliament, I submit, has the duty in such cases to intervene to protect that balance.

Secondly, it is said that this is merely a question of language; that the language of Archbishop Cranmer is not intelligible today; that it is too archaic for common use; that we should put God at his ease by addressing him in more familiar tones. My Lords, the language of the Prayer Book (as of the Authorized Version) is not unintelligible. Not only is it part of our literature – all our literature is impregnated with it, and will lose part of its resonance without it – it is merely a little more stately, more elevated, than our everyday language, and can very easily be learned. We all use different levels of language. We speak differently perhaps in this House and in our homes; and within this House we speak differently before the Throne and in the bar. Religion requires elevation in language in order to inspire depth of feeling. The House of the Lord may deserve a little more profundity even than the House of Lords. The Lord Chancellor has said that the Prayer Book will not be preserved by legislation; but it will be preserved by use, and that is all that we ask for – continued, guaranteed use.

It will be said that this movement in the Church is not confined to the Church of England; that liturgical innovation is a general phenomenon of today: a response to the needs of the time, the demands of the young, the claims of the future. How are we to be sure that this demand for ritual innovation is not like so many other demands of the trendy 1960s? Those of us who live and teach in universities know how quickly such fashions change; but we also know how their former advocates – the unreconstructed trendsetters of yesteryear – though increasingly isolated can, by mere survival in key positions, artificially prolong an increasingly obsolete fashion. It would be a tragedy if the inheritance of the Church were to be sacrificed, as it could be, by the mere artificial prolongation of a dated trend.

For who are the advocates of these innovations? Let us be clear on this. They are not the Church. The Church is the congregation of the faithful, clergy and lay alike, and it includes many who loyally adhere without pedantically subscribing. That is the difference between a Church and a sect. An established Church has a particular duty towards the laity: a duty of tolerance and comprehension. The laity is not to be dragged unwillingly forward along a particular road by a party of activists exploiting their customary loyalty and deference.

I would not venture to use this language on such an occasion merely on my own authority. I am echoing the views of a right reverend Prelate who has written to me and authorized me to quote the words which he says he would himself have used had he been here: 'I fear,' writes the Bishop of

Peterborough, 'that members of congregations and parish councils are pusillanimous when it comes to standing up against the few who have a lust for perpetual innovation.'

I hope your Lordships will allow me, as a historian, to glance back over the history of the Church of England. Our Church obtained its distinctive character in the sixteenth century as the result of a revolt of the laity against a clergy which had lost contact with it. A century later, the same Church of England was in its turn overthrown; its hierarchy abolished, its liturgy suppressed, its property sold, even its cathedrals advertised for scrap. Why? Not because the laity repudiated it, but because even the most loyal of them had been temporarily alienated by the 'innovations' precipitately imposed by a too radical clerical party within it. They stood aside in its hour of danger, and it fell.

How is it, we may ask, that it was, nevertheless, after nearly 20 years of intermission, restored? Because the same laity, during those long years when its outward organization had been destroyed, kept it alive in the catacombs using, as the last and strongest symbol if its continuing life, the Prayer Book of Archbishop Cranmer. After victory, that liturgy, having proved its almost talismanic power, was reassembled in the 1662 Prayer Book, that very Prayer Book which our modern innovators are seeking quietly to destroy. I hope the laity, which as Cardinal Newman wrote is the real measure of the Church – of any Church – will once again prevent such destruction.

Extract from Earl Waldegrave's speech:

If we have doubts, and many people do have doubts, I believe we are entitled in Parliament to legislate so as to ensure that the Church does in fact do what it said it would do if we gave it certain powers. So I, for one, will vote for the Bill. I think we have all the evidence we need to come to a decision in this matter, by reference to two main documents. There are an enormous number of other documents to which we could refer if there were time. The debate in 1974 was a very full debate and it took place at a more humane time; it started at 3 p.m. and finished at 7.30 p.m., and there was no reason why there should be anything but a very full House on that occasion. Then there is the evidence of the ASB – the Alternative Service Book – itself.

Taking the 1974 debate first, I should like to quote some of the things that were actually said. For instance, the most reverend Primate Archbishop Ramsay commented (column 871):

> But in order to conserve both the Church's doctrinal identity and the place of the Book of Common Prayer, and the rights of the laity – all three of these needs, My Lords – there are important provisos built into the Measure and sometimes critics of the Measure have overlooked this.

He then went on to say what the provisos were:

> In the Measure the Book of Common Prayer remains as one of the Church's standards of doctrine.... I believe that this retention of the Prayer Book, both as a standard of doctrine and as a set of forms available when the PCC desires them, is a right means of conserving... the place of the Prayer Book in the Church's standards and the availability of the Prayer Book in the parishes when desired will be alterable only if Parliament were to decide to alter it.

This has been said over and over again ever since that day; but if you go further through that debate you will find at other points the right reverend Prelate the Lord Bishop of Durham, who was courteous enough to answer the speech I made on that occasion, spoke quite clearly about this. I see he is not in his place and I should have warned him that I would refer to something he said.

He said this at column 896:

> This is not to be a new Prayer Book. It is certainly not intended as something which would replace the Book of Common Prayer...The age of little blue and green and pink pamphlets in church cannot go on for ever. Nor can revision, in our generation, go very much further than it has done already.

I am afraid that this is what is so worrying, because the age of little pink, green or blue pamphlets has not come to an end. We have now got the Alternative Service Book, the ASB, available. But this is not going to be like the Prayer Book was, in the pews. You cannot read this book. It is more like a motor manual and it is one of those manuals that covers all the different makes of cars. You have to read down one column to follow whether it is referring to the Allegro and not to the Metro. It is not a prayer book, like the other, and it is not very easily available in the churches. It costs £4.50 a time, with the Psalter in it, and when I finally bought my copy from the bookshop in Wells Cathedral –

Baroness Seear:

My Lords, if I may intervene, it does cost much less in the soft cover.

Earl Waldegrave:

I am grateful to the noble Baroness, my Lords, for telling me there is a cheaper model. But it is not a handy little book that you can use: it is a reference book which tells you all sorts of alternatives. It is a very difficult book to understand at first sight. Of course it has not been in print for very long and I have not had very much time to study it; but you really cannot get on unless you start reading how you are to use it. You need to read page 32, for instance, the general notes, which are called 'distinctions in the text'. It goes on:

> Distinctions in the Text sections of services with numbers in blue may be omitted. Where a number of options are included in a mandatory part of the service, the rubric governing the options is numbered in black, but the texts themselves are numbered in blue. Texts in bold type are to be said by the congregation.

But I cannot find the carburettor! I do not want to be light-hearted, but it is complicated to follow.

It has a Psalter, and the lady who sold me this book told me, 'Mind you, the mice have been at that, too.' I had not realized that it would not be the Psalter that I knew, and that if I looked up Psalms 95 or 121 they would not be the same. This means that we shall not find the Book of Common Prayer bound up in this volume. If we are to have the Book of Common Prayer available and usable, there will have to be two books. That will surely mean the most tremendous confusion, because there are many changes of little words. It is these small changes of little words that are worrying the ordinary layman. Those of your Lordships who have studied this will know that they are trivial alterations. For instance, 'O, come let us sing unto the Lord', is now 'O come let us sing out to the Lord'. It will not scan.

I said that the little pink pamphlets have not gone, as the right reverend Prelate the Bishop of Durham hoped they would go. What is beginning to happen is that a certain section of an alternative service, with the optional words which the incumbent has chosen to use, will be 'roneod' out on the village machine. We in our diocese shall then have to submit what we wish to use to someone in authority – probably at the diocesan office – to see whether we are using the options aright. What will be the result of this? No two churches in England will be having the same service in the same form, and every time the incumbent changes he will alter it. This has been going on for 15 years, while we have had Series 2 and Series 3. No two churches have celebrated Holy Communion with the same Series 2.

So I am afraid that I have to say, from my experience, that the Book of Common Prayer has disappeared and is not in most of the churches now – I am talking of the country churches – in a stack close to the door, or handy when you go in. You will be handed a little pamphlet and a hymn book, or perhaps two hymn books. But we are not going to have what I think so many of us hoped we should have, which is that after the experimentation with the Series 1, 2 and 3, the Synod and the Church, as a whole, would have made up its mind what it wanted to have as alternative services and it would have had them printed and published in one book. In answer to my speech in 1974, the right reverend Prelate the Bishop of Durham said, I recall, that my idea that the Book of Common Prayer and the two alternative services should be printed in the same volume was rather a good one. But we have not got that. A new incumbent was appointed quite recently, and there are three disparate churches, congregations and parochial church councils for the man to wrestle with. He is a young clergyman and he had never used the Book of Common Prayer in his theological college. He was unfamiliar with it. Many of us go from church to church to find that service at eight o'clock on Sunday mornings.

Extract from Lord Beswick's speech:

I venture to take part in this debate with an increased recognition of my own inadequacy. I am not well versed in the theology or the inner politics of the established Church. I fear that I take out from church activities much more than I put in. But I care for the Christian religion. I sincerely believe that we shall not truly solve the economic and social problems which occupy so much of the time of this House until we see the principles of the Christian religion more widely accepted and applied. I want to see the influence of the Church extended and strengthened. As the right reverend Prelate the Bishop of Durham put it, I want the Church to reach out. I would welcome changes in the form of service which genuinely strengthen the authority of the Church and which maintained, widened or deepened its contacts with the world outside: with the infrequent churchgoer; with those, as the right reverend Prelate put it, on the fringe; with those who make up the nation at large, if not the congregation on the Sunday.

I give my opinion, for what it is worth, that the wording of Series 3 does not extend but tends to diminish the area of influence of our Church. The thinness of the language of this new form of service tends to chill and not to warm the relationship with a wider congregation. Some twelve or thirteen years ago, when I had some responsibility for these matters, I recall that there was a suggestion from the Bishops' Benches that we should change the form of service with which we start the proceedings in this House. At the meeting that we had to discuss the matter I asked the most reverend Primate the then Archbishop of Canterbury, 'What is the reason for wanting a change?' I ought not to purport to quote his reply after all these years but I remember very distinctly how I reacted. I said to him 'Why, you will be wanting to change the words in the Lord's Prayer next.' I put it that way because I thought there was nothing less likely than a change in the words of the prayer so widely known and loved. It seemed to me quite inconceivable that anyone – certainly not a member of the Church and absolutely certainly no one who held a high position in the Church – would dream of changing the Lord's Prayer. But such was my innocence; even then, it now seems, there were those who thought they could improve on the words that had been recited over the centuries.

Such insensitivity baffles me. It implies an inability to understand that the sort of wording, the sound of the wording, has become ingrained in our national life and was often more helpful and more influential, indirectly and subtly, than thousands of sermons delivered to dwindling congregations. Many of us here must have warmed by the way those around us at a service on the parade ground or on the seashore or around the war memorial have joined in the recital of the words they knew, of the Lord's Prayer.

The right reverend Prelate [the Bishop of Durham] said he was prepared to agree that the Synod had 'made a mess' of the Lord's Prayer. I was appalled by the expression he used. The noble and learned Lord the Lord Chancellor said he welcomed the statement. I was appalled by it. 'They had made a mess of the Lord's Prayer'! What worries me now is that it is the same line of thought, the same attitude of mind, that made a mess of the Lord's Prayer that wants to substitute the more 'with-it' wording for the measured language of the 1662 Prayer Book.

I am told – and it has been said again today – that the spoken language has changed since 1662, and of course it has, although I remain unconvinced that the 'bed-sit' idiom is superior to, or likely to last as long as, the language of Shakespeare or Cranmer. How often have we heard in everyday situations someone say, 'I have left undone the things which I ought to have done.' The wording in Series 3 Confession is cleared. It has all the clarity of a railway timetable. But it will never be quoted outside the Church, as those 1662 words are occasionally. I wonder whether the right reverend Prelate would tell me if that man in the street to whom he referred would ever quote sentences or expressions out of the Series 3 form of service.

A friend of mine the other day called my attention to a prime example of superfluous wording. There is the line: 'My love is like a red red rose.' One could very easily imagine the authors of Series 3 whipping out the blue pencil and cutting out one of the words in that line. The result would be crisper, more in keeping with modern usage, but the line would never be heard again.

Extract from the Earl of Onslow's speech:

My Lords, three main aspects of the Church of England are

raised in this debate. In my view, they are: is the Church's new literature a worthy successor to Cranmer and Coverdale? Is Parliament the right place to discuss this change, and does it have any power to alter the decision made in 1974? Thirdly, has the Church of England fulfilled its undertaking, given in 1974? I am not a literary critic and I hold no degree; I make no claim to being an intellectual – but I am convinced that the English of the Alternative Service Book is, as one critic has put it, the English of a Treasury civil servant.

In his good and thought-provoking speech, the right reverend Prelate the Bishop of Durham said that the Synod had made a hash of the Lord's Prayer. What a confession to make! The Lord's Prayer is central to the whole worship of the Church of England, and the Synod admits to making a hash of it. The right reverend Prelate went on to say, 'When we have further revision...'. From further revision may the Lord deliver us!

My Lords, the noble Earl, Lord Waldegrave, lost his place when searching for the Venite. I have chosen at random three sections for comparison and I chose the Venite first of all. In 1662, as most of your Lordships will know, the Venite started: 'O come, let us sing unto the Lord: let us heartily rejoice in the strength of our salvation.' Familiar, beautiful and, as the Lord Chancellor said, cadent. It has been changed to: 'O come let us sing unto the Lord. Let us shout in triumph to the rock of our salvation.' I suggest that is less cadent, no more clear and is two words longer; in other words, it is quasi-poetical and arch.

Again, the Te Deum reads: 'We praise thee, O God: we acknowledge thee to be the Lord.' Again, balanced, clear, poetical and with tons of style. The Alternative Service Book offers: 'You are God. We praise you. You are the Lord. We acclaim you.' More words, less poetry, less style and, I suggest, a change for change's sake. Surely God knows that he is God and we do not have to tell him so? The new Creed says: 'I believe in God the Father Almighty, creator of heaven and earth.' Cranmer said 'maker'. Again, why change when there is no qualitative improvement and it is just change for change's sake?

The Second Collect in Evensong for 1662 starts: 'O God, from whom all holy desires, all good counsels, and all just works do proceed...'. Wonderful stuff! It is beautiful! In the Alternative Service Book it says: 'O God the source of all good desires, all right judgements, all just works'. This time there is one word less, but I suggest that "good desires" can be sinful, whereas "holy desires" cannot. A "good desire" could be that you wanted a very good dinner and possibly to eat too much of it.

Incidentally, the Book of Common Prayer makes it mandatory to pray for the sovereign: the alternative Communion Rite A, Series 3, says only that the president may pray for the sovereign. These contrasts really were taken at random, and if I were to continue we should be here all through the night. All the quotations I have used from 1662 are just as understandable, if not more so, on a London housing estate than the Alternative Service Book.

Extract from Lord Vaizey's speech:

I happen to believe that the Church of England has been, and remains, the Church of the people of England. It is not a sect. It happens to be the national Church. I would resist strongly any attempt to disestablish that Church. I believe history shows that from time to time God turns his face against his people, but history also shows that from time to time God turns his face back towards his people. I do not despair that the Church once again might turn itself into the Church of all the people of England.

When I hear these liturgical discussions which have been going on now for practically the whole of my adult lifetime I cannot help feeling that those who engage in liturgical discussions are very similar to those who engaged in the discussions which must have taken place on the bridge of the

Titanic as it sailed towards the iceberg. We have been told time and time again that if we adopted Series 1 or Series 2 or Series 3, the churches would once more be packed with young people. The simple answer is that they are not. All this liturgical experiment and liturgical reform has not for one moment turned the tide of atheism and agnosticism in favour of the Church of England.

What we have seen is that the State would not allow the Church of England to pull down some of its principal glories; namely, the cathedrals and parish churches of which it is privileged to be the guardian. But the State also said that the Church of England would not be allowed to tear up the Book of Common Prayer, of which it is also the guardian. The Book of Common Prayer is not something which is supposed to repose upon a shelf in a muniment room. As was said by one noble Lord, the Book of Common Prayer's value lies in its use. That was quite clearly expressed in the concordat between church and state in 1974.

It is perfectly clear that that concordat has in fact been torn up. I was the only layman present at a conference of clergy where a celebration of Holy Communion in the 1662 rite was conducted, because it happened to be in a royal chapel. We came back and the clergy jeered and sneered. I do not mean that they just condemned it; they fell about with most unholy laughter at what they said was this incredible old-fashioned rubbish that they had had to listen to. I speak literally of the way they were behaving.

The point is that the adoption of all this Civil Service English has not convinced the people on the housing estates that they should come back to church. The people on the housing estates are still staying away from church with all this new liturgy. There is no reason to suppose that the old liturgy would drive even more people away from the Church. The old liturgy itself has been the faith and the language of a large proportion of the English people, and particularly of that large proportion of English people who do not very often go to church. But God is not only interested in those who go to church regularly, or the clergy; God is interested in those who do not go to church; who perhaps only go to church for baptism and for marriage and for burial. But that is what the Church in this country historically has been about and I should have thought that the time has come when we should say, and say openly, to the bishops that what they have been doing in the last twenty or thirty years in the name of the Church has done a great deal of damage to the cause of Christianity in this country and for that reason, with all its imperfections, I shall support the noble Lord in the Lobby tonight.

On the question whether the Bill should be given a second reading, their Lordships divided. The voting was For, 28; Against, 17.

A Warning to the Church

C. H. SISSON

A Bill designed to secure that, subject to certain conditions, at least one main service a month, in Church of England parishes, should be in the form prescribed by the Book of Common Prayer, is certainly an absurdity. It is absurd, almost everyone will say, at this time of day that Parliament should be asked to regulate what the parsons get up to on Sunday mornings. Members of Parliament thought they had washed their hands of such things in 1974, and that was late enough in the day. The promoters of the Bill which had its successful first reading on 8 April, and is to have a second reading this week, are, however, by no means so ingenuous as might appear. The first reading of the Bill attracted a degree of attention – and of parliamentary attendance – which few can have expected. The promoters were thus able to demonstrate that, far from being out of touch with the times, they had a real political sense of what is important to people. There was great ecclesiastical indignation, on the grounds that the matter was important only to a *minority* – which would be an odd and unsatisfactory reason for Parliament *not* concerning itself with any subject. It may be added that the assertion that Anglicans who want the Prayer Book are a minority within the Church is – well, just an assertion.

The more solemn reason given for the indignation of Synod-loving Anglicans (*they*, surely are a minority!) is of

Reprinted from the *Spectator*, 2 May 1981.

course that the regulation of church affairs was put into the hands of the Synod in 1974 and that unsanctified parliamentary hands should no longer touch such matters. One can understand these sentiments on the part of those who thought they had climbed into the Synod as into a spaceship, and pulled up the ladder, but whatever the impression of those inside, such vehicles are controlled from the ground. The privileges Parliament gives, it can certainly take away. It beseems the authorities of the Church of England to remember that in the country at large their membership, however reckoned, is now a minority, and they should not expect from the public a respect they are not prepared to accord to serious elements within their own circles or outside.

It would certainly have surprised the ordinary churchgoer, in 1974, to learn that what was being plotted under the guise of a measure to allow the Church to manage its own affairs, was a complete change in the character of the Church of England. Concern was expressed at the time, by some of the more wary, about the possible fate of the Book of Common Prayer, and even as late as last year, when the Alternative Service Book was going through its final stages in the Synod, assurances were given that the Prayer Book still stood, and that no one therefore should lament its loss. The assurances were, frankly, a pack of lies, and indeed the conduct of the ecclesiastical authorities at large, in relation to the ASB, has been of a kind which would have been unsparingly blasted by any political opposition, if anything so disingenuous were practised – as who shall say it has not sometimes been? – by a government. Nothing could have illustrated better the inept and unhealthy cosiness of the Synod than their utter ignoring of the petition presented to them on the initiative of Professor David Martin. No one expected the *fauteurs* of the ASB to turn tail at the sight of the petition, but that the petition should have been utterly ignored, that no reply of any kind should have been thought necessary, could only be taken to mark a determination on the part of bishops and clergy, to say nothing of the lay ecclesiastical politicians, to turn their backs on responsible outside opinion and behave as if they were a congregation of saints who had no need to notice the vulgar and the damned. That the petition was largely representative of educated opinion, literate and musical, meant that the Synod were in fact turning their backs on that alliance with learning which was one of the glories of the English Church in better days. No wonder the ASB is what it is.

Now that the ASB has been promulgated and widely distributed and the Prayer Book in most places pushed into corners, it is apparently thought safe to be honest. We find, for example, the *Carlisle Diocesan News* saying: 'Diplomacy may have required the unglamorous definition – "Alternative Service Book" – but the truth is that an alternative liturgy is a contradiction in terms.... It is time therefore to abandon political tactics and cover-up titles which suggest that this is no more than an alternative, and that 1662 stands unscathed.' So the people of England have been kidded by these scruffy ecclesiastical politicians, and are now reckoned of so little account, in the councils of the Church, that the little joke can be admitted. No wonder it was felt, when the petition was presented to the Synod, that the presence of outsiders of any sophistication would be an embarrassment. 'For our health's sake,' says the encyclical from Carlisle, 'the blood must be changed.' (The blood is that contaminated by the Book of Common Prayer.) 'What matters now is that the operation should be swift and complete.'

Time for Parliament to intervene? I think it is. Indeed, one may say that the Church of England has begun its course of synodical government by an affront not only to many of its members but to Parliament itself. For did not the authorities of the Church take on the new form of government well knowing, in their inner councils, what they would get up to, but carefully concealing the drift of their politics? Of course neither the promoters of the present Bill, nor those who support it from a distance, expect it to pass into law, and one can imagine the Government being more than a little worried if it faced that possibility. So far from wanting to meddle in such things, the State is delighted not to have to do so. None the less, in the last resort, if clerics are silly enough, in ordinary political terms, if they are dishonest and reckless, they cannot in the end escape retribution from Parliament. That, be it said, goes for other bodies besides the Church of England; it is *not* a peculiarity of the Establishment. For Parliament can do as it likes, and will do, if sufficiently moved. It may be that people now think that the old conflicts between Church and State are something only to be read about in history books. Not at all, as even a short political memory will show. Perhaps it is only in foreign countries, in France or in Poland, that such conflicts can happen? Not at all. We may be sure that, in the last resort, the country which, of all others, roused itself to throw off a foreign ecclesiastical administration and to work out a series of settlements which gave us, after all, a decent history of political liberty, will not stand more than a certain amount of nonsense in the name of religion, whether from the Moonies or anyone else.

The Prayer Book (Protection) Bill is the gentlest of warnings.

Index

Ablutions, 4
Absolution, 51, 62, 71, 75
Act of Uniformity, 131
Acts, 26, 90
Addison, Joseph, 46
Advent, 4
Agnus Dei, 128
Allin, Bishop, 158
Allison, C. F., 38, 39, 51
Altar, 2, 45
Alternative Service Book (ASB), 59, 211, 212, 229
  acclamations, 128
  angels in, 124
  BBC and, 211–12
  burial service, 82, 137–8
  calendar, 83
  canticles, 11, 120, 126
  complexity, 114–15
  copyright, 180, 182, 210
  cost, 82–3, 179, 210, 218
  criticisms of, 59–62, 66, 71–2, 78, 82–4, 88–9, 92–5, 96, 105, 107, 114–28, 131, 133–4, 141, 176, 187, 189, 192, 201, 212–13, 218–19, 223–4
  doctrine in, 50–3, 67, 133, 201
  fighting against, 54
  future of, 81, 93, 94–5, 137, 182
  Gallup poll on, 186–8, 192, 193
  Holy Communion, 84, 88, 127–8, 180, 201; *also under* Rite A, Rite B
  inaccurate claims for, 187–8
  language, viii, 30–1, 51, 68, 85, 92,

Alternative Service Book *continued*
  language *continued*, 117–24, 128, 133, 176, 180, 219, 222, 223–4
  lectionary, 83, 94
  Litany, 128
  Matins, 120
  music, 125, 127–8
  Preface, 115, 117
  printing, 181
  Psalter, 11, 83, 126, 128, 218, 219
  responses, 128
  reviews, 192
  sacraments in, 50
  sales, 80
  society and, 142
  sound of, ix
  spread of, ix
  theology, 200–1
  unnecessary, 116–17
  wedding, 187, 188
  Word v. Sacrament in, 94
American Prayer Book, 48, 53, 149–61, 176
Angels, archangels, 124
Anglican Church in N. America, 156
Anglican Communion, unity through liturgy, 1, 149, 153–4, 175–6
Anthem, 128
Apostles' Creed, 47
Apostolic Constitutions, 2
Aquinas, St Thomas, 96, 97
Arnold, Matthew, 163
Arthur, Bishop, 173
Ash Wednesday, 14
Athanasian Creed, 4–5

Atonement, 61
Auden, W. H., 161, 171
Augustine of Canterbury, St, 135
Augustine of Hippo, St, 52
Austin, George, 201
Australian Church, 163
Australian Liturgical Commission, 169, 173, 174
Australian Prayer Book, An, 162–74
Authorized Version (King James), *see under* Bible

Babington, R. A., 193, 197
Ballantyne, P. S., 196
Banns, 69
Baptism, 137, 211, 226
Basil, St, 48
Baxter, Richard, 3
Beatitudes, 17
Beethoven, 123
Belloc, Hilaire, 169
Benedicite, 65, 120
Benedict, St, 135
Benedictus, 65, 120
Berkeley, Bp George, 117
Beswick, Lord, 220–2
Bible, 9, 63–4, 65, 69, 91, 123, 133, 170, 196, 197
  Authorized Version (AV), x, 22, 23, 31, 57, 64, 111, 112, 116, 118, 120, 151, 154, 167, 171, 181, 182, 187, 188
  Book of Common Prayer and, 74, 78
  Good News Bible, 94, 181
  Jerusalem, 83
  language, viii, 74
  New English Bible (NEB), 31, 32, 111, 112–13, 167, 195
  New International Version, 181
  translation, 111–13
Bishop, D. H., 197, 200
Bonhoeffer, Dietrich, 100, 161
Book of Common Prayer, 67
  (1552), 154
  (1559), 154
  (1927–8), 5, 117, 152, 154, 156, 158–60, 209

Book of Common Prayer *continued*
  Abridgement of, 47
  Americans and, 149–61
  Bible and, 74, 78
  bond of unity, 149, 153–4, 175
  Chichester survey and, 185, 189
  clergy role in, 92, 209–11
  'common', meaning of, 76
  copyright and, 180
  Cranmer and, *see* s.v.
  criticisms of, 59–61, 71–2, 92, 142, 195, 196
  decline of use, ix, 48, 81, 176, 179, 203–5, 207, 209–11, 213, 216, 217, 220, 228–9
  doctrine, viii, x, 48, 50, 68, 217
  exhortations, 114
  explanatory essays, 74–8, 162
  Gallup poll on, 186–8, 192, 193
  General Synod petition, 186, 188, 191, 192
  Holy Communion, 69–72, 84, 90–2, 131, 211, 212
  language, viii, ix, 10, 75, 81, 118, 123, 147, 151, 201, 204–6, 214–15, 222
  literary superiority, 57
  modern revisers of, 49–50, 78, 84–5, 87, 140, 149–61
  need to revise, 9–10, 114, 118
  newspaper letters re, 191–202
  ordination services, 78
  prayers, ix, 73, 78
  Preface, 74, 76, 139; (1549), 132, 139, 154
  preserving, 6, 72, 79, 177, 204, 209
  printers, 181
  spirituality of, x, 75
  thanksgivings, 78
  title, 76
  value, 73, 131–4, 225
Boulard, F., 184
Bouyer, Fr, 164
Brett, George, 196
Bridges, Robert, 118, 119
Brightman, F. E., 5

British Broadcasting Corporation, 211–212
Brook, Stella, 23, 169
Brown, Kenneth, 193, 197
Buchanan, Colin, 85
Burial service, 82, 178, 211, 226
Burkitt, F. C., 5
Burrows, J. E., 196
Busby, C. R., 197
Butler, Bp Joseph, 117
Byrd, William, 28, 126

Calendar, 27, 83
Callistus, Pope, 96
Calvinism, 67
Campbell, Gordon, 171
Candole, Henry de, 7
Canterbury, Abp of, xiv, 158, 175–8, 208, 217, 221
Canticles, 11, 120, 126
Carter, Sydney, 107–8, 109
Cathedrals, 125–6, 177, 225
Ceylon Rite, 6
Chant, Anglican, 126
Charles II, 3, 39
Christ, 42, 44, 45, 46, 70, 108, 170–1
  Ascension, 71
  Body, 142
  'gentleman', 43
  High Priest, 124
  manifestation of, 24–7, 33
  moral, teacher v. Divine Son, 38–9
  New English Bible, language of, 32
  Resurrection, 71, 200
  sacrifice of, 62
  Second Coming, 62, 71
  sin-bearer, 70
Christmas, 60, 211
Church, 24, 37, 142
  as manifestation, 26, 27, 32
  Primitive, 87, 133
Church Militant prayer, 2, 69
Church of England, 68, 82, 117
  Catholic and Protestant, 62
  changing, 12, 21–2, 83, 97, 137
  decline, 137, 199, 202
Church of England *continued*
  Directory and, 136
  disestablishment of, 63, 204, 214, 224
  diversity, 140
  eighteenth-century, 43–8
  fixed service order, 57, 59, 132–3
  General Synod, 186–8, 191–3, 195, 203, 207, 208, 211, 213, 220, 222, 223, 227, 228–9
  ignores wider issues, 106
  leaders, 37, 40
  ministry, 134
  Parliament and, *see* s.v.
  'revised churchmen' of, 49–50
  self-centredness of, 100
  State and, *see* s.v.
  theology of, 38, 40–1
Church of India, Burma and Ceylon, 6
Church of South India, 6, 83
Church's year, 3
Cockerell, David, 110n
Collect for Purity, 69
Collects, 84, 162, 166, 167, 168, 169, 224
Commandments, 69
Commination, 78
Compline, 135
Confession, 51, 62, 67, 70, 71, 115, 120, 180, 212, 222
Confirmation, 50, 123, 158, 211
Consecration, 50
Consecration, prayer of, 3, 71, 91
Cope, J. A., 208
1 Corinthians, 74, 75, 142, 194
2 Corinthians, 27
Cosin, Bp John, 3
Couratin, Canon, 5
Coverdale, Bp Miles, 64, 120–1, 126, 170, 223
Coward, Noël, 172
Cranborne, Viscount, 193, 206–9
Cranmer, Abp Thomas, 86, 96, 171, 189
  Book of Common Prayer and, 74–9, 117, 160, 195–7, 212, 214, 216, 222, 223

Cranmer, Abp Thomas *continued*
  establishment and, 63
  language, 16, 61
  liturgy, 3, 8, 11, 57, 62, 66–9, 71–2, 88, 154, 165, 167, 169, 170, 172, 173
Cromwell, Oliver, 68

Dacre, Lord, 214–16
Dalby, Canon, 200
Dashwood, Sir Francis, 47, 48
Deuchar, Andrew, 192
Directory, 136
Disestablishment, 63, 204, 214, 224
Dix, Gregory, 7–10, 86–7, 117, 212
Donne, John, 34n, 47, 52, 123, 165
Downing, Gerald, 96
Dunlop, Ian, 199
Durant, John, 103
Durham, Bp of, 182, 213, 217, 219–23

Easter, 114
Eastward position, 19, 58, 62
Eliot, George, viii
Eliot, T. S., 47, 56n, 171
Elizabeth I, 154
Elizabeth II, 140
Emerton, John A., 121
Ephesians, 27
Episcopal Church (USA), 5, 37, 38, 48, 52, 53, 55
  Prayer Book revision in, 149–61
Epistle, 69, 145
Eucharist, *see* Holy Communion
Evensong, 64, 75, 77, 93, 116, 118, 120, 126, 224
Every, George, 174n
Eyre, Richard, 185, 189

Fenn, Richard, 187
Fielding, Henry, 46
Foot, Michael, 113
Fraction, the, 10
Franklin, Benjamin, 47, 48
Frere, Bp W. H., 5
Frost, D. L., 119, 121

Galatians, 24, 168
Galileo, 137
Gallup, George, 159
Gallup poll, 159, 186–8, 192, 193
Gardiner, Bp Stephen, 8
Gardner, Helen, 113
Gelineau psalms, 130
General Synod, *see under* Church of England
  Book of Common Prayer petition, 186, 188, 191, 192
Genesis, 104
Genuflection, 62
George I, 47
Glenamara, Lord, 194, 213
Gloria in excelsis, 4, 72, 128
Golden numbers, 114
Good News Bible, 94, 181
Gospel
  liturgical, 69, 128
  as manifestation, 23–8, 32–3
  as message, 23, 31
  Gregory I, Pope, 135
Guildford, Dean of, x
Guitar, 20, 129
Gunpowder Plot service, 1

Hacking, Ian, 109n
Hanson, Professor, 59–60
Hatchett, Marion J., 56n
Hatherly, V. C., 197
Heald, Gordon, 187
Hebert, Gabriel, 7
Henry III, 94
Henry VIII, 141, 163
Herbert, George, 52, 73, 117
Hill, Alec, 192
Hinduism, 100
Hippolytus, 9, 85–7, 88, 90, 92
Hoadly, Bp Benjamin, 46
Hodgetts, Colin, 108
Holder, A. J., 180
Holy Communion, vii, 64, 137
  Alternative Service Book, *see* s. vv.
  Book of Common Prayer, *see* s. vv.
  both kinds, 76
  cathedral Sung, 125

Holy Communion *continued*
- Divine Office and, 10
- early, services, 3–4
- Eucharistic Prayer, 87, 88
- family, 93
- frequency of, 46, 51, 76, 77
- intention at, 144
- manifests Christ, 26
- mid-week, 61
- nature of service, 18, 46–7, 52–3, 69
- New Testament and, 9, 11
- posture in, 62
- privacy of, 27
- seven orders of, 132

Holy Spirit, 10, 26, 158
Hooker, Richard, 21, 117, 131
Hopkins, Gerard Manley, 33
Humble access, prayer of, 71, 91, 164
Hume, David, 44
Hurford, 128
Hymns, 64, 128–30

'I believe' – 'We believe', 20, 21, 69
Immanence, 129
Institution, words of, 3, 71
Intercessions, 145–6
Isaiah, 112
Islam, 100

Jackson, 184
James II, 39
Jasper, R. C. D., 96, 135
Jerusalem Bible, 83
Job, 111
John, Gospel of, 24, 25
John XXIII, Pope, 137
Johnson, Samuel, 47, 52, 70, 73
Jubilate Deo, 65

Kemp, Bp Eric, 184, 185
Ken, Bp Thomas, 39, 118
Kilpatrick, James, 151
King, Martin Luther, 161
King James Bible (Authorized Version), *see under* Bible
Küng, Hans, 185
Kyrie, 128

Lambeth Conferences, 6, 149, 175
Language, 16
- Alternative Service Book, *see under* ASB
- *Australian Prayer Book*, 164–74
- Book of Common Prayer, *see under* BCP
- importance of, 96–9
- liturgical, 11, 20, 29, 197–8
- meaning and, 16, 197–9
- nature of, misunderstood, 197–9
- reality and, 99
- religious, 97–108, 111, 123
- scientific, 123
- theology and, 17–19, 32, 118–19

Latin, 75, 126, 154, 164, 166, 169
Latitudinarians, 40, 47, 48, 50
Laud, Abp William, 2
Lauds, 135
Law, William, 47, 117
Lectionary, 3, 10, 83, 94
Lent, 4, 54, 65
Lewis, C. S., 67
Liddon, H. P., 4
Linskill, Martin, 200
Litany, 4, 128
Liturgical Commission, viii, 10, 81, 96, 124, 135, 137
Liturgy
- aim of, 122–3
- change in, 1–11
- Cranmer's, *see under* Cranmer
- defined, 150
- literary knowledge and, 171
- personal identity and, 12–22
- poetry and, viii, 18, 29, 171, 198
- reform of, vii, 101, 171, 178
- Roman, 6–7, 76, 131, 161
- theology and, 10, 30

Liturgy for India, 6
Lloyd, Trevor, 85
Loane, Sir Marcus, 163
Locke, John, 38–9, 117

Lord Chancellor, 212–13, 215, 222, 223
Lord's Prayer, 3, 69, 71, 116, 187, 188, 212, 221–2, 223
Lossky, Vladimir, 26, 27, 28
Louis, St, 93

MacInnes, Gurney, 196
Mackintosh, Andrew A., 121
Macquarrie, John, 164
Marriage, 50, 178, 211, 226
Martin, David A., 29, 117, 186, 187, 191, 192, 196, 210–11, 228
Mary, Queen, 154
Mary Magdalene, 24
Mass, 6–7, 59, 68–9, 72, 76, 92, 93, 94, 131, 132, 137, 161
Matins, 93, 135, 188
  Alternative Service Book, 120
  Book of Common Prayer, 4, 64–5, 75, 77, 116, 211
Matthew, 24, 31, 32, 167
Mel, Bp Lakdasa de, 6
Merbecke, 127, 130
Methodists, 83, 201–2
Miller, Harold, 85
Milton, John, 126, 170–1
Morris, B., xi
Mozart, 123
Music, viii, 29
  ASB, 125, 127–8
  cathedral, 125–6
  formal v. informal, 130
  guitar, 20, 129
  as manifestation, 28
  parish church, 126–7

New English Bible (NEB), *see under* Bible
New International Version, 181
Newman, Cardinal, 216
Nicene Creed, 69, 126, 128, 180
Non-jurors, 3, 39–40
Notices, 69

Oblation, prayer of, 5
Offertory, 69
Onslow, Earl of, 222–4
Ordination services, 78
Orthodox Church, 5, 19, 60, 83
Oxford Movement, 126

Paisley, Ian, 83
Palestrina, 28, 126
'Parish and People', 7
Parker, Dorothy Mills, 175–8
Parkinson, Simon, 196
Parliament, ix, xi, 136, 141, 142, 209, 215
  Church of England and, 203–4, 207–11, 214–16, 223, 227–30
Parochial Church Council (PCC), 130, 179, 203, 209, 211, 217, 220
Pattinson, Derek, 187
Paul, St, 24, 26, 27, 43, 66, 74, 75, 77, 194, 195, 200
Peace, the, ix, 10, 20, 21, 52, 72
Penitence, 51, 61, 75
Penney, D. J. R., 197
Personal identity, 12–22
Peterborough, Bp of, 216
Philippians, 120
Phillips, C. H., 130
Poetry, viii, 18, 29, 171, 198
Pontianus, Pope, 86
Pope, Alexander, 43
Post-communion, 3, 72
Prayer Book Measure (1965), 131
Prayer Book (Protection) Bill, 204, 206–27, 230
Prayer Book Society, 129, 210, 212
Prayers, 137
  Book of Common Prayer, ix, 73, 78
  Eucharistic, 87, 88
  intercessory, 145–6
  language of, 165
  losing profundity in, 22
  posture in, 19
  State, 69, 78, 224
Presbyterians, 136
Pridham, P., 195
Psalms, 53, 54

Psalter, 10, 11, 47, 64, 74, 78, 116, 120–1, 126, 130, 218, 219
Puritans, 131, 133, 136

Quakers, 173

Rahner, Karl, 184
Ralston, William, 160
Ramsay, Abp Michael, 217
Ratcliff, E. C., 5, 6
Real Presence, 27, 173
Redemption, 61, 67, 68, 70, 200
Reformation, 8, 67, 76, 117, 121, 134
Reith, Lord, 112
Reservation, 5
Responses, 126, 128
Revelation, 132
Ridley, Bp Nicholas, 170
Rite A, 58, 59, 69, 70, 88, 89, 90, 93, 94, 115, 116, 126, 224
Rite B, 70, 83, 88, 89, 90, 93, 94, 115, 116
Robinson, Ian, 23, 31, 101–2
Robinson, Bp John, 99, 100
Rockhampton, Bp of, 168–73
Roman Catholic Church, 83, 87, 131, 164, 201–2
Royal School of Church Music, 130
Rubrics, 1, 4, 6, 10, 76, 77, 126, 127, 219
Runcie, Abp Robert, xiv, 175–8

Sacraments, 10, 42, 45, 48, 50
St Paul's, Dean of, 201
Salvation, 67, 129
Sancroft, Abp William, 3
Sanctus, 166
Sarum use, 76, 154
Savoy Conference, 3
Saward, Michael, 186, 193, 195, 197, 201
Schubert, 126
Scottish Prayer Book (1637), 2
Seear, Baroness, 218
Series 1, 88, 220, 225
Series 2, 88, 201, 210, 219, 220, 225
Series 3, viii, 31, 88, 105, 127, 189, 192, 193–4, 196, 201, 210, 211, 219, 220, 221, 222, 224, 225
Sermon, 69, 75, 123, 144, 221
Shaftesbury, Lord, 51
Shakespeare, 123, 140, 170, 180, 222
Shaw, Geoffrey, 127
Sidney, Sir Philip, 122
Sikhism, 100
Simeon, Charles, 73
Smith, Dan, 109n
Smyth, Charles, 8
Society for the Preservation of the Book of Common Prayer, 157
South Africa, Anglican Province of, 5
Southern, Sir Richard, 90
Southwark, Bp of, 14
State
  Church and, 22, 63, 139, 140–2, 199, 214, 224–5, 230
  prayers for, 69, 78, 224
Steele, Richard, 42, 43
Steiner, George, 29
Sudeley, Lord, 209–12
Sumsion, Herbert, 126
Swift, Jonathan, 117
Sykes, C. G., 200

Tallis, Thomas, 28
Taylor, Bp Jeremy, 117
Te Deum, 17, 64–5, 223
Telfer, William, 7
Thacker, Eric, 197
Thanksgiving, prayer of, 5
Theology
  Alternative Service Book, 62, 180
  Book of Common Prayer, 61, 199, 200
  language and, 17–19, 32, 118–19
  liturgy and, 10, 30
Theresa, St, 52
Thirty-nine Articles, 8, 78
Thomas, R. S., 108–9
Thompson, E. P., 102–4
'Thou' and 'You', 17–18
Tillich, Paul, 99, 146

Tillotson, Abp John, 40, 41, 45
1 Timothy, 26
Townshend, H. L. H., 188, 193
Transcendence, 99, 104, 129, 157
  need to experience, 17, 20
  trend away from, 30
Treasure, Ronald, 197
Trott, Stephen J., 196, 200

Underhill, Evelyn, 150

Vaizey, Lord, 224–6
van Straubenzee, W. R., 207
Vatican II, 164
Vaughan, Henry, 117
Venite, 120, 151, 223
Vespers, 135
Victoria, T. L. de, 28
Voltaire, 117

Waal, Victor de, 12
Waldegrave, Earl, 216–20, 223
Walker, Terry, 208
Wansey, Paul, 199
Ward, Neville, 23
Warnock, Mary, 23
Warren, Paul, 201
Weatherby, Harold, 157
Weelkes, Thomas, 126
Weil, Simone, 52
Wesley, John, 4, 73
Westward position, 19, 20, 58
Willey, Basil, 42
William III, 39
Williams, Isaac, 25
Winslow, J. C., 6
Winstone, P. J., 193
Wittgenstein, Ludwig, 105
Worcester, Dean of, 201
Worship
  congregational, 76
  defined, 150
  language of, ix, 23
  nature of, 129–30
  order in, 77
  purpose of, 196
  'space' and 'place' in, 144–8
  tone of, 129–30
  uniformity sacrificed, 131–2
Worship and Doctrine Measure, 211, 213, 217, 225, 227, 228
Wulfstan, Bp, 29

York, Abp of, 16
York, Dean of, 96, 135
'You' and 'Thou', 17–18, 23